D0983446

Is there no balm in Gilead? Is there no physician there? Finally, Dr. Peter Scazzero's response answers this timeless search for emotional trauma in his book *The Emotionally Healthy Leader*. His approach is a tremendous resource with practical, pragmatic ideas that are revolutionary in their approach to reach far beyond the fluff of spiritual clichés to touch the deepest pains in leadership with salve for the soul.

Bishop T. D. Jakes, Sr.,
C.E.O., TDJ Enterprises,
NY Times bestselling author

Peter Scazzero is one of the world's authorities on emotional health, and his teachings have had a profound impact. His professional approach, borne of many years of study, combines powerfully with his strong Christian faith to offer new hope to anyone seeking to grow and develop the way they live their life.

Nicky Gumbel,
Holy Trinity Brompton, UK;
founder of Alpha Course

The Emotionally Healthy Leader is a profoundly helpful and insightful offering. With remarkable honesty about his own journey, Pete describes key components of healthy Christian leadership, inspiring us to bring our transforming selves to the communities we serve—for the glory of God, for the abundance of our own lives and for the good of many.

Dr. Ruth Haley Barton,
founder and president,
Transforming Center and author of
Strengthening the Soul of Your Leadership

The
Emotionally
Healthy
Leader

Also by Peter Scazzero

Emotionally Healthy Spirituality

The Emotionally Healthy Church

Emotionally Healthy Spirituality Day by Day

The Emotionally Healthy Spirituality Church – Wide Initiative Kit

The Emotionally Healthy Woman
(Geri Scazzero with Pete Scazzero)

The Emotionally Healthy Spirituality (EHS) Course
(includes *The Emotionally Healthy Spirituality Course Workbook*,
The Emotionally Healthy Spirituality Course: A DVD Study,
and *Emotionally Healthy Spirituality Day by Day*)
Available at www.emotionallyhealthy.org

The
Emotionally
Healthy
Leader

How transforming your inner life will
deeply transform your church, team, and the world

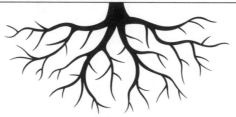

Peter Scazzero

ZONDERVAN®

ZONDERVAN

The Emotionally Healthy Leader
Copyright © 2015 by Peter Scazzero

This title is also available as a Zondervan ebook. Visit www.zondervan.com/ebooks.

This title is also available in a Zondervan audio edition. Visit www.zondervan.fm.

Requests for information should be addressed to:
Zondervan, 3900 *Sparks Dr. SE, Grand Rapids, Michigan 49546*

Library of Congress Cataloging-in-Publication Data

Scazzero, Peter, 1956-
        The emotionally healthy leader : how transforming your inner life will deeply
    transform your church, team, and the world / Peter Scazzero.
        pages cm
        ISBN 978-0-310-49457-7 (hardcover, jacketed)
        1. Clergy—Mental health. 2. Religious leaders—Mental health. 3. Christian
    leadership I. Title.
    BV4398.S295 2014
    253—dc23   2015006570

Cover design: Grey Matter Group
Interior design: Denise Froehlich

Printed in the United States of America

15 16 17 18 19 20 21 22 23 24 25 /DCI/ 20 19 18 17 16 15 14 13 12 11 10 9 8 7 6 5 4 3 2

To Geri

who taught me the meaning and
implications of the word *integrity*

CONTENTS

Part 2
The Outer Life

My Journey through Emotionally Unhealthy Leadership

I grew up in an Italian-American family in a New Jersey suburb just one mile from the skyscrapers of Manhattan. Although we lived within minutes of one of the most diverse cities in the world, our lives were narrowly defined ethnically, socially, and spiritually. When I was about ten, I remember my dad remarking one day that we were Roman Catholics living in a largely WASP town. I was confused because all our friends were Roman Catholic and most of them were Italian. What else could a person be?

My father was fiercely loyal to the church, but my mom was not. She loved gypsies, fortune-tellers, Tarot card readings, and a variety of other superstitions passed down for generations in her Italian family. When we got sick, for example, the first thing Mom did was call "Fat Josie." Fat Josie was a medium who prayed some prayers over us to determine if we had the "eyes," the invisible sign that someone had placed an evil curse on us. She then detailed the necessary steps to remove the "bad luck."

My older siblings and I rejected both the church and Italian superstitions in our teens. My parents were devastated when my brother Anthony quit college to join the Unification Church, founded by self-proclaimed messiah Sun Myung Moon. At sixteen, I was already a committed agnostic, or I too may have followed in my brother's footsteps. Neither of us could have known it at the time, but these early choices set us both on spiritual journeys that continue to this day. My brother remains actively committed to the Unification Church, and I have undergone not just one, but several life-changing conversions.

A Spiritual Journey with Four Conversions

When I tell people I have had multiple conversions, I mean it quite literally. In fact, I've experienced four dramatic conversions, and each one turned my life in a radically new direction.

Conversion 1: From Agnosticism to Zealous Christian Leader

Like many of my friends, I spent most of my teens searching for perfect love in all the wrong places. But everything changed my sophomore year of college when a friend invited me to a concert at a small Pentecostal church near campus. At the end of the concert, the worship leader invited those who wanted to receive Christ to raise their hand. When I tell this story, I often say, "God raised my hand without my permission." It sure felt that way. When the altar call was given, I bolted out of my seat and ran to the front of the church with both hands raised, praising God. I didn't know the difference between the Old and New Testaments, but I did know that I was blind, but now I could see. I also knew without a doubt that God had changed me and set his love upon me. Within nine months, I was president of a Christian group of sixty students, teaching and leading out of whatever I'd learned the week before.

The year was 1976.

I was so profoundly grateful for the love of Jesus, who lived and died on my behalf, that I could not help but share this great news with anyone who would listen, including my family. My father and I especially had many long spiritual conversations. We were sitting in the living room one weekend when I tried again to share Christ, but he remained skeptical.

"Pete, if this Christianity and Jesus you are talking about are true," he said, "then why haven't I ever heard of this 'personal relationship' thing?"

He paused for a moment, and I could see a mix of anger and sadness on his face as he looked out the living room window. "And why didn't someone talk to your brother before he destroyed his life ... before he destroyed our family?" He looked back at me and made a sweeping gesture with his hands. "Where are all these Christians you are talking about? How is it that I'm fifty-six years old and I've never met one?"

I didn't say anything because I knew the answer. Most Christians, especially those who grew up in evangelical homes, were insulated from our Italian-American world. Although my father later gave his life to Christ, I never forgot that conversation. It ignited a fire in my bones, and I set out to bridge that gap, sharing the gospel with anyone who would listen.

My career in ministry leadership continued when I joined the staff of InterVarsity Christian Fellowship, an interdenominational ministry that works with students on university campuses. I traveled around New York City and New Jersey, doing open-air preaching and mobilizing students to share Christ with their friends. In my three years on staff, I witnessed many lives radically changed by Jesus Christ. At the same time, I was developing a burden for the church. I wondered what might happen if the richness and vitality of what I had seen with students could be experienced by people in a local congregation. How might the glory of Christ spread even farther if an entire church could be radically changed and mobilized?

So off I went to prepare for church leadership, with three years of graduate study at Princeton and Gordon-Conwell seminaries. During that time, I married Geri, a friend of eight years who also was serving full-time with InterVarsity. Shortly after graduation, we moved to Costa Rica for one year of Spanish language study. I had a vision that we would return to New York to start a church that would bridge racial, cultural, economic, and gender barriers.

When we returned to New York, I served for a year as an assistant pastor in a Spanish-speaking immigrant church and taught in a Spanish seminary. During this time, Geri and I not only perfected our Spanish but were immersed in the world of 2 million undocumented immigrants from around the globe. We became friends with people who had fled death squads in El Salvador, drug cartels in Colombia, civil war in Nicaragua, and implacable poverty in Mexico and the Dominican Republic. It was just the preparation we needed for starting a new church in a working-class, multiethnic section of Queens where more than 70 percent of the 2.4 million residents are foreign born. It also shaped our understanding of the power of the gospel and the church, and how much the largely invisible poor have to teach the prosperous North American church.

In September 1987, forty-five people attended the first worship service of New Life Fellowship Church. God moved powerfully in those early years, and it wasn't long before the congregation had grown to 160 people. After three years, we launched a Spanish-speaking congregation. By the end of our sixth year, attendance at the English service had reached 400, and 250 were attending the Spanish service.

It was an exciting and rewarding experience for a young pastor. People were coming to Christ. The poor were being served in new, creative ways. We were developing leaders, multiplying small groups, feeding the homeless, and planting new churches. But all was not well beneath the surface, especially in my own life.

Conversion 2: From Emotional Blindness to Emotional Health

My soul was shrinking.

We always seemed to have too much to do and too little time to do it. While the church was an exciting place to be, there was no longer any joy in ministry leadership, just an endless, plodding duty of thankless responsibilities. After work, I had little energy left over to parent our daughters or to enjoy being with Geri. In fact, I secretly dreamed of retirement—and I was only in my mid-thirties! I also began to question the nature of Christian leadership. *Am I supposed to be miserable and pressured so that other people can experience joy in God?* It sure felt that way.

I struggled with envy and jealousy of other pastors—those with larger churches, nicer buildings, and easier situations. I didn't want to be a workaholic like my dad or other pastors I knew. I wanted to be content in God, to do ministry in the unhurried pace of Jesus. The question was, *How?*

The bottom began to fall out in 1994 when our Spanish-speaking congregation experienced a church split. I will never forget the shock I felt the day I walked into the Spanish service and two hundred people were missing—just fifty remained. Everyone else had left to start another church. People I had led to Christ, discipled, and pastored for years were gone without so much as a word.

When the split occurred, I accepted all the blame for the problems that led up to it. I tried to follow Jesus' model of remaining silent when accused, like a lamb going to slaughter (Isaiah 53:7). I repeatedly thought, *Just take it, Pete. Jesus would.* But I was also full of conflicting and unresolved emotions. I felt deeply wounded and angry at the assistant pastor who had spearheaded the split. Like the psalmist, I was devastated by the betrayal of someone "with whom I once enjoyed sweet fellowship" (Psalm 55:14). I was full of rage and hate, feelings I couldn't get rid of no matter how hard I tried to let go and forgive. When I was alone in my car, curse words came out of my mouth almost involuntarily: "He is an @#&%!"

I was now the "cursing pastor." I did not have a theology for what I was experiencing. Nor did I have a biblical framework for sadness and grief. Good Christian pastors are supposed to love and forgive people. But that wasn't me. When I shared my predicament with fellow pastors, they were afraid I was sliding into an abyss of no return. I knew I was angry and hurt, but at a deeper level I remained unaware of my feelings and what was really going on in my interior life. My larger problem now was not so much the aftermath of the split, but the fact that my pain was leaking out in destructive ways, and I couldn't control it. I angrily criticized the assistant pastor who had left. I told Geri I wasn't sure I wanted to be a Christian anymore, let alone the pastor of a church! The most helpful counsel I received was a referral to a Christian counselor.

Geri and I made an appointment and went, but I felt humiliated, like a child walking into the principal's office. In our sessions, I blamed my problems on anything and everything I could think of—the complexities of life and ministry in Queens, the unrelenting demands of church planting, Geri, our four small children, spiritual warfare, other leaders, a lack of prayer covering. It did not yet occur to me that my problems might have their roots in something to do with me.

I somehow managed to keep life and ministry going for another year before I finally hit rock bottom. On January 2, 1996, Geri told me she was quitting our church.[1] That was the end of any illusions I may have had about my innocence in the mess that had become my life. I notified church elders about Geri's decision and acknowledged my uncertainty about what should happen next. The elders suggested that Geri and I attend a one-week intensive retreat to see if we could sort things out. So we packed our bags and spent five full days with two counselors at a nearby center. My goal for the week was to find a quick way to fix Geri and end our pain so we could then get back to the real business of life and ministry. What I did not anticipate was that we would have a life-transforming encounter with God.

This was my second conversion and, much like the first, I had the experience of knowing I had been blind and suddenly received my sight. God opened my eyes to see I was a human *being*, not a human *doing*, which gave me permission to feel difficult emotions such as anger and sadness. I became aware of the significant impact my family of origin was having on my life, my marriage, and my leadership. Although I initially felt shocked by it all, the awareness also offered me a newly discovered freedom. I stopped pretending to be somebody I was not and took my first steps to be comfortable being Pete Scazzero, with my unique set of strengths, passions, and weaknesses. And Geri and I discovered the importance of love as the measure of maturity and reprioritized our schedules to place our marriage before ministry.[2]

However, this second conversion also introduced me to painful realities I could no longer deny. I was an emotional infant trying to raise up mothers and fathers of the faith. There were large areas of my life that remained untouched by Jesus Christ. For example, I didn't know how to do something as simple as being truly present or listening deeply to another person. While I was a senior pastor of a large, growing church who had been trained in two leading seminaries, attended the best leadership conferences, and been a devoted follower of Christ for seventeen years, I was stunted emotionally and spiritually.

For nearly two decades, I had ignored the emotional component in my spiritual growth and relationship with God. It didn't matter how many books I might read or how much I devoted myself to prayer, I would remain stuck in repeated cycles of pain and immaturity unless and until I allowed Jesus Christ to transform aspects of my life that were deep beneath the surface.

I discovered that my life is a lot like an iceberg—I was aware of only a fraction of it and largely unaware of the hidden mass beneath the surface. And it was this hidden mass that had wreaked havoc on my family and on my leadership.

It wasn't until I understood that these beneath-the-surface components of my life had not been transformed by Jesus that I discovered the inseparable link between emotional health and spiritual maturity — that it is not possible to be spiritually mature while remaining emotionally immature. In the months and years that followed, Geri and I changed much about the way we did life and ministry.

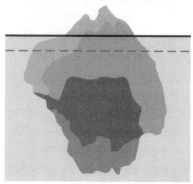

Iceberg Model
What Lies Beneath the Surface

We began by working a five-day week, not a six-and-a-half-day week. Leading out of our brokenness and weaknesses became a core value. Loving well was now the most important task among all our work for God. We slowed down the pace of ministry at New Life. As we journeyed deep beneath our own icebergs, we invited our leaders to join with us. The result was nothing short of a Copernican revolution — in my journey with Christ, in my family, and in my leadership.[3] New Life Fellowship Church blossomed.

Conversion 3: From Busy Activity to Slowed-Down Spirituality

When I first became a Christian, I fell in love with Jesus. I cherished time alone with him while reading the Bible and praying. Yet, almost immediately, the activity of my life ("doing" for Jesus) began to eclipse the contemplative dimension of my life ("being" with Jesus). I had learned early on about the importance of daily devotions to nurture my relationship with Christ, but especially as I entered ministry leadership, a daily quiet time was simply not enough. It wasn't long before I was engaged in more activity *for* God than my being *with* God could sustain.

My third conversion happened in 2003–2004 when Geri and I took a four-month sabbatical. I had been reading about monastic movements since my seminary days, and now we had the time and space to actually learn from them. We visited a number of monasteries (Protestant, Orthodox, and Roman Catholic) and embraced the monastic rhythms of solitude, silence, Scripture meditation, and prayer.

By the time the sabbatical was over, Geri and I had made radical adjustments to slow down the pace of our lives. Spending time in solitude and silence, praying the Daily Office, and practicing weekly Sabbath became our core spiritual disciplines. We experienced such joy and freedom — in our walks with Christ and in our marriage — that we wondered if perhaps God might be calling us to leave the intensity of New York City and move to a more peaceful place. But it soon became clear that these disciplines were in fact the foundational practices we needed in order to remain in Queens and continue leading the church.

As we began to teach about contemplative spirituality (which I define as slowing down to be with Jesus), integrating it with what we'd already been teaching about emotional health, great power and life were unleashed into our entire church. In every ministry — from small groups to Sunday services and equipping events — people experienced a radical resurgence of their life in Christ. And I experienced a resurgence in my leadership.

I stopped praying for God to bless my goals and started praying for his will.

I learned to wait on the Lord for the Lord himself — not for a blessing.

I worked less. God worked more.

I embraced a more balanced view of God as both immanent and transcendent, and I recognized and affirmed his work both within and beyond us.

I began to measure ministry success by the quality of people's transformed lives rather than by attendance and giving alone. The impact was so astounding that I felt compelled to write about what God was doing in our midst. The result was the publication in 2006 of *Emotionally Healthy Spirituality*. The church was growing. Lives were being changed. I felt stronger personally and professionally. But one unconquered continent of my iceberg remained untouched, which was leadership itself.

Conversion 4: From Skimming to Integrity in Leadership

While New Life was flourishing on many levels, there remained a significant disconnect between what I had learned about emotional and spiritual health and my leadership role as senior pastor. Specifically, although I was applying the principles of emotionally healthy spirituality (EHS) to my personal life, our family, our small groups and discipleship efforts in the church, I wasn't applying the same principles to my leadership. I was aware of the need to embed EHS more deeply into the organization, but I didn't know how. As I read books and attended seminars, it became clear to me that few others had done this level of integration. So I didn't either — for years.

I avoided making personnel decisions, managing staff and key volunteers, writing thoughtful job descriptions, taking time to plan for meetings, or following through on project details. On the rare occasions when I did do these things, I did so reluctantly. I saw things that clearly needed to be done, but I wanted someone else to do them.

Because I felt overwhelmed by too many things to do and attend to (sermons, pastoral decisions, leadership training events, crises among staff and congregants), I rushed and skimmed my way through some of the more difficult responsibilities of leadership.

- I avoided meetings I knew would be hard or stressful.
- I massaged the truth when being completely honest was too uncomfortable.
- I avoided performance evaluations when someone was doing a poor job.
- I failed to ask difficult questions or speak up when something was clearly wrong.
- I walked into important meetings without having taken time to be clear on my goals and agenda, or to be thoughtful and prayerful about decisions.
- I failed to allow adequate time to follow through on my commitments, which meant I dropped a lot of balls and made it difficult for staff to do their best work.
- I struggled to take the time I needed for silence and abiding in Jesus during intense planning and meeting days.
- Perhaps worst of all, I consistently disregarded the painful indicators that my life and my ministry might not be going as well as I hoped or imagined.

All of these behaviors came to a head in 2007 when several difficult events converged and broke my twenty-year leadership denial. Among them, I had to acknowledge that the church itself had hit a wall. Although we had grown in numbers and incorporated emotional health and contemplative spirituality into the lives of our people, the executive functioning of the church had gone on largely as before. And it was now obvious that addressing this failure had to begin with me.

Even so, I wanted someone else to come in and "get the house in order," to do the dirty work of hiring, firing, redirecting, and leading the church through the painful changes before us so I could continue to focus on the enjoyable things like preaching and teaching. But in choosing to avoid these difficult leadership issues, both my integrity, and that of our church, was at stake. I finally admitted the truth to myself: the greatest deterrent preventing New Life Fellowship Church from becoming what God intended was *me*.

Once again, I had to take a hard look beneath the surface of my life—this time at the hidden mass of pain and failures related to my role as a leader. As I began to consider the changes I needed to make, I soon realized that applying the principles of emotionally healthy spirituality to the tasks of leadership and building a healthy organizational culture would be far more complex than I had imagined. It was a process that led to an intense and sustained exploration of my inner life and, ultimately, to a fourth conversion.

Common wisdom in leadership practice is to delegate areas of weakness to those who have strong skills in that area. But I knew this wasn't what I needed. Instead, I made the weakest area of my leadership a key focus of my work by formally incorporating the responsibilities of executive pastor into my job. Crazy, right? But I was determined to learn how to perform this role, at least for a season. I canceled speaking engagements outside of New Life, established a teaching team, said no to a book contract, and signed up for a round of intensive counseling to sort through my own beneath-the-iceberg blockages—everything that was getting in the way of being a healthy and effective leader.

Over the next two years, I learned some key skills, many of which did not come easily. In the process, I made mistakes that hurt people. At the same time, I also developed greater courage and a willingness to have difficult conversations, to follow through on my commitments, and to gather data and facts before making important decisions. I learned that being misunderstood and having a few people leave the church as a result of my decisions was less important than losing my integrity. And even though it was often very painful, I learned to not only acknowledge the truth but to seek it out regardless of where it led me.

I was not and am not a gifted executive pastor. Yet, by investing myself in that role for a time, God was able to address issues within my character that needed to be transformed if the church was to go forward. And it was specifically through the crucible of leadership that God peeled off layers of my false self and taught me to integrate beneath-the-surface transformation with the tasks and responsibilities of leadership.

You Will Be Challenged

The Emotionally Healthy Leader was born out of the struggles and growth I experienced following my fourth conversion in 2007. I have kept a careful journal during these past eight years, chronicling my questions, internal struggles with God, mistakes, and occasional successes. Even so, I was sorely tempted not to write this book. I remain profoundly aware that I am a broken companion on this journey. I write honestly from the hard lessons of my failures. I wish I had known in my twenties, thirties, and forties what is described here.

Every page of this book was written with you — the Christian leader — in mind. As I wrote, I often imagined myself sitting across the table from you over coffee, asking you to tell me about your hopes as well as your leadership struggles and challenges. Drawing on my conversations with the many pastors and leaders I have coached, mentored, and counseled over the years, I imagined you might say something like this:

> *I want to be a better leader. I'm open and eager to learn, but I don't know where to start.*

> *I know something's not right. I feel like it's only a matter of time before something bad happens.*

> *I can't go on this way. I've hit a wall and I need help to make sense of what went wrong so I can get back on my feet and lead differently.*

I'm stuck in an environment I can't change. I'm a mid-level leader in a negative situation, and I feel powerless to change it.

I'm doing the best I can, but I'm not having an impact. I'm running programs but not changing lives. I feel plateaued and stagnant.

I'm too overwhelmed by work to enjoy life — with God, myself, and others. I'm missing out on the joys of life because of the crushing demands of leadership.

Do you relate to any of these statements? If so, then you are an excellent candidate for taking your next steps in leadership growth and transformation. As you read the pages that follow, I hope you will be sobered by the truths you may discover about yourself and your leadership, but I don't want you to despair about the possibilities for your future. I am living proof that it really is possible to tear down old ways of thinking about Christian leadership and make room for the new. I want you to be stretched theologically, emotionally, and spiritually as you discover new insights from Scripture for your life and leadership.

If you take this book seriously, it will require a lot from you — hard work, perseverance, vulnerability, humility, and a willingness to change. To be sure, you will be challenged. But my prayer is that the challenge will be matched by a compelling vision for how things might be different if you embrace the courageous choices that will allow God to transform you and your leadership. I hope you soon find yourself beginning to think things like this:

Wow, leading can be way better than I imagined.

I feel like I've walked through a door into a new world and I never want to go back.

It's hard to face up to the ways I've failed, but I have renewed hope in leading again.

I finally feel like I'm growing. I'm going somewhere and I can't go back to the way I led and lived before.

My excitement for serving as a leader has been rekindled!

By sharing my story and the hard lessons I've learned along the way, I hope to offer you the unique and personal perspective of one pastor who has been deeply engaged in a local church for more than twenty-eight years. For twenty-six of those years, I served as senior pastor; for the last two, I have been a teaching pastor and pastor-at-large. Our church in Queens, New York, represents a lower-middle-class, poorer population with people from more than seventy-three nations around the world. It is not a cushy situation by any means, but it has been a rich and fertile field for growth and transformation—personally and in my leadership.

This book is written out of my passion to see the church be faithful and fruitful in her mission for the long term. However, if we hope to transform the world with the good news of Jesus, we must begin by embarking on a personal journey, one that will lead us through a deep, beneath-the-surface transformation in our own lives. On the pages that follow, I offer a road map of sorts for that journey, complete with specific ideas and practices to help you discern God's next steps for you. It's a road map not just for pastors, but for every Christian leader. Whether you are a senior pastor, executive pastor, church staff person, an elder/deacon board member, a small group or ministry leader, a denominational or para-church staff person, a missionary, or marketplace leader, I pray you will find here truths and guidance that will not only help you to become more effective in your role but also to be personally transformed.

How to Read This Book

The chapters in the book are gathered into two parts, one focused on the inner life, and one focused on the outer life. In part 1, we'll explore the four core tasks of the inner life every leader must undertake: facing one's shadow, leading out of marriage or singleness, slowing down for loving union, and practicing Sabbath delight. If we hope to build strong ministries and organizations, these practices and values must deeply inform our spirituality.

In part 2, we'll build on the foundation of an emotionally healthy inner life by exploring four core outer-life tasks we routinely deal with in the course of leadership. These include planning and decision making, culture and team building, power and wise boundaries, endings and new beginnings.

The Emotionally Healthy Leader isn't a quick read. It is meant to be read prayerfully and carefully. I invite you to keep your journal or a pad of paper with you, making notes and writing down questions as God speaks to you. If you want to maximize the impact of what you read, I encourage you to invite at least one other person — ideally your whole team — to read and wrestle through it with you.

My hope is that this book offers you a door into a whole new way of viewing yourself and a radically new way of leading. Just as our father Abraham was called, I believe each of us is called to leave our familiar country and follow God's invitation to the unknowns of new territory — one full of promise. My prayer is that you will meet the living God in new and fresh ways as you journey through these pages, discovering, like Abraham, that the Lord has gone ahead of you, preparing riches and revelation that will not only transform you but also those you lead.

CHAPTER 1

THE EMOTIONALLY
UNHEALTHY LEADER

W hat first comes to mind when you think of an emotionally unhealthy leader? Or perhaps a better question might be, *Who* first comes to mind? Is it a boss, a staff member, a colleague? Or perhaps you? How would you describe this person? Is it someone who is chronically angry, controlling, aggressive? Or perhaps someone who is avoidant, inauthentic, passive? While emotionally unhealthy leadership expresses itself in all these ways and many more, the foundational definition of an emotionally unhealthy leader is perhaps both simpler and more multifaceted than you might expect:

> The emotionally unhealthy leader is someone who operates in a continuous state of emotional and spiritual deficit, lacking emotional maturity and a "being *with* God" sufficient to sustain their "doing *for* God."

When we talk about emotionally unhealthy Christian leaders, we are referring to the emotional and spiritual deficits that impact every aspect of their lives. *Emotional deficits* are manifested primarily by a pervasive lack of awareness. Unhealthy leaders lack, for example, awareness of their feelings, their weaknesses and limits, how their past impacts their present, and how others experience them. They also lack the capacity and skill to enter deeply into the feelings and perspectives of others. They carry these immaturities with them into their teams and everything they do.

Spiritual deficits typically reveal themselves in too much activity. Unhealthy leaders engage in more activities than their combined spiritual, physical, and emotional reserves can sustain. They give out *for* God more than they receive *from* him. They serve others in order to share the joy of Christ, but that joy remains elusive to themselves. The demands and pressures of leadership make it nearly impossible for them to establish a consistent and sustainable rhythm of life. In their more honest moments, they admit that their cup with God is empty or, at best, half full, hardly overflowing with the divine joy and love they proclaim to others.

As a result, emotionally unhealthy leaders skim when building their ministries. Rather than following the apostle Paul's example of building with materials that will last — gold, silver, and costly stones (1 Corinthians 3:10 – 15) — they settle for something like wood, straw, and mud. They build with inferior materials that will not stand the test of a generation, let alone the fire of final judgment. In the process, they obscure the beauty of Christ they say they want the whole world to see. No well-intentioned leader would set out to lead this way, but it happens all the time.

Consider a few examples from the everyday lives of leaders you may recognize.

Sara is an overwhelmed youth pastor who needs help, but she always finds a reason to avoid enlisting a team of adult volunteers who could come alongside her and expand the ministry. It's not because she lacks leadership gifts, but because she is defensive and easily offended when others disagree with her. The youth group stagnates and slowly declines.

Joseph is a dynamic worship leader who nevertheless keeps losing key volunteers because of his lateness and spontaneity. He doesn't see how his "style" alienates people who have different temperaments. Thinking he is just being "authentic" and true to who he is, he's not willing to make changes or accommodate other styles and temperaments. The quality of music and effectiveness leading people to the presence of Jesus at weekend services diminish as volunteers with gifts in music and programming drop out of the worship team.

Jake is the volunteer director of the small group ministry at his church. Under his leadership, the ministry has begun to flourish — four new groups have formed in the last three months! Twenty-five people, previously unconnected, now meet every other week to share their lives as they grow in Christ together. Beneath the excitement, however, cracks are beginning to show. The group leader in the fastest-growing group is new to the church and appears to be taking the group in a different direction than the larger church. Jake is worried, but he avoids talking to him, fearful the conversation may not go well. Another small group leader has mentioned in passing that things aren't going well at home. In yet another group, one troublesome member is talking way too much, and the group is rapidly losing people. The group leader has asked Jake for help, but he is trying to avoid getting involved. While greatly loved by most, Jake is conflict averse. He secretly hopes the issue will somehow resolve itself without involving him. Over the next six months, three of the four new small groups close.

The list of examples could go on and on, but I think you get the point. When we devote ourselves to reaching the world for Christ while ignoring our own emotional and spiritual health, our leadership is shortsighted at best. At worst, we are negligent, needlessly hurting others and undermining God's desire to expand his kingdom through us. Leadership is hard. It involves suffering. But there is a big difference between suffering for the gospel as Paul describes (2 Timothy 2:8) and needless suffering that is a result of our unwillingness to honestly engage difficult and challenging leadership tasks.

Four Characteristics of the Emotionally Unhealthy Leader

The deficits of emotionally unhealthy leaders impact virtually every area of their lives and leadership. However, the damage is especially evident in four characteristics: low self-awareness, prioritizing ministry over marriage/singleness, doing too much for God, and failing to practice a Sabbath rhythm.

They Have Low Self-Awareness

Emotionally unhealthy leaders tend to be unaware of what is going on inside them. And even when they recognize a strong emotion such as anger, they fail to process or express it honestly and appropriately.

They ignore emotion-related messages their body may send—fatigue, stress-induced illness, weight gain, ulcers, headaches, or depression. They avoid reflecting on their fears, sadness, or anger. They fail to consider how God might be trying to communicate with them through these "difficult" emotions. They struggle to articulate the reasons for their emotional triggers, their overreactions in the present rooted in difficult experiences from their past.

While these leaders may have benefited from personal and leadership inventories such as the Myers-Briggs Type Indicator, StrengthsFinder, or the DiSC profile, they remain unaware of how issues from their family of origin have impacted who they are today. This lack of emotional awareness also extends to their personal and professional relationships in their inability to read and resonate with the emotional world of others. In fact, they are often blind to the emotional impact they have on others, especially in their leadership role. Perhaps you'll recognize this dynamic in Sam's story.

Sam, age forty-seven, is senior pastor of a church whose attendance has plateaued. It's Tuesday morning and he's sitting in his usual place at the head of the table for the weekly staff meeting. Also around the table are Sam's ministry assistant, the assistant pastor, the youth director, the children's pastor, the worship leader, and the church administrator. After opening in prayer, Sam updates the team on the attendance figures and finances for the past nine months. It's a topic that's been on the agenda before, but this time there's a sharpness in Sam's demeanor, and everyone in the room knows he's not happy.

"How are we going to buy a new building so we can reach more people for Christ if we aren't growing now?" he asks. Everyone is suddenly quiet as a painfully tense atmosphere fills the room. "We've added only twenty people since January, not nearly enough to meet our goal of seventy-five adults by the end of the year."

Sam's frustration and anxiety are palpable. Sam's assistant tries to ease the tension by mentioning how the bad weather this past winter almost shut down the church on two Sundays. Surely, that had an impact on the numbers. But Sam quickly dismisses her comment, noting the issues are much deeper than that. Though he hasn't come right out and said it, it's clear Sam blames the staff for the shortfall.

Sam feels justified in forcing the difficult questions and confronting the hard data. *I'm just trying to help us be good stewards of God's resources,* he tells himself. *We are paid with the tithes of people. We all need to work hard and smart to earn our salaries. Hey, there are volunteers around here who give ten to fifteen hours a week for no pay at all!* But even he is a little surprised by how angry he feels and the harshness in his tone.

Still, it hasn't occurred to him that his heightened frustration might have anything to do with an e-mail he got the day before. Someone from out of town sent him a link to a news article about the rapid growth of a church plant just ten miles away and asked if Sam knew the new pastor. Sam's stomach immediately knotted and his shoulders tightened when he read it. He knew better than to compare and be competitive when it comes to ministry, but he couldn't help but resent the new pastor and his success. Though he can't admit it even to himself, he also felt inse-cure—afraid some of the younger families might leave to be part of a more exciting church.

After giving everyone around the table a week to identify three ways to improve programs and performance, Sam dispenses with the rest of the agenda and abruptly ends the meeting. He has no clue how his lack of self-awareness is negatively impacting him, his staff, and the church.

They Prioritize Ministry over Marriage or Singleness

Whether married or single, most emotionally unhealthy leaders affirm the importance of a healthy intimacy in relationships and life-style, but few, if any, have a vision for their marriage or singleness as the greatest gift they offer. Instead, they view their marriage or single-ness as an essential and stable foundation for something more import-ant—building an effective ministry, which is their first priority. As a result, they invest the best of their time and energy in becoming better equipped as a leader, and invest very little in cultivating a great mar-riage or single life that reveals Jesus' love to the world.

Emotionally unhealthy leaders tend to compartmentalize their mar-ried or single life, separating it from both their leadership and their relationship with Jesus. For example, they might make significant lead-ership decisions without thinking through the long-term impact those decisions could have on the quality and integrity of their single or mar-ried life. They dedicate their best energy, thought, and creative efforts to leading others, and they fail to invest in a rich and full married or single life. Consider the story of Luis.

Luis, a twenty-seven-year-old youth pastor, serves on staff at a small but fast-growing church—in the last three years, attendance has grown from 150 to almost 250 people. It's past 10:00 p.m. on a Thursday night and Luis is working late—again. The weeknight student Bible study he teaches wrapped up almost an hour ago, but he's still at his desk sending e-mails and catching up. On top of his regular job, he's taken on the responsibility for launching a number of new community outreach initiatives as a follow-up to their record-setting Easter attendance. When Luis first started working at the church three years ago, he thought the intense pace would eventually settle down, but it hasn't. If anything, it's only gotten faster.

Luis loves his job, and he doesn't mind taking on the extra projects, but his hours are starting to become an issue at home. Throughout their four-year marriage, his wife, Sofia, has always been his biggest cheerleader, affirming his gifts and encouraging him to follow God's call into ministry. But lately she's been less supportive. She even admitted she sometimes feels jealous of his job and wonders if he loves the church more than he loves her. He reasons that maybe she's just tired. Their first baby is due in six months, and it's been a difficult pregnancy. Maybe that's the reason she's lost sight of how important this work is.

Luis wonders, *How can I give less than my best to the church when people's lives and eternities are at stake? She has to understand that.* As he finally closes his laptop and turns off the lights, Luis breathes a prayer: *God, please ignite Sofia with a new vision for what you are doing in the church.* He doesn't realize he is hurting his spouse and that his prayer for her isn't going to change that.

They Do More Activity for God than Their Relationship with God Can Sustain

Emotionally unhealthy leaders are chronically overextended. Although they routinely have too much to do in too little time, they persist in saying a knee-jerk yes to new opportunities before prayerfully and carefully discerning God's will. The notion of a slowed-down spirituality—or slowed-down leadership—in which their *doing for Jesus* flows out of their *being with Jesus* is a foreign concept.

If they think of it at all, spending time in solitude and silence is viewed as a luxury or something best suited for a different kind of leader, not part of their core spiritual practices or essential for effective leadership. Their first priority is leading their organization, team, or ministry as a means of impacting the world for Christ. If you were to ask them to list their top three priorities for how they spend their time as a leader, it's unlikely that cultivating a deep, transformative relationship with Jesus would make the list. As a result, fragmentation and depletion constitute the "normal" condition for their lives and their leadership. You may recognize yourself or someone you know in Carly's story.

Carly is a thirty-four-year-old worship leader at an 800-person church. She grew into this role beginning as a volunteer musician ten years ago when attendance was less than 100 people. In addition to leading a volunteer worship team and planning weekend services, Carly oversees the programming team. It's a huge job involving dozens of volunteers as well as four paid staff, but somehow she makes it look easy. In fact, she's so good at what she does that every year Barry, the assistant pastor and her supervisor, challenges her to take on more responsibilities.

Lately, however, Carly hasn't been keeping up. She's showed up late for meetings, missed a couple minor deadlines, and neglected to return important phone calls. Even with these recent misses, she trusts that things must be okay because her work at church is flourishing. But in her more honest moments, she has doubts. *How can things be going so well on the outside when I feel like I'm dying on the inside?*

Between morning meetings, the semi-regular crises of people on her team, and things to do at home, she doesn't have much time for herself or a lot of energy left over to spend time with God in prayer or Scripture. Every week it's a battle just to get to the grocery store, cook some semi-healthy meals, exercise, and do a few loads of laundry. The speeding ticket she got last week is an accurate reflection of her life—she's going way too fast. "I feel like I'm so swamped building the church and creating environments for others to meet God," she told Barry recently, "that I wonder if I lost Jesus somewhere along the way. I need something to help me feel connected to God again."

Barry was sympathetic and understanding. He suggested a few books that had been helpful to him and offered to pay for Carly to attend an upcoming training conference for worship leaders. But no book or conference will address the underlying issues in Carly's life or give her what she really needs — time to slow down for God, for others, and, most importantly, herself.

They Lack a Work/Sabbath Rhythm

Emotionally unhealthy leaders do not practice Sabbath — a weekly, twenty-four-hour period in which they cease all work and rest, delight in God's gifts, and enjoy life with him. They might view Sabbath observance as irrelevant, optional, or even a burdensome legalism that belongs to an ancient past. Or they may make no distinction between the biblical practice of Sabbath and a day off, using "Sabbath" time for the unpaid work of life, such as paying bills, grocery shopping, and errands. If they practice Sabbath at all, they do so inconsistently, believing they need to first finish all their work or work hard enough to "earn" the right to rest. Notice this dynamic in John's story.

John is a fifty-six-year-old denominational leader responsible for overseeing more than sixty churches. He hasn't had a real vacation — the kind where you don't check e-mail or write anything — for several years, let alone practiced a weekly Sabbath. It's early Saturday morning and he's having coffee with Craig, a longtime pastor friend, before heading to the office to catch up on e-mails and write a monthly report that was due last week.

"John, you look beat," Craig says. "When was the last time you took a day off and really rested?"

" 'We can rest when we get to heaven.' At least that's what my seminary professor used to say thirty years ago. God is always working, and we're supposed to join him in that work, right?"

But it's clear that John is tired nearly to the point of exhaustion.

"I know you love your work," Craig replies, "but what else in your life right now gives you joy and delight?"

After a moment of silence with his head down, John utters quietly, "It's been so long since I've had time to even think about such a question, I don't know what to say."

After another long silence he adds, "But what am I supposed to do? All the pastors and denominational leaders I know work like this."

"Really?" Craig responds with a gentle smile. "That's your excuse?"

"Okay," John answers, "you're right. I'll go back to trying to take Mondays off."

An hour later at the office, John takes a look at his calendar and realizes he's booked with appointments and writing deadlines for five of the next six Mondays. *Who am I kidding?* he thinks. *Taking a day off every week just isn't practical for me right now. I'll just have to catch some down time whenever my schedule allows for it.* But chances are that John's schedule will never allow for it. And the occasional day off will not be enough for him to develop the rhythm of work and rest he needs in order to be a healthy and effective leader for his team and the churches he oversees.

At the beginning of this chapter, I asked what or who came to mind when you think of an emotionally unhealthy leader. So how do the four characteristics we just explored line up with your initial ideas? Did you recognize yourself in any of the descriptions? Perhaps you're thinking, *Yes, I relate to most of these characteristics.* Or maybe you're still somewhat skeptical, thinking, *That's just the nature of leadership. I know people who are a lot more unhealthy than the people you just described, but are still effective leaders.* While it's true that none of the characteristics or stories appear to be especially dramatic, over time these leaders and the ministries they serve will pay a heavy price if such unhealthy behaviors continue unchecked.

If we can agree that the long-term consequences of unhealthy leadership are a threat to the health and effectiveness of the church, the question we have to ask ourselves is, *Why do we persist in unhealthy patterns?* You would think the church and its leaders would be all for healthy leadership and whatever it takes to achieve it. But the truth is that there are parts of church leadership culture that actually work hard against it. If you decide to be intentional about pursuing emotionally healthy leadership, you're going to face some "friendly fire." You're going to have to do battle with what I call the four unhealthy commandments of church leadership.

How Healthy Is Your Leadership?

Being an emotionally unhealthy leader is not an all-or-nothing condition; it operates on a continuum that ranges from mild to severe, and may change from one season of life and ministry to the next. Use the list of statements that follow to get an idea of where you're at right now. Next to each statement, write down the number that best describes your response. Use the following scale:

5 = Always true of me
4 = Frequently true of me
3 = Occasionally true of me
2 = Rarely true of me
1 = Never true of me

_____ 1. I take sufficient time to experience and process difficult emotions such as anger, fear, and sadness.

_____ 2. I am able to identify how issues from my family of origin impact my relationships and leadership — both negatively and positively.

_____ 3. (If married): The way I spend my time and energy reflects the value that my marriage — not leadership — is my first priority.

(If single): The way I spend my time and energy reflects the value that living out a healthy singleness — not leadership — is my first priority.

_____ 4. (If married): I experience a direct connection between my oneness with Jesus and oneness with my spouse.

(If single): I experience a direct connection between my oneness with Jesus and closeness with my friends and family.

_____ 5. No matter how busy I am, I consistently practice the spiritual disciplines of solitude and silence.

_____ 6. I regularly read Scripture and pray in order to enjoy communion with God and not just in service of leading others.

_____ 7. I practice Sabbath — a weekly twenty-four-hour period in which I stop my work, rest, and delight in God's many gifts.

_____ 8. I view Sabbath as a spiritual discipline that is essential for both my personal life and my leadership.

_____ 9. I take time to practice prayerful discernment when making plans and decisions.

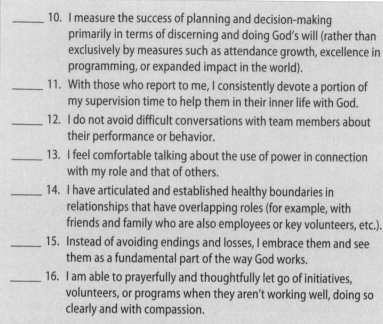

_____ 10. I measure the success of planning and decision-making primarily in terms of discerning and doing God's will (rather than exclusively by measures such as attendance growth, excellence in programming, or expanded impact in the world).

_____ 11. With those who report to me, I consistently devote a portion of my supervision time to help them in their inner life with God.

_____ 12. I do not avoid difficult conversations with team members about their performance or behavior.

_____ 13. I feel comfortable talking about the use of power in connection with my role and that of others.

_____ 14. I have articulated and established healthy boundaries in relationships that have overlapping roles (for example, with friends and family who are also employees or key volunteers, etc.).

_____ 15. Instead of avoiding endings and losses, I embrace them and see them as a fundamental part of the way God works.

_____ 16. I am able to prayerfully and thoughtfully let go of initiatives, volunteers, or programs when they aren't working well, doing so clearly and with compassion.

Take a moment to briefly review your responses. What stands out most to you? Although there is no definitive scoring for the assessment, at the end of the chapter (page 46) are some general observations that may help you understand more about where you're at.

Wherever you find yourself, the good news is that you *can* make progress and learn to become an increasingly healthy leader. In fact, God has specifically wired our bodies and neurochemistry for transformation and change — even into our nineties! So even if the truth about the current state of your leadership is sobering, don't be discouraged. If someone like me can learn and grow through all the failures and mistakes I've made, it is possible for anyone to make progress in becoming an emotionally healthy leader!

Four Unhealthy (and Unspoken) Commandments of Church Leadership

Every family has "commandments" — those unspoken rules about what is okay and not okay to say and do. Growing up, we naturally absorb and follow these rules that govern the way our families do life. If our families were places of warmth, safety, and respect, then we absorb those qualities like the air we breathe. They inform our understanding of ourselves and the way we interact with the world. If our families were instead places where coldness, shame, put-downs, and perfectionism were the norm, we naturally absorb these qualities, and they too inform the way we view ourselves and how we engage the world.

In the same way, we have been birthed into a church family that has its own unhealthy and largely unspoken commandments about leadership. If you want to become an emotionally healthy leader, sooner or later you will have to resist the pull of one or more of these commandments.

Unhealthy Commandment 1: It's Not a Success Unless It's Bigger and Better

Most of us have been taught to measure success by external markers. In the context of the church, we typically measure things like attendance, baptisms, memberships, people serving, number of small groups, and financial giving. And let's be clear—numbers aren't all bad. In fact, quantifying ministry impact with numbers is actually biblical. Jesus commands us to make disciples of *all* nations. More than once, the book of Acts uses numbers to describe the impact of the gospel— about 3,000 baptized (Acts 2:41), about 5,000 believers (Acts 4:4), crowds of men and women coming to faith (Acts 5:14). We have a whole book in the Bible called Numbers. Naturally, I and virtually every pastor I know desire to see our churches grow in numbers and add people for the sake of Christ.

But let's also be clear: There is a wrong way to deal with numbers. When we use numbers to compare ourselves to others or to boast of our size, we cross a line. When King David commissioned Joab to conduct a census of all the fighting men, the results for his leadership were disastrous. Motivated by pride, David placed his trust not in God, but in the size of the Israelite army. His focus on numbers was idolatrous, and the Lord brought a severe plague of judgment across all of Israel for this sin (1 Chronicles 21; 2 Samuel 24). Seventy thousand people died.

Numerical growth is what the world equates with power and significance. It is an absolute value—bigger is *always* better. If you run a big company or organization, people esteem you more than they do the owner of a one-person start-up. If you are a millionaire versus a person on public assistance, you can expect people to treat you with greater deference. If you work at a church, the size of your team or your ministry affects the way people view you.

When it comes to the church and numbers, the problem isn't that we count, it's that we have so fully embraced the world's dictum that bigger is better that numbers have become the *only* thing we count. When something isn't bigger and better, we consider it — and often ourselves — a failure. What we miss in all this counting is the value Scripture places on *internal* markers. What constitutes failure in the eyes of the world isn't always a failure in the kingdom of God.

For example, Jesus' stunning success in teaching and feeding the 5,000 at the beginning of John 6 is followed just a few paragraphs later by a corresponding numerical failure: "At this point many of his disciples turned away and deserted him" (John 6:66 NLT). Jesus didn't wring his hands and question his preaching strategy; he remained content, knowing he was in the Father's will. He had a larger perspective on what God was doing.

Success isn't always bigger and better.

The teaching of Jesus is that we are to abide in him *and* abound in fruit (see John 15:1 – 8). It's not about choosing one or the other — abounding in growth *or* abiding in Jesus. What abiding and abounding looks like will differ depending on our unique leadership callings. Cloistered monks who spend most of their time in prayer and offering spiritual direction will bear a different kind and quantity of fruit than I will as a pastor of a church in New York City.

Perhaps the best biblical text about this issue is found in Luke 10. Jesus sends out seventy-two disciples two by two. When they return, they are excited to report significant numerical impact and that the demons submit to them in his name. Jesus affirms their activity of kingdom building, but he also reminds them of something more important: "Do not rejoice that the spirits submit to you, but rejoice that your names are written in heaven" (Luke 10:20). In other words, he wants them to remember that their joy comes from their relationship *with* him, not their achievements *for* him.[1]

How then do we resist obeying this bigger-is-better commandment? The only way, I believe, is to slow down our lives for a relationship of deep, loving union with Jesus (more about this in chapter 4), and to have a few trusted companions who protect us from self-deception. When I find myself thinking "bigger and better," I often ask myself this question: "Am I casting this vision of growth from my own ambitions or from the mouth of the Lord?" (see Jeremiah 23:16–20).

Unhealthy Commandment 2: What You Do Is More Important than Who You Are

What we do matters — to a point. Whether you're a board member, pastor, ministry or small group leader, a worship team member, greeter, children's ministry volunteer, or a marketplace leader, your competency and skill set to do that task are vitally important. And, hopefully, you want to develop your skills and increase your effectiveness.

But who you *are* is more important than what you *do*. Why? Because the love of Jesus in you is the greatest gift you have to give to others. Who you are as a person — and specifically how well you love — will always have a larger and longer impact on those around you than what you do. Your *being with* God (or lack of being with God) will trump, eventually, your *doing for* God every time.

We cannot give what we do not possess. We cannot help but give what we do possess.

We can give inspiring messages about the importance of spiritual transformation and enjoying the journey with Christ. We may quote famous authors. We may preach rich truths out of Scripture and craft clever blogs and tweets. But if we have not lived the truths we teach and been transformed by them personally, the spiritual transformation of those we serve will be stunted. I am not saying there will be none. Just not much.

Trust me, I know.

I spent the early years of my pastoral career giving sermons I did not have time to patiently and thoughtfully live. I thought, *How can any leader possibly take in all the truth they teach each week and still keep up with all the demands of leadership?* I didn't work sufficiently on my interior life or consider how my family of origin impacted who I was as a leader. I wasn't willing to sit with a mature mentor or counselor to look at my beneath-the-surface issues. I was too busy building the church, making things happen. I figured as long as I was using my gifts for God and the fruit of my leadership was evident, all was good—even if my inner life was filled with chaos and anxiety.

I was wrong.

Inevitably, my interior life was reproduced in my exterior ministry. How could it not be? Especially when I couldn't see that who I was on the inside with God was more important than what I did for God.

Jesus' identity was firmly rooted in *being* the beloved of the Father before he ever engaged the *doing* of public ministry. In the first thirty years of his life, Jesus did nothing extraordinary. Nonetheless, before his public ministry began, the Father said to him, "You are my Son, whom I love; with you I am well pleased" (Luke 3:22).

The three temptations the devil posed to Jesus after his forty days in the wilderness focused specifically on this issue of doing versus being (Matthew 4:1–11). Two of the three temptations begin with the words, "If you are the Son of God ... [*do* something]." The third offers a bribe to get Jesus to "bow down and worship [Satan]." The evil one was intent that Jesus' *doing*—not his *being* with God—be the foundation of his life and ministry. And that is, I believe, among the first temptations the evil one poses to every leader. When we succumb to it, we rush headlong into initiatives God never asked us to undertake and, slowly, we become disconnected from the Father's love.

What do we do to resist the influence of this commandment? Repeat after me: *What I do matters. Who I am matters much more.* Remember Jesus' priority of being with the Father. Watch for the internal signs that you are exceeding your limits, doing more for God than your abiding relationship with him can sustain (for example, lack of peace, irritability, rushing). Make it your first priority and goal to seek his face and to do his will each day.

Unhealthy Commandment 3: Superficial Spirituality Is Okay

For years, I assumed. I assumed that anyone who attended church and listened to biblical teaching—in our church and others—would experience transformation. I assumed that gifted worship leaders were as passionate for Christ in private as they were passionate for him in public worship. I assumed pastors, administrative staff, missionaries, board members, and para-church workers routinely devoted them-selves to nurturing a deep, personal relationship with Jesus.

I assumed wrong.

Now I don't assume anything. Instead, I ask.

I ask leaders to tell me about how they are cultivating their rela-tionship with God. I ask questions like: "Describe to me your rhythms, how you study Scripture apart from preparations, when and how much time you spend alone with God." I ask them how they structure their time with God and what they do. The more I've asked these questions of pastors and Christian leaders around the world, the more alarmed I have become. Most leaders don't have good answers.

The problem is that in most settings, as long as leaders are doing their jobs (volunteer or paid), everyone is pleased. If their ministry is growing, we are thrilled. Who are we to judge if someone's relationship with Christ is superficial or lacking? I agree we don't want to judge, but we do want to be discerning. Just because we have the gifts and skills to build a crowd and create lots of activity does not mean we are building a church or ministry that connects people intimately to Jesus.

I love the Lord's instruction to Samuel, "The LORD does not look at the things people look at. People look at the outward appearance, but the LORD looks at the heart" (see 1 Samuel 16:7). In other words, we don't look simply on the outside; we are concerned about the heart, beginning with our own.

Consider this historical example. In the seventh century, the church in Arabia and North Africa appeared prosperous. They had a rich history going back to the first century. They were theologically sophisticated, boasted well-known leaders and bishops, and exercised considerable influence in the culture. Nonetheless, Islam advanced over these Christian churches in a very short time. Most church historians agree the church as a whole was beset by a superficial spirituality that was unable to withstand the intense assault of this new religion. Local churches were divided from each other over minor doctrinal points, refusing to recognize the presence of Jesus in those with whom they dif-fered. Moreover, they failed to translate the Scriptures into Arabic, the language of the people. As a result, while attendance was strong and the financial giving stable, people were not grounded in Jesus. Their lack of a spiritually solid foundation as churches led to a rapid collapse under the weight and pressure of an advancing, intolerant Islam.[2]

How can we overcome the lure of this deadly commandment?

We slow down. We commit ourselves to learning from the contemplative tradition and writings of leaders through church history. And we apprentice ourselves to the wider global church, to believers who, though different from us in some ways, have much to teach us about such things as solitude, silence, and stillness with God as we labor to bring the good news of Jesus to the world around us.

Unhealthy Commandment 4: Don't Rock the Boat as Long as the Work Gets Done

In the late sixth century BC, the prophet Jeremiah condemned the leaders of God's people for tolerating a false peace and security. "They dress the wound of my people as though it were not serious," the prophet lamented. " 'Peace, peace,' they say, when there is no peace" (Jeremiah 6:14). I imagine these ancient leaders were much like we are. They avoided and even denied the existence of problems and conflict because they didn't want to rock the boat.

Thousands of years later, not much has changed in this regard. Too much of contemporary church culture is characterized by a false niceness and superficiality. We view conflict as a sign that something is wrong, so we do whatever we can to avoid it. We prefer to ignore difficult issues and settle for a false peace, hoping our difficulties will somehow disappear on their own.

They don't.

For years, I turned a blind eye to staff issues I should have been engaging promptly and directly — everything from sloppy preparation, lack of approachability, judgmentalism, failure to spend time with God, marriages that were not doing well, to name a few. My first concern, so I reasoned, was to keep the church moving, and wading into the muddy waters of conflict and hard conversations felt like lurching to an abrupt and unwelcome stop. But as we all learn sooner or later, I discovered that I couldn't build God's kingdom with lies and pretense. I found out the things I ignored eventually erupted into much bigger problems later. We have to ask the painful, difficult questions we prefer to ignore or the church will pay a much larger price later.

The apostle Peter had no qualms about rocking the boat even in the midst of a revival meeting. He confronted Ananias and then his wife Sapphira when they pretended to be something they were not (Acts 5:1–11). When Barnabas sold a field and donated all the proceeds to the church, Ananias and Sapphira followed suit—but with one difference. They made a pretense of donating everything from the sale while secretly keeping back part of the money for themselves. When confronted, they even lied about it. They pretended to be something on the outside they were not on the inside and paid for the lie with their lives. Right there in church, they both died on the spot. It is an excruciating story, but a very effective lesson for leaders about the need to engage rather than avoid conflict and difficult conversations.

I often wonder what might have happened to this 5,000-member church if Peter had allowed this kind of lie to go unchallenged in the name of not rocking the boat. Would such posturing and pretending have spread into families, leadership gatherings, worship services, and community outreach? Would the church have had the strength of character and maturity to continue following God's will as the book of Acts describes? Would the Holy Spirit's power have been quenched and the advance of the church stalled? Fortunately, we don't have to speculate. Peter's refusal to tolerate a false peace laid a solid foundation for the integrity and the future of the church.

So do you see why being aware of and resisting these commandments is so important?

If we allow ourselves and our leadership to be formed by these faulty, unspoken commandments—even in small ways—we increase the likelihood of devastating, long-term consequences. Odds are good we will damage ourselves—physically, spiritually, emotionally, and relationally. We may well damage our families and friends because they get only the leftovers of our attention and energy. And we will damage the people we serve by failing to bring them into spiritual/emotional maturity so they can offer their lives to the world. I could have avoided so much needless pain and wasted years if I had been aware of and resisted these commandments in the early years of my ministry.

Learning to Be an Emotionally Healthy Leader Takes Time

"So then, where do I go from here?" you may be asking.

The rest of the book is an invitation to go on a journey into becoming an emotionally healthy leader — a leader who can build an emotionally healthy ministry for the sake of Christ in the world. That is no small task. In fact, if you decide to set out on this path, you will most likely experience times of confusion, fear, and grief. It's a state I know well. I can also tell you that your fears might take the form of whispers from that accusing and self-protective voice inside you:

You don't know what you are doing.

Do you realize what could happen if you take this road?

Okay, sure, you can try to be emotionally healthy, but no one will respect you, and the church will shrink to nothing.

Why should you try to do leadership this way? Other leaders aren't and they seem to be doing just fine!

Face it: this isn't going to work for you.

You don't have time for this right now. Try it later, when things settle down.

I know that voice well. So trust me when I tell you not to listen to it. Know that God invites you to take only one step at a time, one day at a time. God also understands that growth and change take time. In my experience, even relatively simple changes sometimes take years to fully implement (see "The Five-Stage Process of How We Learn and Change," page 46). God sees your present leadership context and challenges and he knows what you need — not only to meet the challenges but to grow into a stronger leader because of them. While the journey can feel lonely at times, that too may be part of God's process of teaching you to wait on him and to trust in him. You can expect God to send key people and resources your way at just the right time to help you take your next step. He *always* has done that for me. And be sure to invite others to pray with you and support you along the way.

Most importantly, remember that the Holy Spirit who lives within you will guide you into all truth and grant you supernatural power from outside yourself. Over the years, there have been many times I felt overwhelmed because I lacked the maturity, wisdom, or character to overcome the leadership challenges I faced. It was precisely at those times when God would remind me, *Do not be afraid ... with [humans] this is impossible, but not with God; all things are possible with God* (Joshua 1:9; Mark 10:27).

With that said, let's get started.

The Five-Stage Process of How We Learn and Change

Benjamin Bloom, a great educational psychologist, along with a team of thinkers, developed a brilliant taxonomy that describes how people learn in different domains. This has been adapted and revised many times over the last sixty years, and continues to be a standard in many educational systems around the world.[3] Bloom distinguishes five levels of knowing, or "getting," a value. We tend to think in one of two ways: I know something or I don't know something. For example, I value caring for the poor or I don't value caring for the poor. What we don't always understand is it takes a long time — and many small incremental steps — to really "get" a new value. In fact, it requires moving through five distinct levels.[4]

Let me illustrate this with my own journey of coming to value slowing down my life to spend more time with Jesus.

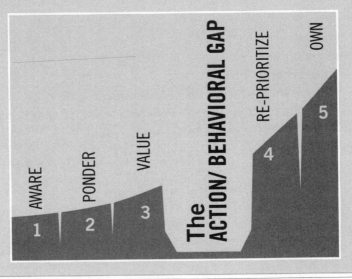

1. *Awareness: "Slowing down is an interesting idea."* I first thought about this in a serious way in 1994 when I was experiencing pain in both my personal life and in my leadership.

2. *Ponder: "Help me understand more about slowing down."* When I started the emotionally healthy journey in 1996, I read books, listened to messages on slowing down, and preached about it in sermons.

3. *Value: "I really believe it is important for everybody to slow down."* I dabbled in a few new behaviors like Sabbath, solitude, and one-day retreats with God, but my actions and behaviors didn't fundamentally change. For years.

4. *Prioritize: "I am shifting my entire life around as I slow down to be with Jesus."* When I took my second sabbatical in 2003 – 2004, I reprioritized my time, energy, and schedule in order to integrate this new value for a four-month period. It helped me to kick-start a new way of leading and living out this value. It was life changing.

5. *Own: "All my decisions and actions are based on this new value."* Moving from *prioritizing* to *owning* took me another six to eight years. I had a lot of work to do to integrate this value with the demands and challenges of pastoring New Life. While I still fail at times, slowing down to be with Jesus now informs all I do. My entire body feels it when I, or others around me, violate this value.

You'll notice that the chart highlights the large gap between levels three and four — *value* and *prioritize*. Why? Because that is the point that requires a radical, often difficult shift. Many leaders love the ideas and principles of emotionally healthy spirituality. However, moving from *valuing* to *prioritizing* is a formidable challenge. I understand why.

So let me encourage you. The changes you seek won't happen overnight, but they will happen. Take your time. Read slowly. Entrust yourself to God's care and ask him to lead you into the next step in your process. Thousands of leaders around the world are on the journey with you and have already begun to experience powerful transformation in both their personal lives and their leadership.

Stay with it, taking one step at a time. Neither you, nor those you lead, will ever be the same.

Understanding Your Healthy Leadership Assessment

If you took the leadership assessment on pages 34–35, here are some observations to help you better understand the condition of your leadership right now.

If you scored mostly ones and twos, your leadership is more unhealthy than healthy, and you are likely functioning emotionally at the level of a child or infant. If that sounds harsh, you can at least take comfort in knowing you are far from alone. This was where I found myself after seventeen years as a Christ-follower, with a seminary degree, and eight years of pastoral experience. And most pastors I mentor are in a similar place. Growing up into spiritual and emotional adulthood takes years, even decades, not days or months. So take a deep breath. Relax. You are not alone.

If you scored mostly twos and threes, you have begun the journey, but you are likely functioning emotionally at the level of an adolescent. Your Christian life may be primarily about *doing*, not *being*, and you are feeling the effects of that on your soul. You have yet to apply personal values — such as slowing down to be with Jesus or prioritizing your marriage/singleness — to the way you lead your team. You are aware of your strengths, weaknesses, and limits, but more work probably is needed in this area. Consider how God may be inviting you to a more robust inner life and deeper spiritual practices so you can take your team and ministry to another level. Expect to be challenged personally as well as in your leadership in a number of crucial areas as you read.

If you scored mostly fours and fives, your leadership is more healthy than unhealthy, and you are likely functioning emotionally at the level of an adult. You have a healthy sense of your strengths, limits, and weaknesses as a leader. You are able to assert your beliefs and values without being adversarial. You protect and prioritize your relationships with your spouse (if applicable), friends, and family. You have a good sense of your identity as a leader and how to relate to those around you. And you are well on your way to integrating your *doing* for God with a solid base of *being* with him. Expect greater clarity and insights, both for yourself and those you lead, as you continue to apply these principles to your life and leadership.

Part 1

The Inner Life

Leading a church, an organization, or a ministry that transforms the world requires more than the latest leadership strategies and techniques. Lasting change in churches and organizations requires men and women committed to leading from a deep and transformed inner life. We lead more out of who we are than out of what we do, strategic or otherwise. If we fail to recognize that who we are on the inside informs every aspect of our leadership, we will do damage to ourselves and to those we lead.

There are many issues we might identify as important to developing and transforming the inner life of a leader. I've chosen to focus on four that have emerged as foundational, both in my own life and in two decades of mentoring other leaders. I've discovered that to lead from a deep and transformed inner life, you must:

- Face Your Shadow
- Lead Out of Your Marriage/Singleness
- Slow Down for Loving Union
- Practice Sabbath Delight

Building a ministry, a church, or a nonprofit is a lot like building a skyscraper. First you dig down for the foundation, and then you build up. The foundation in this case is your inner life. The quality and durability of the building — the team or organization you lead — will be determined by how carefully this foundation is laid. Let me illustrate this.

The island of Manhattan consists almost entirely of bare granite, a very hard and strong type of rock. To carry the weight of a 75- or 100-story skyscraper, builders use foundation anchors called "piles." Piles are concrete or steel columns hammered into the ground until they penetrate solid rock.

For especially tall buildings, some piles are driven twenty-five stories below ground. The heavy weight of the skyscraper is then distributed through each of the piles. Together they support the structure's enormous weight. If foundation piles are drilled and driven in poorly, cracks will eventually appear in the structure. Entire buildings may lean. Then they must be torn down or lifted completely so the piles can be reset — a costly and time-consuming process.

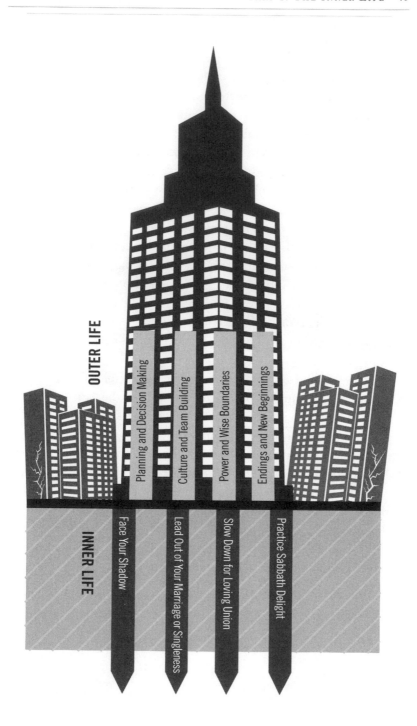

OUTER LIFE

Planning and Decision Making

Culture and Team Building

Power and Wise Boundaries

Endings and New Beginnings

INNER LIFE

Face Your Shadow

Lead Out of Your Marriage or Singleness

Slow Down for Loving Union

Practice Sabbath Delight

In 1996, God used brokenness in my life to teach me that emotional health and spiritual maturity are inseparable. At that point, I began to hammer some new piles into my spiritual foundation. But I soon discovered that unless these structural supports were deeply drilled into the granite of my soul, the above-the-surface levels of my life and my leadership remained vulnerable. What I needed was a deep foundation (inner life) that could effectively support my leadership (outer life).

As a leader, I had been formed in a certain way. For example, I learned about things like planning and decision making or culture and team building by watching and serving with other leaders. From them I learned to do certain leadership tasks in a "standard" way. However, without the solid foundation of a deep inner life, even the best leadership practices were only marginally effective for me.

The dysfunction and wounds hardwired into my brain and body proved to be much harder ground than I anticipated. It would take many years of starts and stops, trial and error, and returning to the unfinished drilling before I had the foundation that enabled me to write these pages.

Mature spiritual leadership is forged in the crucible of difficult conversations, the pressure of conflicted relationships, the pain of setbacks, and dark nights of the soul. Out of these experiences, we come to understand the complex nature of our inner world. Moreover, as we develop new practices and rhythms robust enough to withstand the pressures that leadership exerts on the inner life, we naturally become stronger and more effective leaders. And we move on from simply affirming truth and wisdom to owning and applying what we know.

Enough said.

Let's begin the process of drilling by looking into your inner life for placement of the first pile — Face Your Shadow.

Chapter 2

Face Your Shadow

Most leaders search out books on leadership to discover new tools, ideas, or skills. We are charged with the task of knowing what to do next, knowing why it is important, and then bringing the necessary resources to bear to make it happen. Yet the first and most difficult task we face as leaders is to lead ourselves. Why? Because it requires confronting parts of who we are that we prefer to neglect, forget, or deny. Here is how author and educator Parker Palmer describes this experience:

> Everything in us cries out against it. That is why we externalize everything — it is far easier to deal with the exterior world. It is easier to spend your life manipulating an institution than dealing with your own soul. We make institutions sound complicated and hard and rigorous, but they are simplicity itself compared with our inner labyrinths.[1]

The following two stories illustrate the complex and demanding nature of what it looks like to walk the "inner labyrinths" Palmer describes — to face our shadow as Christian leaders — and why it is so easy to avoid it altogether.

Sean, the business leader

Sean is a successful and gifted Christian leader. Charismatic, entrepreneurial, hard-working, and smart, he seems to succeed in everything he touches. After pastoring a church for ten years, Sean founded a for-profit company to serve other pastors. Within a few short years, the organization had eleven employees and was flourishing. He brought in a partner and set himself up in a role within the company that he had always dreamed of having.

Sean's business partner did a great job of running the day-to-day operations, but that actually created another problem: Sean was miserable and bored. So he started another business. His coping mechanism was to stay busy by starting new projects, but chaos inevitably followed because he never finished anything he started. Eventually, his business partner was fed up trying to clean up Sean's messes and told him how impossible he was to work with. Any spiritual rhythms and disciplines Sean once practiced had long since disappeared. He had accountability partners and a lot of friends, but he was now drinking—a lot. And he was constantly nervous. Nervous enough to fly to New York City to meet with us at New Life.

This is how Sean describes his story:

> When I gather with other visionary leaders like myself, it's electric. We dream, talk, plan, and imagine a better world. I love it! But I've begun to notice something that's not so great about it. We love to talk about living on the edge and the excitement they feel for the next adventure, but all I know is that I am completely addicted to the adrenaline rush of what's next! And nobody at the gatherings I attend talks about the fallout from that kind of leadership.
>
> I've achieved financial success and expanded my ministry, but my pace is unmanageable and I feel crippled by anxiety. You would think that the more you have the less you fear, but the opposite is true. The more I achieve, the more worries I have. The pressure that comes from having to meet payroll and keep the momentum going is wearing on my soul—if there is any soul left at all at this point.
>
> I know I push hard. I promote even harder. I constantly start more stuff. I come up with more ideas. And the talents God has given me to serve the church now consume me. I thought success would take pressure off my soul. It only made things worse.
>
> On a typical day, this is what life is like for me:

I overcommunicate on social media.

I check stats about the business all the time.

I don't sleep well because my mind is always racing.

I live in panic mode.

I have a short fuse.

I am in a hurry ALL. OF. THE. TIME.

I constantly pressure my team to work smarter and harder.

I quickly write people off.

I am always looking for the next idea or activity.

People around me—my wife, my kids, my friends, my colleagues—are catching the fallout from all this. All my relationships feel like they are about to crack.

So what do I do? I try to keep performing and producing while somehow working on my soul at the same time. But it's not working. I can't just quit work and become a monk, so there has to be a way, right?

While Sean's story may appear extreme, I can assure you it's not. I routinely talk with Christian leaders whose lives are just as chaotic and driven. Sean has a long way to go, but he's taken the first step by allowing himself to experience the sharp pain of confronting aspects of himself he has previously worked hard to avoid. After decades of ignoring his "inner labyrinths," he feels disoriented. That is to be expected. But thankfully, he has taken his first step.

The impact of the shadow in Sean's life isn't hard to spot. I suspect, however, that more leaders might relate to this next story about Jason and the way his shadow remained cloaked by contemporary Christian culture.

Jason, the pastor

Jason has been the pastor of First Congregational Church—185 members strong—for the last five years. Recently, both his wife and a close friend have been encouraging Jason to assert himself more strongly in making ministry and leadership decisions. Jason agrees that he should, but he is also afraid of displeasing or disappointing people. His outgoing, friendly personality, along with his good listening skills, camouflage his allergic reaction to any kind of conflict.

After five years, however, the ripple effects of this aversion are now being felt throughout the church. For example, when Jessica volunteered to be the children's ministry director, Jason was concerned about her lack of experience and her tendency to be easily offended. Nevertheless, he agreed because he didn't want to disappoint or hurt her. But within a year, he was doing part of her job to keep the ministry moving and smoothing over tensions volunteers experienced in interacting with her. The church board, along with most parents, knew Jessica was not suited for this role. An elephant of a problem was now in the room, but nobody wanted to address it.

Jason also wants to launch a contemporary worship service at 11:00 a.m. and move the present 10:00 a.m. service to an earlier time. He wrote up plans to formally propose this shift at a board meeting, but suspected that two of the six members would be strongly against it. Jason never did propose the change or initiate a discussion about the future of the church. The church continues to lose young people.

Jason's inability to say no, to disagree, or to risk disappointing others has its roots in his family of origin and the way he and his family related to one another. The unspoken rules he grew up with went something like this:

Do not make others upset.

You are responsible for your parents' happiness.

When you are sad or mad, keep it inside.

This led Jason to be less than honest and overly involved in the feelings of other people. Now this painful family legacy is crippling his leadership. When a church board member recently asked Jason to have breakfast, he felt a sense of dread.

"Why do you always have to make it so that no one can have anything against you?" the board member asked.

Jason felt as if he had been punched in the stomach.

He knows he can't avoid dealing with his conflict aversion much longer. What he may not realize is that the board member actually handed him a gift. The question now is, what will Jason do with it?

In order to uproot the source of his intense aversion to conflict, Jason will have to face up to the complex and demanding nature of his shadow. Unlike Sean, who has taken his initial steps by reflecting on the way his inner chaos manifests externally in his work, Jason has avoided that journey — and his church is suffering the consequences.

Jason, at this point, is aware he has a problem, but he has yet to acknowledge how serious and how pervasive it really is. The verdict is out on how he will respond to his board member's perceptive observation. Fortunately, it's been my experience that once leaders understand what the shadow is and realize they're not alone — that we all have shadows — most will courageously face it. In the process, they also discover God's grace and the Holy Spirit's wind at their back.

So let's turn our attention to defining and unpacking this elusive notion that is the *shadow*.

What Is the Shadow?

Everyone has a shadow. So what is it?

Your shadow is the accumulation of untamed emotions, less-than-pure motives and thoughts that, while largely unconscious, strongly influence and shape your behaviors. It is the damaged but mostly hidden version of who you are.

The shadow may erupt in various forms. Sometimes it reveals itself in sinful behaviors, such as judgmental perfectionism, outbursts of anger, jealousy, resentment, lust, greed, or bitterness. Or it may reveal itself more subtly through a need to rescue others and be liked by people, a need to be noticed, an inability to stop working, a tendency toward isolation, or rigidity. Aspects of the shadow may be sinful, but they may also simply be weaknesses or wounds. They tend to appear in the ways we try to protect ourselves from feeling vulnerable or exposed. This means that the shadow is *not* simply another word for sin. If that makes you think the shadow is hard to pin down, you're right. "The shadow, by nature, is difficult to grasp," write psychologists Connie Zweig and Jeremiah Abrams. "It is dangerous, disorderly and forever in hiding, as if the light of consciousness would steal its very life."[2]

Robert Louis Stevenson's infamous story *Dr. Jekyll and Mr. Hyde* helped me to understand my own shadow as something that lies concealed just beneath the surface of my more respectable self. During the day, Dr. Jekyll leads a polished, well-respected life with many friends, but at night he roams the streets as the violent Mr. Hyde. While he initially enjoys the ability to indulge his shadowy Mr. Hyde side, over time Dr. Jekyll loses his ability to control going back and forth between his two identities. Increasingly, he becomes the dark Mr. Hyde at the most inopportune times. The story ends when Jekyll finally realizes he will soon become the evil Hyde forever and ends his own life. While Stevenson casts the shadow side of Dr. Jekyll as blatantly evil — which is not how we are describing our shadow — I especially relate to Dr. Jekyll's efforts to avoid, at all costs, facing up to the reality of his shadow.

So how does the shadow reveal itself in leadership? Here are a few examples:

- Many of us have gifts in speaking and in mobilizing people. That is good. The shadow side of these gifts may be an insatiable need for affirmation. Even public sharing of repentance and failure may be motivated by an unconscious hunger for approval. It is also not uncommon for those of us with gifts of public speaking to use them to distance ourselves from close relationships.

- We value excellence. That is good. The shadow side emerges when the pursuit of excellence crosses into perfectionism that makes no allowances for mistakes. Our perfectionism becomes one way we silence our own inner voices of shame.

- We are zealous for God's truth and right doctrine. That is good. The shadow emerges when our zeal prevents us from loving those who disagree with us. It is driven by our own insecurities and fears about feeling competent and "right."

- We want to see the church maximize its potential for Christ. That is good. However, the shadow takes over when we become so preoccupied with achieving objectives that we are unwilling or unable to listen to others and create an unsustainable pace for those serving with us. The shadow motivation might be a desperate need to receive praise from others for our work.

- We love to serve. That is good. The shadow reveals itself when we hide ourselves in the kitchen at social events to avoid talking to people. It is our way of protecting ourselves from getting close to others.

- We accept a new assignment in a different city. That is good. The shadow emerges when, before we leave, we pick a fight with another leader at our current assignment over issues that never bothered us before. Why? Because it's easier than acknowledging the sadness we feel and saying, "I will miss you."[3]

These are all general examples, so allow me to share a recent personal example of my own shadow in action. Fair warning, it's not a pretty picture.

Geri and I were sitting down for one of our occasional two-person staff meetings. I had an agenda of four to five items, the first of which was to get input from Geri on a revised mission statement for our organization, Emotionally Healthy Spirituality. I had been pondering the statement and soliciting input from different people for over three months. I thought I would pass it by Geri briefly to get her opinion.

We were sitting on separate couches facing each other as I handed her the revised mission statement.

She stared down at the paper. "Let me think about this ... I'm not sure," she said.

A jolt of tension ran through my body, but I tried to hide my annoyance.

"This is a three-minute item," I said tersely. "Actually, I am looking for you to say that this is fantastic, not to suggest a total revision."

Geri, noting my impatience and annoyed tone, remained silent.

After pausing for a moment, she said, "I think I would change this to ..." Then she stopped.

The tension between us was palpable.

"Pete, what's going on inside you right now?" Geri asked. "What are you feeling?"

I knew this was not going to be good.

"And where is this coming from?" she continued. "I've seen you do this with other people in meetings. And it's not good. I mean, you are writing a book, you know, called *The Emotionally Healthy Leader*."

Geri was calm. I was not. Part of me wanted to attack her, defend myself, or scream.

A heavy silence filled the air.

I closed my eyes and took a deep breath. A part of my shadow was exposed, and I could see it—again.

I had not crossed the line into sin — yet. But I was seriously considering it. I took a breath and thought about her question. I sent an SOS to the Holy Spirit asking for power and self-control.

"Geri, right now I am anxious, impatient, frustrated," I finally said. "I just wanted to spend a few minutes on this and hear you say, 'This is awesome,' or, 'Perhaps change one word.' I didn't want any more. So my question really wasn't honest or clear."

"Where does *that* come from?" Geri asked.

I allowed the heavy silence to fill the room.

"I'll tell you where it comes from," I finally uttered. "My *family.* They are in me. All of it is in me — the impatience, the anxiety, the failure to take the time to clearly think through what I'm asking! When you didn't immediately say it was great, all I could think of was the constant negative feedback in my family when I was growing up."

It was painful to see this so clearly — and not for the first time.

Even so, I thanked God for the grace that I *could* see it, which kept me from attacking Geri or defending myself. And I was grateful for the grace that kept me from allowing my shadow to cross the line into sin.

I asked Geri's forgiveness, and we took a tea break. Ten minutes later we were moving on to item number two on the agenda of our little staff meeting.

Part of what enabled me to recover in the moment was a healthy biblical theology that reminded me that I am more than my shadow.

How Healthy Is Your Approach to Your Shadow?

Use the list of statements that follow to do a brief assessment on how you relate to your shadow. Next to each statement, write down the number that best describes your response. Use the following scale:

5 = Always true of me
4 = Frequently true of me
3 = Occasionally true of me
2 = Rarely true of me
1 = Never true of me

 1. I take time regularly to experience and process my anger, fear, and sadness with God and others.

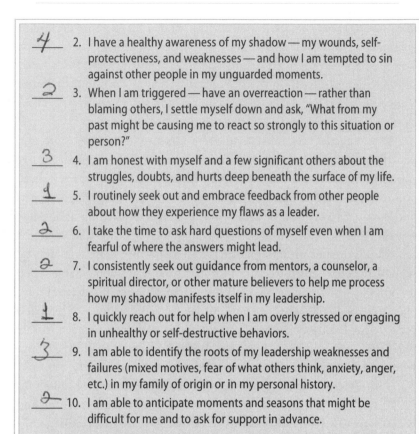

_4_   2. I have a healthy awareness of my shadow — my wounds, self-protectiveness, and weaknesses — and how I am tempted to sin against other people in my unguarded moments.

_2_   3. When I am triggered — have an overreaction — rather than blaming others, I settle myself down and ask, "What from my past might be causing me to react so strongly to this situation or person?"

_3_   4. I am honest with myself and a few significant others about the struggles, doubts, and hurts deep beneath the surface of my life.

_1_   5. I routinely seek out and embrace feedback from other people about how they experience my flaws as a leader.

_2_   6. I take the time to ask hard questions of myself even when I am fearful of where the answers might lead.

_2_   7. I consistently seek out guidance from mentors, a counselor, a spiritual director, or other mature believers to help me process how my shadow manifests itself in my leadership.

_1_   8. I quickly reach out for help when I am overly stressed or engaging in unhealthy or self-destructive behaviors.

_3_   9. I am able to identify the roots of my leadership weaknesses and failures (mixed motives, fear of what others think, anxiety, anger, etc.) in my family of origin or in my personal history.

_2_ 10. I am able to anticipate moments and seasons that might be difficult for me and to ask for support in advance.

Take a moment to briefly review your responses. What stands out most to you? Although there is no definitive scoring for the assessment, at the end of the chapter (pages 79 – 80) are some general observations that may help you understand more about where you're at. Even if your score isn't what you hoped, give yourself credit for having taken the assessment in the first place. That is actually a significant step forward in growing into a more effective and healthy leader. Spiritual and leadership maturity is a marathon, not a sprint — allow yourself to take it one step at a time.

You Are More than Your Shadow

When it comes to understanding and facing up to the shadow within, many Christian leaders fall into one of two extreme views. The first extreme view says, *I am totally bad. I am terribly sinful and no good thing dwells inside me* (see Romans 7:18). The other extreme declares, *I am totally good. I am a new creation in Christ, a saint who is wonderfully and uniquely made* (see 2 Corinthians 5:17; Psalm 139:14). Both views have elements of truth in them, but holding to one without the other leads us into a biblical distortion. To have a healthy perspective on the shadow, we have to hold both together in a healthy tension.

At any given time, most of us are a mixture of these tensions and contradictions. For example, at times I am vulnerable and open. Other times, I am defensive. I am loving and I am also, at times, prejudiced and unkind. I am a hard worker when it comes to preparing sermons and writing; I may also be lazy when it comes to learning about new technologies or setting aside time for extended solitude and silence. I am calm in certain situations like public speaking; I become anxious when I have too much to do in too little time. I am dependable when it comes to work, leadership, and my responsibilities at church. I have been undependable when it comes to taking responsibility to plan and prepare for family vacations. I am teachable and open to learn from a wide variety of sources. I have also been rigid and closed in learning from certain Christians with whom I don't agree.

God invites us to integrate these coexisting realities into our self-understanding and leadership. We recognize we have a treasure, and we are a treasure, but it dwells in a jar of real clay (see 1 Corinthians 4:7).

If we buy into the lie that the shadow is what is most true about us, we may well be overwhelmed and potentially throw up our hands, believing there is nothing we can do. And this has grave consequences. Yet, we can't ignore the shadow without paying a price.

You Know It's Your Shadow When You ...

- Act out inappropriately when under pressure.
- Don't want someone to succeed because they've hurt you.
- Are triggered by a person or circumstance and say things you later regret.
- Disregard your spouse or coworker when they bring up a difficult issue about you and your behavior.

- Keep doing the same thing over and over even though the consequences remain negative.
- Are angry, jealous, and envious — a lot.
- Do and say things out of fear of what other people think.
- Get busier rather than more reflective when you are anxious.
- Tend to idealize others who seem to have been given special gifts by God, forgetting they too have a shadow and are broken like you.
- Make negative comments to others about those who frustrate you rather than go to them directly.

The Consequences of Choosing to Ignore Your Shadow

Facing the shadow is a formidable task. The self-protective part of us can be very creative in finding what appear to be legitimate and justifiable ways to avoid it. However, over the years, I've found that these maneuvers can be categorized into a few major categories—denial, minimizing, blaming yourself, blaming others, rationalizing, distracting, or projecting anger outward. Regardless of the defensive shield we default to, the consequences of choosing to ignore the shadow are devastating.

Your Shadow Will Undermine the Best of Who You Are

Studies indicate that EQ (emotional quotient) is so critical that it accounts for 58 percent of performance in all types of jobs.[4] In fact, emotional intelligence in the workplace trumps almost every other factor—IQ, personality, education, experience, and gifts—when it comes to effective performance for leaders.[5] When we consider God's desire that Christ be formed in us and his great concern for our character, the implications for us are more far-reaching. Consider a few examples of how this plays out in different leadership settings:

- William is a gifted and effective pastor, but the chaotic nature of his family of origin drives him to dominate and control environments—whether at home or at work. Leaders and staff routinely move on from the church because of a lack of opportunity to exercise their gifts and learn from their mistakes.

- Christine is an outstanding executive director of ministries — organized, detailed, and a quick learner — in a rapidly growing church. But she is so highly sensitive to criticism and the appearance of failure that it negatively impacts her ability to work with her team of mostly entrepreneurial leaders. She is growing increasingly resentful of her job description changing every six months as more and more of her responsibilities are being spread out to others.

- Evelyn has a God-given gift to mentor students and lead the young adult ministry at her church. She is in constant motion, launching new initiatives to expand the work, but she is unaware how her drive to achieve comes partially out of a family script that says, *You are worthless unless you do something great.* Half her volunteers grow tired trying to keep up with Evelyn and drop out after two to three months.

Sadly, the leaders in these examples are ignoring their shadow and reaping negative consequences as a result.

Although I first became aware of and began to work on my shadow in 1996, it wasn't until 2007 that I fully recognized the depth of its impact on my leadership. This gridlock was broken when I finally confronted the hidden motivations that drove my shadow behaviors, particularly around issues relating to hiring and letting go of staff. In the process, three primary issues emerged.

The first revolved around validation. When I preached and led from up front, I received a lot of affirmation. People moved toward me. They said nice things to me. When I spoke painful truths or made a difficult decision, people moved away from me. They avoided me or said unkind things about me behind my back. (In most cases, this was more my imagination than reality.)

I wanted very much to prevent people moving away from me. The roots of this go back to my family of origin. Neither of my parents possessed the emotional resources to adequately affirm their four children. They never received affirmation themselves. As a result, I lived with an emotional hole and a deep need for acceptance and approval. When I understood the connection between the lack of affirmation in my childhood and my intense need to prevent people from moving away from me,

I gained insight, at least partially, about why I so consistently avoided difficult conversations. The problem was that my avoidance had moved well beyond a personal concern and was now impacting the whole church.

The second issue concerned lying and truth telling. By this point in New Life's history, we had nearly twenty staff as well as a Community Development Corporation that housed a health center, food pantry, and other ministries. New Life had become increasingly complex. I am strong in preaching, teaching, and vision casting. I am not strong in administration, budget management, hiring and firing, and detailed strategic planning. I focused on what I was good at and ignored, as much as possible, the executive functions I was not so good at.

I wasn't being honest — with myself, the staff, or the church. I did not give staff honest feedback about their performance lest they feel bad. I avoided asking difficult questions, fearful it might lead to answers I didn't want to hear. I gave the impression things were sometimes better than they were. I appeared happy when I was not.

The third issue related to pessimism about my ability to provide strong organizational leadership. Since 1923, my family has owned an Italian bakery in New York. It remains chaotic and poorly run. I absorbed the message that the Scazzeros are good talkers (exaggerating and embellishing in casting vision), but not good at running an effective organization. So I excused my failure of executive leadership of New Life, saying, "I'm just not good at that." I couldn't even imagine changing the family commandment of chaos and its ingrained patterns of disorganization. I could practically hear my mother's voice, "You can't do that. You don't know what you're doing."

Like most pastors and leaders, I gravitated to the things I liked, such as teaching an extra summer class on the book of Revelation, rather than take the time to really think about staff, budgets, and supervision meetings. In the short term I soothed my anxiety, but in the long term I only increased it. As a result, my shadow undermined, over time, even the strengths and gifts I brought to my role as a leader.

Your Shadow Will Limit Your Ability to Serve Others

The degree to which you recognize and engage your own shadow is the degree to which you can free others to face theirs. I don't look for people's shadows, but they are increasingly obvious to me. How is that possible? Because I know mine!

One of my favorite sayings comes from a story in *The Desert Fathers* about a fourth-century monk named John the Short. A jealous fellow monk once approached John as he was teaching at the front of the church.

> [The monk] said, "John, your cup is full of poison."
>
> John answered, "Yes ... it is. But you said that when you could only see the outside; I wonder what you [would] say if you saw the inside."[6]

John the Short is not defensive in his response. He does not attack the monk or fire off verbal chaff to deflect the conversation away from himself. He courageously admits his vulnerability and what he knows to be true about himself. Like the apostle Paul, he affirms, "I am the worst of all sinners" (see 1 Timothy 1:16). Acknowledging, rather than denying the reality and depth of the shadow, is one indication of emotional and spiritual maturity. In John the Short's case, he didn't retreat into a self-protective shell and stop serving others. Rather, he remained open and vulnerable to those who criticized him.

If our desire is to lead and serve others, we have to come to grips with this plain, hard fact: the degree to which we ignore our shadow is the degree to which our loving service to others is limited. You'll recognize this dynamic in Charles's story.

Charles is a gifted, para-church worker with an impressive resume. He published three books on poetry before he graduated from a top university. Charles is a "super" leader with a great future—charismatic, well-spoken, and creative—a sought-after speaker. Charles is also a member of the small group that meets in our basement. Whenever he shared something in our group, however, something always seemed off. I wasn't sure what it was, but his statements seemed empty—even if the words and his accomplishments were impressive.

Charles and I sat together one Sunday afternoon to talk about how his family of origin had impacted who he is today. The week before, our group had talked about the shadow aspects of ourselves that are fearful, protective, defensive, manipulative, and self-promoting. Charles talked about the number of men in his family who lived double lives, pretending to be someone they were not. Then he talked about the rural small town where he was raised, what it was like to make it in the big city of New York, and how everyone back home was so proud of his accomplishments.

"Charles," I said, "it seems that you have built so much of your life around being a speaker, author, poet, rapper, a leader who has made it, but who are you *really* ... beneath all that?"

He grew quiet. Looking wistfully at the floor, he said, "Pastor Pete, I'm not sure."

A few months later, Charles and I met again. He said, "After identifying the issues in my family and how they impact me today, God helped me to recognize my shadow. I looked at my poetry books, my accomplishments, and the perfect life story I had constructed. And I felt like God was inviting me to make a choice. I could try to revise and polish my story even more to present myself perfect and happy. Or I could allow God to redeem and restore me."

He paused briefly and then smiled. "I chose redemption ... and you know what? It's already starting to change the way I write and speak. I don't know where it's all going, but it feels great."

Your Shadow Will Blind You to the Shadow of Others

In his book *The Denial of Death*, cultural anthropologist Ernest Becker observes that we have a universal human need for heroic figures who are less helpless or broken than we are. We assume God has smiled upon them, granting them special gifts, intelligence, and wisdom. They appear to have triumphed over the hardships of life. They dazzle us with their self-confidence.

When we refuse to confront our own shadow, we will either be blind to or fail to take into account the shadows of others. This blindness causes us to idealize certain people, as if they don't have a shadow like the rest of us. We often feel worse about ourselves as a result, falling into a quicksand of morbid introspection in which we sink even deeper under the weight of our own shadow. Or at times we might judge others because of their imperfections, cruelly gossiping about them out of our own jealousy and insecurity. We forget that they too have a shadow that leaves them feeling as inadequate and vulnerable as we do.

So when someone puts you on a pedestal, idealizing you and projecting onto you qualities that appear to distinguish you and set you apart from the rest of fallen humanity, remember that they may despise you someday when they eventually realize you too have a shadow. As Becker writes, we are all just a *"homo sapien*, standard vintage."[7]

Jesus was deeply aware of the shadow in those who followed him. After Jesus threw the money changers out of the temple and many people believed in him, Scripture tells us, "Jesus would not entrust himself to them, for he knew all people" (John 2:24). Jesus knew that belief alone was no cure for the shadow. We need look no further than the apostle Peter for proof—the apostle who had boldly declared Jesus the Messiah, then readily denied Jesus three times after his arrest.

So we need to be mindful of the potential consequences of choosing to ignore the shadow. However, there are also positive blessings found when we follow God's paths.

The Gifts of Choosing to Face Your Shadow

God offers us wonderful gifts when we choose to courageously face our shadow. And by wonderful, I mean painful but worth it—the kind of gifts that might be called severe mercies. Although the thought of facing our shadow may initially fill us with fear, once we choose the path that leads us into our shadow, we find God is waiting for us there, offering us at least two magnificent gifts.

You Break the Shadow's Hidden Power

One of the great truths of life is this: *You cannot change what you are unaware of.* However, once we acknowledge our shadow—both its root causes and expressions—her power over us is diminished, if not broken. Exposing the shadow to the light of Jesus is the first, and most important, step we must take in order to receive this gift.

The apostle Paul was one of the most brilliant minds of his day. He led with power as an apostle, prophet, evangelist, pastor, and teacher. He received amazing visions and revelations from God. In spite of persecution, death threats, and a steady stream of adverse circumstances, he experienced unsurpassed success in planting churches throughout the

Roman Empire. Yet the intensity of his opponents and the pressure of carrying the weight of the churches surely tested Paul's character. We do not know the nature of Paul's shadow, but I suspect he may have been headstrong with a potential to be overbearing, intolerant, and violent (consider his persecution of the early church).

Paul spoke openly about how God humbled him and made him weak through a "thorn in my flesh" (2 Corinthians 12:7). We don't know if this was a physical ailment, the agony of being persecuted and misunderstood, or a spiritual temptation with which he struggled. We do know, however, that it tormented and discouraged Paul. It also empowered him to lead out of weakness and vulnerability. In this sense, it was a gift — one of the ways God helped him to face and break the power of his shadow. Paul himself refers to his weakness as a paradoxical source of strength:

> *Three times I pleaded with the Lord to take it away from me. But he said to me, "My grace is sufficient for you, for my power is made perfect in weakness." Therefore I will boast all the more gladly about my weaknesses, so that Christ's power may rest on me.... For when I am weak, then I am strong.*
>
> (2 Corinthians 12:8–10)

Paul's shadow was not a source of shame. Instead, it became a source of healthy boasting, providing a means through which Jesus' power and life flowed through him.

In the same way, once I recognized some of my shadowy tendencies — to seek validation inappropriately, to skim on the truth, to believe the worst about myself as an organizational leader — I was determined *not* to follow these self-defeating inclinations. And so I openly acknowledged them to those close to me. I reminded myself of all the strengths God had already developed in me. Much like David reminding Saul, and himself, that with God's help he had already killed the lion and the bear and so could fight Goliath (1 Samuel 17:36–37), I identified and rehearsed my small victories up to that point to remind myself of God's faithfulness and power.

I also met with wise mentors and counselors who coached me in the executive functions of leadership — hiring, transitioning people, strategic planning, budget planning, managing large projects, etc. I set aside time not only to create specific goals but to think through the steps and time required to reach those objectives. It was a painstaking but transformative process for both me and for New Life. I did these tasks over and over again until they became more natural to me. In the process, the shadow's hidden power over these areas of my life and leadership was broken.[8]

You Discover the Shadow's Hidden Treasures

Through the prophet Isaiah, God promises, "I will give you hidden treasures, riches stored in secret places" (Isaiah 45:3). This promise is especially true when we choose to enter the dark places of the shadow and allow those places to become tools in our service to God. Abraham Lincoln's life offers a beautiful illustration of this gift.

Lincoln struggled with serious depression from a very young age. In his twenties, neighbors sometimes took him into their homes for a week or two at a time to watch over him lest he take his own life. In his twenties and thirties, he had three breakdowns and dared not carry a pocketknife. As a country lawyer with only one year of formal schooling, Lincoln had a history of defeats in running for public office. When he was eventually elected president, he was derided as a country bumpkin and a disgrace. He had to sneak into Washington, DC, for his inauguration because of the number of people who wanted him dead.

In the early years of his presidency, Lincoln's failures and setbacks were a source of vicious public ridicule. His military generals performed poorly in the early stages of the Civil War. When Willie, his favorite child, died at age eleven, Lincoln was devastated. By the time the Civil War ended (1865), one of every five men between the ages of fifteen and forty had died in the conflict—529,000 men (in a country of 32 million) lost their lives. Virtually every family had been touched by agony and loss.

And yet Lincoln's personal and spiritual development during those years was astounding. He made it clear that God had *not* taken sides in the Civil War, articulating his view that the war was a consequence of the sin of slavery. He called for nine national days of fasting and prayer. When the war ended, Lincoln harbored no hatred or need for revenge against his former enemies, offering forgiveness and reconciliation to the Confederate officers and soldiers who surrendered.

How was this possible? In his book *Lincoln's Melancholy*, author Joshua Wolf Shenk describes how Lincoln was able to integrate his melancholy and his failures into a larger purpose. Shenk argues that it was, in fact, Lincoln's suffering and weaknesses that later fueled his greatness and propelled his personal transformation.

> Observers have long noticed how Lincoln combined sets of opposite qualities. Harriet Beecher Stowe [author of *Uncle Tom's Cabin*] wrote that he was unsteady but strong, like a wire cable that shakes in storms but tenaciously moves toward its end. Carl Sandburg described Lincoln as "steel and velvet … hard as rock and soft as drifting fog." As these metaphors indicate, Lincoln not only embraced contrasts — self-doubt and confidence, hope and despair — but somehow reconciled them to produce something new and valuable. In this lies the key to his creative work as president — and an enduring lesson. Living a good life often requires integrating a bundle of contrasts into a durable whole.[9]

Lincoln's lifelong journey required integrating his many gifts and talents with his failures, weaknesses, and depression. What was Lincoln's shadow? We cannot know for sure, but perhaps it was his tendency for despair and self-hatred. It may have been a desire for public recognition and approval. This could, perhaps, explain his failure to remove incompetent Union generals in the early years of the Civil War.

Whatever Lincoln's shadow, it is clear that his willingness to acknowledge and integrate all of himself is what enabled him to serve and lead a nation in great danger of falling apart. He did not need to demonize the opposition by dividing the nation into heroes and villains. He had learned to hold that tension and complexity within himself. His heartbreak had opened up for him a greater capacity for joy as well as suffering. As a result, he led a fractured nation through a civil war that could have destroyed it and is considered by many to be America's greatest president.

You and I may not be like Abraham Lincoln or be forced to face his leadership challenges, but we can still follow in his footsteps by choosing to embrace our shadows. There really are only two options when it comes to the shadow. We can ignore it until we hit a wall, with pain so great we have no choice but to face up to it. Or we can be proactive, courageously looking at the factors that contributed to its formation.

Four Pathways for Facing Your Shadow

As you no doubt have surmised, the process of facing the shadow requires both courage and hard work. I often liken it to the task of breaking up permafrost. Permafrost is frozen soil, at least eighteen inches thick, with a temperature that has remained below freezing for more than two years. In some places in Siberia, the permafrost can extend to 5,000 feet below the surface. Northern Alaska has permafrost depths of 2,400 feet. Our shadow at times can seem just as permanent as the deepest permafrost.

In the marketplace, businesses have come to rely on the field of emotional intelligence to help leaders manage their emotions and minimize the negative impact they might have on their teams and organizations.[10] Our concern here, however, is with more than just managing and minimizing negative impact. What we are after is long-term inner transformation into the image of Christ for the sake of the world. If that's a challenge you're prepared to undertake, then I trust that, while you may still feel somewhat cautious, you are ready to take one or more of the next steps.

1. Tame Your Feelings by Naming Your Feelings

Neuroscientists now confirm that growing up in family environments where feelings are not expressed leads to underdevelopment in parts of the brain. This damages our ability to work and love well. The good news is that the damage isn't permanent. Using brain imaging, researchers have documented how our brains are rewired when we learn to name our feelings. Even at the cellular level, something powerful is tamed and changed within us when we recognize and identify our emotions.[11]

You can begin to name your feelings by writing in a journal as part of your time with God. You might prayerfully consider and respond to questions such as these:

What am I feeling? And what am I feeling about that feeling?

What am I sad about? Glad about? Angry about? Anxious about?

Where in my body am I feeling tension or stress (e.g., shoulders, neck, stomach)? What might this be telling me about what is going on inside me?

I spent the first seventeen years of my Christian life denying my feelings, especially the more difficult emotions like anger, sadness, and fear. I fell into a superspiritual, unbiblical theology that considered such emotions sinful. I failed to recognize all the biblical examples that clearly demonstrated otherwise. Jesus, our Messiah and God, did not deny his anger and sadness. The prophet Jeremiah wrote an entire book, Lamentations, expressing his deep anguish over the destruction of Jerusalem. And King David, a man after God's own heart, expressed the full gamut of emotions before the Lord. In fact, two-thirds of his psalms are laments or complaints![12]

When I began the journey of emotionally healthy spirituality in 1996, I wrote in a journal almost every day as part of my prayer time. This proved to be a foundational discipline for me because it allowed me to exercise my long dormant "feeling" muscles. Three to four times a week, I paused to reflect on the emotions I had experienced the previous day. Those "feeling" workouts strengthened my routine awareness of my emotions. Soon I got better at identifying my feelings in the moment so I didn't have to wait until the next day to acknowledge them. I also experienced a greater freedom and peace because I was no longer suppressing them. While initially it was difficult, with consistent practice, identifying and naming my emotions became as natural as breathing.

After identifying my feelings, I made it a habit to reflect on *why* I might be experiencing each emotion. For example, "Why might I be angry when I think about meeting that person from our church? Is it her apparent forcefulness? Is it that I am afraid I will give in to pressure and make an unwise decision I will later regret?" Again, I wrote my responses in a journal. Once I could name my feelings and identify their source, I could then take appropriate action, such as, graciously saying no to an invitation, asking difficult questions, or waiting before making a final decision.[13]

2. Use a Genogram to Explore the Impact of Your Past

In our work with leaders over the past nineteen years, Geri and I have discovered that constructing a genogram is one of the most compelling and effective ways of helping people to identify and face their shadow. A genogram is a visual tool to document the history and dynamics of our family relationships, and their impact on us, over three to four generations. Constructing a genogram helps us examine unhealthy patterns from the past that we bring into our present leadership as well as our relationship to Christ and others. To give you an example, here is my own genogram:

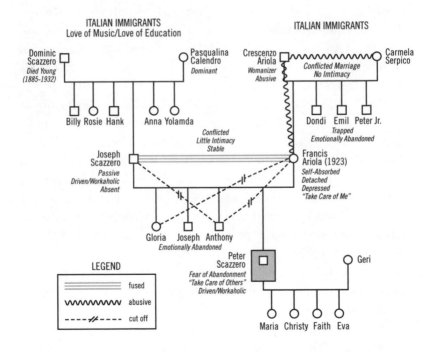

At New Life we like to say, "Jesus may be in your heart, but Grandpa lives in your bones." As you can see from my genogram, the proverbial "grandpas" cast a long shadow over the generations in my family. That's why it's so important to be aware of generational patterns in our family history if we want to face up to our shadow. Consider the stories of Ben and Juan.

Ben, an accountant and leader in his church, always seemed to become oppositional in conversations. He responded to every question as if it were a challenge. Regardless of the topic—whether it be a program for an upcoming event, a pastoral dilemma, the arrangement of the office, or a biblical truth—Ben's tone was combative. He knew it was a problem, but he couldn't seem to change his behavior. It wasn't until he completed a genogram that he recognized why he felt hostile when questioned, especially if the questioner was a person in authority.

As a child, he had been severely punished every time he did something wrong, even if it was very minor. He learned early on to defend himself against any potential accusation of error or weakness. When he realized how the roots of his behavior extended back to his family of origin, he was able to start making changes.

Juan is a leader who lives and works at a breakneck speed. "Successful people are driven," he says. "From the moment I get up until the moment I go to bed, I want to be fully scheduled and going from one thing to another. There's no greater high." You might think Juan is simply young and ambitious, but if you could see his genogram, you would have a larger context for his behavior. His father was an immigrant who told Juan that he owed his parents a debt for all the suffering they had endured in order to bring him to the United States. Decades later, that message lives on in his bones. Once Juan saw it, he realized how far he was from living the love of God in the gospel. It catapulted him into a journey not only to revisit his relationship with his parents but to change his pace of life and the way he works. He will tell you that it has reduced his stress level 50 percent. The change is even evident in his physical appearance—he no longer looks haggard and rushed, but settled and at peace.

As we have worked with leaders like Ben and Juan over the years, Geri and I developed a tool called "Genogram Your Family." If you're ready to take a life-changing step, you can access this tool on our website, www.emotionallyhealthy.org/genogram. Completing a genogram will take you beyond a conceptual or motivational level to a place of practical application. Watch the online video and use the worksheet,

"Genogram Your Family," on page 313 to diagram your family history. This will help you discover previously unexplored areas of your life and shadow. For additional guidance, you can also work through the material in "Sample Questions to Ask in Constructing Your Genogram" (below).

Sample Questions to Ask in Constructing Your Genogram

The following questions are ones we ask to help people get beneath the surface and identify how the past might be impacting the present. As you read through the questions, try to consider them especially from the perspective you had as a child between the ages of eight to twelve.

1. Describe each family member in your household with three adjectives and identify their relationship to you (parent, caregiver, grandparent, sibling, etc.).

2. Describe your parents' (or caretakers') marriage(s) as well as your grandparents' marriage(s).

3. How were conflict, anger, and tensions handled in your extended family over two or three generations?

4. Were there any family "secrets" (such as an unwed pregnancy, incest, mental illness, or financial scandal, etc.)?

5. What was considered "success" in your family?

6. How did ethnicity or race shape you and your family?

7. How would you describe the relationships between family members (conflicted, detached, enmeshed, abusive)?

8. Were there any heroes/heroines in the family? Any villains or favorites? Why were these individuals singled out in this way?

9. What generational patterns or themes do you recognize (addictions, affairs, abuse, divorce, mental illness, abortions, children born out of wedlock, etc.)?

10. What traumatic losses has your family experienced? (For example, sudden death, prolonged illness, stillbirth/miscarriage, bankruptcy, divorce?)

11. What insights (one or two) are you becoming aware of that help you to make sense of how your family of origin, or others, impacted who you are today?

> 12   What are one or two specific ways this may be impacting your leadership?*
>
> When you explore your past with a genogram, you expose your shadow to the light of Jesus. Then by God's grace, you can break its power over you and integrate its hidden treasures into your leadership.
>
> *Adapted from Scazzero, *The Emotionally Healthy Church*, 98–99.

3. Identify the Negative Scripts Handed Down to You

A negative script is an internalized message from the past that shapes our conscious and unconscious behaviors in the present. Even if we have put these scripts out of our minds, our bodies remember them, especially if they are connected to traumatic experiences. That's why, even decades later, some events can trigger a disproportionate response — they evoke the memory of being in an overwhelming situation. Reflecting on the past enables us to identify and change these negative scripts that were handed down to us.

My mom, for example, was deathly afraid of risk and of being shamed by others. She passed this on to her four children. When I was about eleven, I remember telling my mom I wanted to learn to repair car engines. She then repeated a refrain she often used when I tried something new: "You can't do that. You don't know what you're doing. You'll mess things up." That's a negative script. As an adult, I've had to check myself more than once and ask, "Is this risk I'm considering a step of faith for God or an effort to prove Mom wrong?"

A negative script could develop out of almost any kind of experience. See if you recognize yourself in any of these examples:

- Dan is a highly accomplished doctor who earns a very good salary. He also serves on the church board. He struggles with perfectionism and workaholism that hurt his relationships at both work and church. One day when he was ten, he came home with an A on his report card and was punished by his father for not getting an A+. His dad sat Dan in his room and drilled him on vocabulary words since that is where he got two answers wrong. Dan's negative script? *Get it right — all the time. And don't make mistakes!*

- Allison's parents divorced when she was seven. She remembers the day her parents sat across the table from her and her brother to tell them the news. "I love you and will be there for you," her father promised. The problem came six months later when he remarried and started a new family. She and her brother rarely saw their dad over the next twenty years. Her cautious and careful approach to life is both an expression of prudence and of a negative script: *Don't trust people.*

- Jiao's parents immigrated to the United States from China. They left behind their language, culture, family, and jobs to make a better life for Jiao and her three brothers in New York. They worked twelve-hour days, six and a half days a week, and had only one message for their children, "Study. Make it in America." Toward this end, Jiao excelled at school and graduated at the top of her high school class. Her negative script: *Your worth and value are based on your performance and achievements.*

- In Joseph's family, there was a lot of yelling and screaming. His father had an affair at one point, and Joseph, the oldest sibling, served as the intermediary to calm his mom down. He was the peacemaker in the family. Now Joseph is a pastor. He avoids conflict and angry people, withdrawing until the unpleasantness passes. His script: *Conflict is dangerous and bad.*

- Nathan was raised in a Christian home where his dad repeatedly said to him, "God has a special destiny and plan for your life, but if you step out of his will, he will judge you harshly." So Nathan devoted himself to being responsible and productive. His script: *God has something for me to do and be, and I better not screw that up.*

As you read through the examples, what came to mind? Did you recognize any negative scripts of your own?

Once you identify one or two of the negative scripts handed down from your family, the next step is to prayerfully reflect on them—alone and then with others whom you trust. Why? So you can take prayerful and practical steps to replace them with scripts you write that are anchored in the truth of what God says about you.

4. Seek Feedback from Trustworthy Sources

Without wise feedback from trustworthy sources—therapists, spiritual directors, trusted colleagues, and mentors—I would not have been able to recognize, much less face, my shadow. Often, we need to step outside of our church in order to draw on additional resources such as these, especially in the case of a therapist or a spiritual director. This reduces any potential conflict of interest or tension that too often arises in dual relationships (we'll talk more about this in chapter 8).

You will need different types of feedback at different points in your life and leadership journey. If you have the opportunity, I encourage you to do a "360" (360-degree feedback), a tool that enables you to receive feedback from those all around you—supervisors, peers, coworkers, and people who report to you.[14] You get the benefit of a combined perspective about your teamwork, communication, leadership, weaknesses, and skills. While this tool focuses specifically on you in the workplace, a number of Christian leaders have found it exceedingly helpful in facing their shadow. Another helpful tool that has benefited many leaders, including our staff at New Life, is the Enneagram, a typology that uses nine personality types to help people identify and understand the forces that motivate their behavior.[15]

As leaders we have the power to project our shadow and its effects on other people. For this reason we have a stewardship responsibility to honestly face our shadow. Seeking feedback and help from others is not optional. It's essential. However, always keep in mind that not all feedback is created equal, especially when feedback comes in the form of a harsh rebuke.

I've received many, many rebukes in my life. The most helpful came from people who enjoyed intimate walks with God and were sensitive to their own shadow. They spoke to me not out of condemnation but out of their own brokenness. They loved me enough to speak to me thoughtfully. I received their words as a gift. By pointing out aspects of my shadow that were beyond my awareness, they served God's growth process in my life.

The least helpful rebukes came from those who were mean-spirited or thought they were being helpful, but were not. They were unaware of their own shadow motivations. In my early days, their sharp criticism did me more harm than good.

Author and pastor Gordon MacDonald has shared with me about his experience with that second kind of rebuke, the rebuke from a person who does not speak in love. He recounts one particularly painful rebuke almost twenty years ago when a well-known Christian leader turned to him in the car and said, "Gordon, I sense a root of bitterness in you."

Gordon kept driving, but his body tightened. He remembered his father as a bitter person, and he had worked hard throughout his life not to be like him. The leader's comment cut deep. Silence marked the rest of their car ride.

"I went home to think about it," he said. "Then I gathered three of my friends and told them what the man said. I asked for their help to assess the rebuke."

Over the next month, the friends met together without Gordon and reviewed all the times they had been with him. One of the friends then gave him their report: "We have met and we want you to know we have not seen any bitterness in you."

"I thank God for those trusted friends," Gordon concluded. "Otherwise, I would have assumed this man was right, when he wasn't, and spent more nights wrestling with something that was not my issue."

When leaders ask about how to seek feedback, I always recommend the safety of asking for input from a variety of sources—a spiritual director, a counselor, a mentor, a good friend, a board member. I routinely seek input from all of these sources at certain times, depending on the intensity of the season in which I find myself. Feedback from one source might be biased (positively or negatively), but getting input from different parts of the body of Christ will keep us in the safety zone of a broad, balanced perspective. I take advantage of that whenever possible.

When a person has come at me with a particularly biting critique that cuts deep, I bring that to the people I trust whom God has placed around me. In my case, these people have been on the New Life elder board. Some have seen my shadow for years. They have been a gift to me in my most difficult moments.

Keep these four pathways for facing your shadow before you and commit to following through on at least one of them as a first step: tame your feelings by naming your feelings, use a genogram to explore the impact of your past, identify the negative scripts handed down to you, seek feedback from trustworthy sources. These pathways will serve you well on the journey of facing your shadow. But most important is to stay close to Jesus in this process. He is your anchor as you navigate these challenging waters.

Staying with Jesus as You Face Your Shadow

Each time you make a choice to face rather than ignore your shadow, you follow Jesus to the cross. It is often an experience of nakedness, vulnerability, pain, scourging, loneliness, fear, and darkness that whispers this will lead only to despair and death. There are seasons when God uses these experiences to strip us, exposing yet another layer of our shadow. The most important task during such times is to wait on the love of the Father as Jesus did while hanging on the cross. Remain. Endure. Abide. Like Jesus.

As you wait, you anchor yourself in the truths that God's love and grace are true and that resurrection is a certainty. Based on personal experience, I can promise that you will be reborn into a new place of maturity in Christ. You will become more compassionate, more vulnerable, more broken, and more loving. Each time you pass through a season of facing your shadow, you will be transformed even more into the image of Jesus.

Understanding Your Shadow Assessment

If you took the shadow assessment on pages 59–60, here are some observations to help you reflect on your responses.

If you scored mostly ones and twos, your relationship with your shadow is just beginning. Most likely, your leadership has been focused almost exclusively on doing Christ's work in the world with only a limited focus on your interior life. This may have been a scary or difficult assessment for you. If so, don't worry. You can begin slowly with one of the pathways for facing your shadow. God will lead you at a pace that works for you.

If you scored mostly twos and threes, you have likely already begun to face your shadow and now God is inviting you to the next level of awareness and growth. Your challenge will be to take the necessary steps to truly go deep beneath the surface of your interior life. As a starting place, I encourage you to do the "Genogram Your Family" skill (visit www.emotionallyhealthy. org/genogram). Ask God for wise, trusted companions for your journey. You can expect God to teach you how to lead out of your weaknesses, like the apostle Paul did, so Christ's power might rest on you in new and fresh ways.

If you scored mostly fours and fives, you likely have a healthy awareness of your shadow. That is wonderful. You have integrated facing your shadow in your leadership and now no longer experience the negative consequences of ignoring your shadow. You may even have discovered the shadow's hidden treasures for your leadership. You can expect new levels of discovery as you continue to engage your shadow. And, by God's grace, you can be an instrument in his hands to gently serve others in discovering and facing their shadows.

CHAPTER 3

LEAD OUT OF YOUR
MARRIAGE OR SINGLENESS

My friend Sam, a seminary professor, was in China recently visiting several friends. Among them was a woman named Li, lead pastor of a 5,000-member church. They met for lunch at a quiet restaurant on a sunny, spring day and began their conversation by sharing the latest news about their families. But within just a few minutes, Pastor Li began to weep. In fact, she repeatedly burst into sobs throughout the remainder of their two-hour lunch. She was desperate to pour out her soul, and Sam was just as desperate trying to understand what she was saying through her tears and his limited grasp of Mandarin Chinese. Gradually, the truth emerged.

Pastor Li was exhausted. She preached six times each Sunday and had not had a day off, much less a vacation, in seven years. In addition, she taught a course in systematic theology at a nearby seminary. Her one assistant pastor was not allowed to preach because he was not ordained.

At one point in the conversation, her cell phone rang and she took a call from a parishioner. Sam waited patiently, sipping his coffee. Ten minutes later, she returned to the conversation.

"My cell phone is on 24/7," she complained. "It is on all night long so people can reach me." Her eyes once more welled up with tears.

Sam encouraged her to turn off her phone at night so she could sleep. Pastor Li grimaced and replied harshly, "Suppose someone needs my help at 2 a.m.!"

Sam also learned that Li's husband lived five hours away in a nearby city where he taught full-time in a seminary. They saw each other for just one day every two weeks. Her two teenage boys were in the United States attending school. She saw them once or twice a year at most. She felt terrible about that, but with all her responsibilities, she didn't have time to raise them.

"This is not a good situation," Sam said kindly. "Can we talk about some changes you—"

Pastor Li cut him off.

"You think *my* situation is bad?" she said, pointing her finger at Sam. "Let me tell you about another pastor from a different city. His wife and son are living here and attend our church. But he pastors in a city twenty hours away by train. He is so busy that he comes home only once a year for the Chinese New Year. He stays for one night, but then he returns to his church."

"What?" Sam said, shocked by what he was hearing.

"No, it gets worse," Pastor Li replied. "He has so much to do, he feels guilty for taking time away. There is so much need. Last year, as he was about to board the train to leave his family for another year, his young son ran after him, crying and begging him, 'Please stay here, Daddy.'"

Pastor Li's voice grew soft. "Do you want to know what the father did?" she asked, looking down at her shoes. "He kicked his son and said, 'Devil, get thee behind me.' Then he pushed his son away and got on the train."

Sam was stunned.

"You see, Sam," Li concluded with resignation in her voice, "what you don't understand is that it is wrong if we don't sacrifice everything for the gospel."

Li's story may strike you as extreme—and it is. But the truth is, her perspective is not all that different from what I absorbed in more subtle ways in my own formation as a leader. The mind-set I picked up went something like this: *As Christian leaders, we routinely deal with life-and-death issues in people's lives. If we lead in the church, we are engaged in work with eternal ramifications. If we lead in the nonprofit sector, we are called to be the hands and feet of Christ to a world beset by a host of*

*ills—poverty, inadequate health care, addiction, family breakdown, and
more. Wherever we lead, we are ultimately seeking to build Christ's kingdom
and extend his love through our efforts. What could be more important?
How could we even think about withholding ourselves when the world is in
such desperate need?*

Does that line of thinking sound familiar?

Interestingly, the question of how a leader's singleness or marriage
fits into this sacrificial call to leadership wasn't discussed much, but I
did pick up a few messages about it along the way.

"Double Your Ministry for God"

I attended four different student mission conferences in my twenties.
The purpose of such conferences was to encourage and equip students
to devote their lives to serving Christ somewhere around the world or
to meet a critical need in North America. I have a vivid memory of one
conference, especially, during which one of the speakers thundered, "If
you are going to marry, make sure you marry someone who doubles
your ministry and doesn't cut it in half!"

Nobody had said it quite that bluntly before, but that was pretty
much the message I had already picked up about Christian marriage
and singleness. My young friends and I walked away with a clear
understanding that our priority in life was to extend the kingdom of
God. If we should marry, then it needed to be in service of that objective. On the plus side, many conference speakers did emphasize the
importance of not being unequally yoked to a partner who did not share
our commitment to Christ. It was a good caution, but a thin foundation
for integrating marriage or singleness with ministry leadership.

So I prayed for a woman who would double my impact for God.

God answered that prayer when I met Geri. We had been friends
for eight years prior to falling madly in love. We both were former
InterVarsity Christian Fellowship staff workers and deeply committed
to Christ. After we married, we gave our lives to serve Jesus through
church planting in New York.

Fast-forward eight years. The church we planted was growing and
people were coming to faith in Christ. While it was also true that I had

too much to do in too little time, I accepted it because it was the normal state for every pastor and leader I knew. But it was during this time that Geri's sadness developed into a full-blown depression as she found herself raising our four girls by herself. Even when she expressed her concerns, I didn't take her condition too seriously. *She is the strongest Christian I know*, I thought. *She can do this.*

Finally, one of her statements got my attention: "Pete, my life would be easier if we were separated. At least then you would have to take the kids on the weekends."

But I'm doing God's will, I reassured myself. *And I'm sure doing better than my father did.* I also reminded myself that our marriage was better than many others around us. I unconsciously wished Geri would be more cooperative and supportive of my ministry, but, of course, I would continue to do what I needed to do to get the job done. And so I offered an olive branch.

"Geri, let's find babysitters for the girls and go away overnight to a bed-and-breakfast."

The problem was that, even as I made the offer, I partially resented it. On the surface, at least, I couldn't help but think that instead of doubling my ministry for God, Geri was now cutting it in half!

No overnight getaway, date night, or coming home on time every night for a month could heal our growing disconnect. Our theology of marriage and leadership, if we had one, was defective. It would take much more than the Band-Aid of a weekend getaway to fix what was wrong.

After Geri quit the church (not the marriage, fortunately) in January 1996, we did in fact go away for a five-day intensive retreat with two Christian counselors. I went to fix Geri. Geri went to fix the church. God seemed intent to fix our marriage — and our marriage was the last place I expected to meet God. But toward the middle of the week, we learned a simple skill we now call "incarnational listening."[1] I do not remember the precise content of the conversation. What I will remember forever is *seeing* Geri and *being seen* by Geri. It was what Jewish philosopher Martin Buber called an I-Thou moment. God entered into the sacred space between us. We were dumbstruck with wonder.[2]

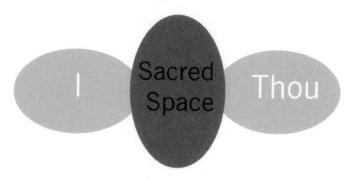

I had been a Christian for more than seventeen years at that point, but nothing prepared me for the glory of God that filled the space between us. While I did not have a theological framework for what happened, I knew we had tasted a bit of heaven. And I realized for the first time that it was God's will for Geri and me to lead out of our marriage. This was the moment that launched the global movement and ministry we now call Emotionally Healthy Spirituality, or EHS.

I informed Geri that I was committed to leading out of the joy of our marriage, out of the overflow of our cup running over with love for one another. And if I could not maintain the boundaries necessary to keep the pressures of church leadership from negatively impacting our marriage, I would gladly resign my position.

"Okay," she said cautiously, though it was clear she was skeptical.

I wanted her to know how serious I was. "Honey, I know that living in New York City is hard for you. If, at any point, you feel like you no longer want to be here, I will take that as God speaking to both of us. I will leave New Life, and we can seek out whatever God has for us to do next."

Even I was astounded at what I was saying. But I meant every word.

Two months later, we took a three-and-a-half-month sabbatical to begin building a relationship that would enable us to return to New Life and take the first steps in discovering how to sustainably lead out of our marriage. Ultimately, this set us on an unexpected journey over the next nineteen years of studying Scripture and researching available literature for insights on how to integrate marriage or singleness with leadership. Our discoveries profoundly altered our relationship with Jesus, along with every aspect of how we led at New Life.

Understanding Marriage and Singleness As Vocations

Every Christian has the same primary calling or vocation: *We are called to Jesus, by Jesus, and for Jesus.* Our first call is to love him with our whole being and to love our neighbor as ourselves. Biblical writers use many analogies to describe our relationship with God (shepherd/sheep, master/slave, parent/child), but marriage is perhaps the most comprehensive and "least inadequate"[3] (Ezekiel 16; Mark 2:19–20; Revelation 19–22).

In ancient times, marriage included two events, the betrothal and the wedding. During the betrothal phase, the man and woman were considered husband and wife (think of Mary and Joseph), but the marriage was not consummated until after the wedding. When we receive Jesus as Lord and Savior, we are effectively *betrothed* to him. This marriage will be consummated when we see him face-to-face at the end of our earthly life.

We work out this marriage to Jesus through our secondary callings, or vocations, as single or married persons.

Throughout the history of the church, Christians have tended to elevate the importance of one over the other. For the first 1,500 years of the church, singleness was considered the preferred state and the best way to serve Christ. Singles sat at the front of the church. Marrieds were sent to the back.[4] Things changed after the Reformation in 1517, when single people were sent to the back and marrieds moved to the front — at least among Protestants.[5]

Scripture, however, refers to both statuses as weighty, meaningful vocations. We'll spend more time on each later in the chapter, but here is a brief overview.

Marrieds. This refers to a man and woman who form a one-flesh union through a covenantal vow — to God, to one another, and to the larger community — to permanently, freely, faithfully, and fruitfully love one another. Adam and Eve provide the clearest biblical model for this. As a one-flesh couple, they were called by God to take initiative to "be fruitful ... fill the earth and subdue it" (Genesis 1:28).

Singles. Scripture teaches that human beings are created for intimacy and connection with God, themselves, and one another. Marriage is one framework in which we work this out; singleness is another.

While singleness may be voluntarily chosen or involuntarily imposed, temporary or long-term, a sudden event or a gradual unfolding, Christian singleness can be understood within two distinct callings:

- *Vowed celibates.* These are individuals who make lifelong vows to remain single and maintain lifelong sexual abstinence as a means of living out their commitment to Christ. They do this freely in response to a God-given gift of grace (Matthew 19:12). Today, we are perhaps most familiar with vowed celibates as nuns and priests in the Roman Catholic or Orthodox Church. These celibates vow to forgo earthly marriage in order to participate more fully in the heavenly reality that is eternal union with Christ.[6]
- *Dedicated celibates.* These are singles who have not necessarily made a lifelong vow to remain single, but who choose to remain sexually abstinent for as long as they are single. Their commitment to celibacy is an expression of their commitment to Christ. Many desire to marry or are open to the possibility. They may have not yet met the right person or are postponing marriage to pursue a career or additional education. They may be single because of divorce or the death of a spouse. The apostle Paul acknowledges such dedicated celibates in his first letter to the church at Corinth (1 Corinthians 7).

Understanding singleness and marriage as callings or vocations must inform our self-understanding and the outworking of our leadership. Our whole life as a leader is to bear witness to God's love for the world. But we do so in different ways as marrieds or singles. Married couples bear witness to the *depth* of Christ's love. Their vows focus and limit them to loving one person exclusively, permanently, and intimately. Singles — vowed or dedicated — bear witness to the *breadth* of Christ's love. Because they are not limited by a vow to one person, they have more freedom and time to express the love of Christ to a broad range of people. Both marrieds and singles point to and reveal Christ's love, but in different ways. Both need to learn from one another about these different aspects of Christ's love.

This may be a radically new concept for you, but stay with me. God intends this rich theological vision to inform our leadership in ways few of us may have considered. Before exploring the connections between leadership and marriage or singleness, it's important to understand the way marriage and singleness are commonly understood in standard practice among leaders today.

How Healthy Is Your Ability to Lead Out of Your Marriage or Singleness?

Use the list of statements that follow to do a brief assessment on your ability to lead out of your marriage or singleness. Next to each statement, write down the number that best describes your response. Use the following scale:

5 = Always true of me
4 = Frequently true of me
3 = Occasionally true of me
2 = Rarely true of me
1 = Never true of me

Leading Out of Your Marriage

_____ 1. I see my marriage as a prophetic sign of God's love for the church and the world.

_____ 2. I consider the quality and integrity of my marriage as the most important gospel message I preach.

_____ 3. I place the highest priority on investing time and energy to build a healthy marriage that reveals Christ's love to the church and the world.

_____ 4. I experience a direct connection between my oneness with Jesus and my oneness with my spouse.

_____ 5. A key factor for me in discerning God's will in major ministry initiatives is the impact it will have on my marriage.

_____ 6. I am aware of how issues from my family of origin impact my ability to be emotionally available in a healthy way to my spouse as well as to those I serve.

_____ 7. I do not overfunction as a leader at the expense of my marriage.

_____ 8. I make what is important to my spouse important to me regardless of my leadership responsibilities.

_____ 9. The fruit I bear in ministry overflows out of the richness of my marriage.

_____ 10. I am comfortable articulating a biblical vision for marrieds and singles on how each serves to bear witness to God's love.

Leading Out of Your Singleness

_____ 1. I see my singleness as a prophetic sign of God's love for the church and the world.

_____ 2. I believe the quality and integrity of my singleness is the most important gospel message I preach.

_____ 3. I place the highest priority on investing time and energy to build a healthy singleness that reveals Christ's love to the church and the world.

_____ 4. I experience a direct connection between my oneness with Jesus and my relationships with close friends and family.

_____ 5. A key factor for me in discerning God's will in major ministry initiatives is the impact it will have on my ability to live a whole, rich, and healthy single life.

_____ 6. I am aware how issues from my family of origin impact my ability to be emotionally available in a healthy way to my close friends, family, and those I serve.

_____ 7. I do not overfunction as a leader at the expense of living a healthy and balanced single life.

_____ 8. I make what is important to my close friends and family important to me regardless of my leadership responsibilities.

_____ 9. The fruit I bear in ministry overflows out of the richness of my close relationships with family and friends.

_____ 10. I am comfortable articulating a biblical vision for marrieds and singles on how each serves uniquely to bear witness to God's love.

Take a moment to briefly review your responses. What stands out most to you? Although there is no definitive scoring for the assessment, at the end of the chapter (page 116) are some general observations that may help you understand more about where you're at.

If your responses aren't what you'd hoped, you are not alone. The integration of marriage and ministry was one of the most neglected parts of my leadership for my first seventeen years as a pastor. Wherever you find yourself, the great news is that a little awareness and making a few changes can have an immediate and positive impact not only in your personal life but on those you lead.

The Role of Marriage and Singleness in Standard Practice

I attended two excellent theological seminaries and routinely traveled to the best Christian leadership conferences offered in the United States. At no point during that time was the issue of integrating marriage and singleness into leadership addressed. Perhaps a well-known speaker might encourage those of us who were married to have a date night, a special evening with our children, or a well-planned vacation, but that was pretty much the extent of it. Sexuality was not talked about except for the occasional warning, "Don't do it outside of marriage." It was assumed, for example, that married leaders knew how to have a life-giving sexual relationship with their spouse. And little, if any, effort was ever made to acknowledge or include spouses at leadership events. Over time, the unspoken message I got about marriage and leadership went something like this: *Pete, seek first the kingdom of God. Build the church and everything else will be added to you. That includes a blessed marriage and family. You need a stable marriage (or single life) in order to have a strong, stable ministry.*

So it's not surprising that my first priority was to be an innovative pastor with a growing ministry. As long as I was not having an affair, not dabbling in pornography, and not married to someone who complained about me publicly or threatened to leave me, I was okay. For single leaders, the same principle applied. *Keep it together morally, but your first priority is to build the ministry and extend the kingdom of God.*

If little equipping was given to help married leaders, even less was provided for single leaders. The connection between singleness and leadership was rarely, if ever, mentioned. But the not-so-subtle message behind the silence was loud and clear: *You would have a broader, more effective ministry if you were married.* In some cases, single leaders were even considered suspect, the underlying message being, *What's wrong with you that you're still single?*

Among Christian leaders today, the default thinking about marriage and singleness in standard practice goes something like this:

- A leader's highest priority is to build an effective and successful ministry to reveal Jesus' love to the world. We give our best time and energy to achieve that objective. Marriage or singleness is important, but secondary on the priority list.

- A leader's connection or oneness with Jesus is separate from his or her connection to a spouse (if married) or close friends and family (if single).
- How a decision might impact a leader's marriage or singleness is a secondary rather than primary consideration in ministry discernment and decision making.
- Leaders need to get as much training and equipping as possible to improve their leadership skills. They should get training and equipping for marriage or singleness if they have problems or a crisis.
- Christian leaders need sound doctrine and a foundational theology, but they can't be experts on everything. There are more essential things to know and understand than a theology of marriage, singleness, or sexuality.
- Christian leaders don't need to be overly concerned about marriage or singleness of their team members. Senior leaders, in particular, should know how to care for these aspects of their lives by the time they get into higher levels of leadership.

I've stated them rather bluntly, but do any of these perspectives sound familiar to you? Do you recognize some of your own default thinking in the mix?

Within the Christian community, this pervasive disconnect between leadership and one's vocation (as married or single) is so pronounced — and yet so pervasively considered "normal" — that only a powerful theological vision from God can reverse and redeem this dangerous state of affairs. But in order to live out a new vision, we need to understand what it means to do so in practical terms — to rearrange our lives and leadership in ways that enable us to truly lead out of our marriage or singleness.

Leading Out of Your Marriage

In 1996 when Geri and I began researching the connection between marriage and leadership, the scarcity of theological thinking around marriage, particularly with regard to sexuality, shocked us. We continued to deepen our own marriage and sexuality, but we were keen to identify and understand the differences between Christian and secular marriage—especially for leaders. Eventually, we identified three foundational qualities we believe must inform the marriage or single life of the emotionally healthy Christian leader.

We'll explore the qualities for both, beginning with marriage. If you want to lead out of your marriage, then you must make marriage—not leadership—your first ambition, your first passion, and your loudest gospel message.

Marriage Is Your First Ambition

The word *ambition* is defined as "a strong desire to achieve something." That seems like a reasonable thing to have, right? And we all do have ambition of one kind or another. But in the church, *ambition* is a word from which we tend to distance ourselves. We connect it negatively with things like a competitive spirit or the "selfish ambition" of the divisive church faction to which Paul refers (Philippians 1:17). Yet, ambition can be a good thing, especially when it motivates a pursuit of the good, the true, and the beautiful.

The first ambition for married Christian leaders must shift from leading our church, organization, or team to loving our spouse passionately. We must cultivate a strong desire to make visible the invisible—the love of Jesus for his church—in and through the love we have for our spouse. We then lead out of the overflow of this love. In other words, out of the giving and receiving of love in our relationship, we have extra "give away" love. It overflows from the nurturing, connection, and sense of well-being we receive from one another.[7]

When Christians marry, we make a covenantal vow to love our spouse faithfully, freely, fruitfully, and forever. From this point on, every significant decision we make is to be informed by that vow. The pace of the church or organization we serve, the commitments we make, and the focus of our heart's passion are all to be informed by that vow. To put it bluntly, if you are married, it is no longer an option for you to live as if you were single. Why? You made a vow to be married. Yes, it is sometimes painful to connect to your spouse, but in the long term, it is even more painful not to.

This means the first item on your leadership job description is to conduct your life in such a way that your demeanor and choices consistently demonstrate to your spouse that he or she is loved and lovable. You make what is important to him or her important to you.[8] That means I awake each day and ask myself, *What is important to Geri today? How can I be present to her in a way that reflects Jesus' love?*

My tendency is to be distracted and self-absorbed in doing the ministry work I love, whether it is pastoring at New Life, teaching about emotionally healthy spirituality, or writing books. With marriage as my first ambition, I am led to prioritize things I might otherwise put off or minimize — taking a hike with Geri on a rainy day, cooking a healthy meal together, helping out with things that need to be done around the house. And all of these actions stand in stark contrast to what I observed in both my family growing up and in the leadership models from my early ministry days. Doing these things does not come naturally or easily to me. In fact, the changes necessary to truly lead out of marriage don't come naturally to most of us. I saw this, for example, in a friend of mine who planted a church in a nearby city.

Philip worked hard, and within five years the church he planted had grown from a core group of twenty-five to more than three hundred. The problem was that Philip was routinely working eighty to ninety hours a week.

"My day started about 5 a.m.," he shared with me one afternoon. "There were times I slept only three to four hours a night. I was out at least four to five evenings a week. Sometimes I was out every night. I took two to three vacations a year, but only for one week, and that lasted Monday through Friday." Philip paused and took a deep breath. "Since I was the only pastor, I returned to preach every Sunday. So it wasn't really a vacation because I still had to think about preparing for the sermon. I was gaining weight and not sleeping much. My wife thought it was her duty to cooperate with what God was doing, so she never complained. After putting our three children to bed, she spent most nights alone at home watching television."

One Sunday evening, after a particularly grueling weekend that included speaking at a weekend retreat, preaching two services, hosting a newcomers' dinner in his home, and a late-night counseling appointment for a troubled couple, Philip felt exhausted and despairing. His only thought was, *I want to die. I don't want to live anymore.* God finally had Philip's attention. Within a few days, he had consulted the church board and made arrangements for a two-month sabbatical. This led him into the journey we call "emotionally healthy spirituality." Three years later, this is how Philip describes his ministry and marriage:

> One of the ways I know I'm in a healthy place now is that I actually love being a husband and father more than being a pastor. My marriage is my most important ministry now, which really goes against the grain of my Korean culture. It has forced me to slow down. I frequently say no to speaking at outside conferences and retreats. I'm out only one or, at most, two nights a week. Susan and I put our children to bed by 9:00 p.m. and then spend our evenings together. Initially, it was hard because Susan had spent so many years not having me around. So, even though I was staying home at night, we didn't know how to connect. Eventually, we learned.
>
> But there has been pushback from some in the church. Just last week, one of our leaders said to me, "You are *never* around." When she said that, my first thought was, "Do I need to work harder?" Then I reminded myself that I still do work hard, but in comparison to how much time I was spending at the church before, I understand how it could seem like *"never"* to her. I think I'm beginning to understand what it means to lead out of my marriage.

Philip's greatest fear, he confided, was that the church would shrink if he made this shift. The opposite has actually proven true. The church has continued its steady growth. The difference now is that Philip is content and enjoying the process of being a pastor and leader.

Marriage Is Your First Passion

Passion, according to the *Oxford English Dictionary*, is "a strong and barely controllable emotion." If marriage, not leadership, is our first passion, then married Christian leaders should be among the most "in love" couples in the church. That means our passion — the focus of that strong and barely controllable emotion — is not devoted to pursuing leadership goals or achievements, but to our spouse.

When we think of marital love, we tend to emphasize things like commitment and loyalty. As a result, a Christian couple may go to church and serve together, but too often end up with only a vaguely detached sense of devotion to one another. This is a far cry from God's desire for the covenant of marriage.

God loves us with a faithful, persevering, *agape* love. Yet his covenant love for us is also characterized by *eros*, the Greek word for a love that expresses itself in sexual passion. This means God's love for us is fiery and wild with delight. He is crazy about us! Consider the following Scriptures that express this aspect of God's love for us:

> *"He will take great delight in you ... [he] will rejoice over you with singing."*   (ZEPHANIAH 3:17)

> *He ran to his son, threw his arms around him and kissed him [repeatedly, in Greek].*   (LUKE 15:20)

> *"How can I give you up ...? My heart is changed within me; all my compassion is aroused."*   (HOSEA 11:8)

> *"Father, just as you are in me and I am in you. May they also be in us."*   (JOHN 17:21)

Do you see the passion in God's love for us?

This same passion is to be reflected in every Christian marriage, but especially in the marriages of those in leadership. We are to love our spouse as God does—with commitment and passion. In doing so we model the love of Jesus for our teams and those we serve.

Most couples are passionate when they are engaged. We cannot stop thinking of each other. Day and night we wonder how to give ourselves to our future spouse. We are sexually attracted to him or her. We are drawn out of our selfishness into an other-centered focus. This passion, however, is not meant to diminish as the years and decades pass; rather, God intends it to deepen and mature. Passion is actually central to our marital vocation. It is meant to point to something beyond us, to offer people a taste and picture of the same passionate love God has for the world.

Sadly, most couples become less passionate and less sexual after they marry, especially when one spouse is consumed with leadership tasks. Very few of us have been equipped to have a passionate, flourishing marriage. We expect that it will happen naturally. It does not. It must be cultivated.[9] The question, then, is *how*. How do we cultivate a passionate marriage, especially in the context of leadership?

There are three things that enable Geri and me to make our marriage, rather than ministry, our first passion: praying for passion, making passion an intentional spiritual practice, and affirming one another.

We pray for greater passion. Geri and I pray regularly, alone and at times together, for greater passion. I initially tried to remain passionate without prayer and found I was unable to sustain it in my own strength. Prayer released the Holy Spirit's power in our marriage, and that has made all the difference. Resisting the temptation to become apathetic in our passion requires a power from outside us. We ask God for grace to *live in love*[10] each day, seeking to be present to one other in the way that God is present to us. Prayer has changed everything in this regard.

Through prayer, the Holy Spirit keeps us thinking about each other throughout the day. Prayer also keeps us focused on the heart of God and his love for the world. Our prayer is that others might see our passionate love for one another, experience a revelation, and say, "Wow, that is how Jesus loves me!"

We make cultivating passion an intentional spiritual practice. We are committed to regular physical nakedness and union as a spiritual practice and declaration of the first importance of our marital vocation. We seek to set aside twenty minutes each day to be naked and without shame in each other's arms (Genesis 2:24). The goal is not sexual intercourse. We simply want to be passionately connected to one another—physically, spiritually, emotionally, and intellectually.

This twenty-minute spiritual practice also serves to cultivate an atmosphere of sexual attraction between us. Marriage is different than every other relationship. We are more than best friends with similar values. We are more than coworkers for Christ. What makes our marriage distinct is our sexual relationship. We intentionally "make love" outside the bedroom (tender touches, thoughtful gestures, surprise gifts, appealing dress) as well as inside the bedroom. This skin-to-skin practice spills over into our whole life, permeating all of our days and activities.

Are we always 100 percent successful in these efforts? No. Our rhythms are interrupted, for example, by vacations with family, holidays, health setbacks, seasons when we travel and speak. Regardless, with marriage (not leadership) firmly established as our first passion, it's naturally something that's constantly in our thoughts and in our hearts.

We talk about passion, plan for passion, and pray for passion. And we add to our thoughts about passion and our regular twenty-minute discipline one final important practice — affirmation.

We intentionally affirm one another. During our spiritual practice of regular physical nakedness, we intentionally affirm one another. It's been said that you find what you look for — look for faults and you will find faults, look for beauty and you will find beauty. Regular, sincere affirmation is one of the greatest gifts one spouse can give the other. When we look for goodness and beauty in one another and speak honest words of life over one another, we become God with skin on for the other. Affirmations heal wounds, cover shame, and communicate how God sees us — as infinitely valuable and lovable. A steady stream of criticism, on the other hand, sucks the life out of us and out of our relationships. It is one of the great killers of passion.

When I intentionally share with Geri the qualities I find attractive about her — be they physical, emotional, spiritual, or relational — not only do I feel differently about her, she feels closer to me and safe with me. Receiving words of affirmation from Geri can be challenging for me sometimes because they were so rarely given in my family of origin. But God has used her words to remind me of the gospel and how God sees me. Intentionally affirming your spouse — especially when you know his or her faults better than anyone on earth — is one of the greatest gifts you can give. It also serves as an enormous contributor to greater passion.

God knows we are at our best when we are living in an atmosphere of passion for one another. We are more generous, more patient, and more forgiving. When we can't get enough of each other, we see the world in full color, not black and white.

Marriage Is Your Loudest Gospel Message

Most Christian leaders believe that the loudest message we preach to the world comes through our words, or perhaps our service to others in Jesus' name. In the early years of ministry, I considered planting a church and preaching sermons to be my loudest gospel message.

When I say that *marriage* is a leader's loudest gospel message, I mean that a Christian marriage points beyond itself to something more important—to Christ. As such, marriage is a sign and a wonder. When Jesus turned water into wine, it is referred to as the first of his miraculous signs. The miracle pointed to Jesus the Messiah as the best wine that was saved until the fullness of time in history. Much more was happening in Cana than simply water becoming wine. The miracle pointed to Jesus as *the wine* that never runs out, that always satisfies, and that now overflows in extravagant abundance.

The apostle Paul makes this same connection in what may be his most important statement on marriage:

> *"For this reason a man will leave his father and mother and be united to his wife, and the two will become one flesh." This is a profound mystery—but I am talking about Christ and the church.*
> (EPHESIANS 5:31–32)

Paul understands earthly marriage as more than two people coming together to have children and enjoy a great life. It is more than a foundation for our leadership. He sees marriage as a sign and wonder in two distinct ways. As mentioned earlier, marital love makes visible how God loves the world—totally, faithfully, freely, and fruitfully. For Christians, the love between spouses is meant to reveal how God loves the world. Earthly marriage points to our eternal destiny when we will be perfectly united in and fulfilled by his love. The apostle Paul views earthly marriage as a prophetic sign of the Marriage Supper of the Lamb (Revelation 19–22). That is why Jesus said there is no marriage in heaven. Once we arrive, the sign will no longer be needed (Matthew 22:30); we will have reached our destiny, marriage to Christ, and will enjoy a wedding celebration that will last forever.

So what does this mean in practical terms? How do Christian leaders make marriage the loudest gospel message we preach?

When I moved from a nonvocational view of leadership (I am a leader who happens to be married) to a vocational view (I lead *out of my marriage*), several things changed. I gained a heightened awareness of myself first as Geri's husband, not as Pastor Pete. I embraced

God's call to be "God with skin on" for Geri, seeking to be present and responsive to her as I am to my own body. My definition of leadership success was transformed beyond merely growing the church to nurturing a passionate marriage that overflows to the rest of the world. My need to have my lovability affirmed through ministry achievement dissipated as I more fully experienced Geri's deep love for and delight in me. In the initial baby steps of this new journey, I restructured my leadership priorities so that the top of my weekly to-do list looked something like this:

- Spend time alone with God (listing times and spiritual practices for the week)
- Invest in Geri and our marriage (listing times and specific actions for the week)
- Everything else at New Life Fellowship (message prep, staff meetings, board meeting prep, etc.)

Making marriage our loudest gospel message didn't mean Geri and I suddenly began to do everything together. We did not and do not. But once I set my heart on making what is important to Geri important to me, things changed. Perhaps the biggest shift in me was an increase in my awareness of, and my ability to be present to, Geri first, especially at New Life services. In the past, once I arrived at church for weekend services, I wouldn't think much about Geri or touch her if she was nearby. The people I was there to serve came first. But for Geri, those were some of the moments that mattered most. Initially, it was a conscious effort to walk across a room to put my arm around her, hold her hand in the midst of worship, or hug her in the foyer after service. Now seeking Geri in a crowd is a natural extension of our oneness and love. She loves it and, to my surprise, others notice as well. I am keenly aware of how we preach the love of Christ through our marriage when we are in public — even if I am not teaching publicly.

It's no exaggeration to say that these were dramatic changes, all of which pushed me to bring my best leadership energy first to our marriage and then to my role as a pastor. Investing in our marriage became core to my leadership for New Life, not an "extra." It also helped me to understand more about what it means to lead out of singleness.

Leading Out of Your Singleness

In the same way that we need a robust spirituality of vocational marriage, we also need a rich spirituality of vocational singleness if the church is to mature into all God intends. But before we explore what it means to lead out of one's singleness, I need to acknowledge the limitations I bring to writing on this topic.

To begin with, I'm not single. Although I was a dedicated celibate from age nineteen to twenty-eight, I write as someone who has now been a married pastor for thirty-one years. I have not experienced the challenges and complexities of serving for decades as a single leader. I do not know what it is like to be treated with suspicion or as a second-class citizen because of my singleness. I also come from a Protestant tradition that, for the most part, has largely failed to develop a biblical theology of singleness, let alone its practical application in the church. And while I have studied Christian singleness over the years and talked with hundreds of singles about their experiences, I remain profoundly aware of how much I do *not* know.

Despite these limitations, I write to advance a meaningful and much-needed conversation about this topic within the church. I earnestly hope single leaders will be encouraged to take their rightful places of leadership in the church, and that married leaders will exhibit a much greater sensitivity to the issues and concerns of singles so that all of us, together, can advance the cause of Christ in the world.

Having acknowledged my limitations, I feel confident in stating that if you want to lead out of your singleness, then there are three things you must do: be intentional about the kind of single God has called you to be, make a healthy singleness (not leadership) your first ambition, and make singleness your loudest gospel message.

Be Intentional about the Kind of Single God Has Called You to Be

An increasing number of leaders in the body of Christ today are single. There was a time when the term *single* referred almost exclusively to young adults who had not yet married. Today, it might just as readily refer to a forty-year-old divorced dad, a sixty-five-year-old widow, or a thirty-three-year-old man who chooses to be a vowed celibate. This means we have more and more Christian leaders who need to be intentional about choosing their vocation as either a vowed or dedicated celibate.[11]

Vowed Celibates

Today, most of those who practice vowed celibacy serve in Roman Catholic and Orthodox religious orders and churches. Sadly, vowed celibacy is seldom talked about or considered a valid calling in most Protestant churches.[12] Slowly, however, this is changing. In the last two hundred years, there has been something of a rediscovery of the biblical teaching around vocational celibacy and a resurgence of its practice in the Protestant church around the world.[13]

It was Jesus who first acknowledged the notion of a vowed or consecrated celibacy. And he did so at a time and in a culture that would have found it shocking. Jewish history, culture, and even Old Testament teaching up to that point provided no real place for intentionally single people.[14] In fact, it was so taken for granted that a Jewish man would marry that there was no Hebrew word for bachelor. Some rabbis taught that to be unmarried at age twenty was considered a sin. Carrying on the family name through the eldest son was literally considered a matter of life and death. Nothing was worse than the extermination of the family name.[15] The pressure from family, synagogue, and culture to marry was enormous. So keep that context in mind as you read these words from Jesus:

> *"Not everyone can accept this word, but only those to whom it has been given. For there are eunuchs who were born that way, and there are eunuchs who have been made eunuchs by others — and there are **others have renounced marriage because** of the kingdom of heaven. The one who can accept this should accept it.*
> MATTHEW 19:11 – 12, EMPHASIS ADDED

> *Jesus replied, "You are in error because you do not know the Scriptures or the power of God. **At the resurrection people will neither marry nor be given in marriage;** they will be like the angels in heaven."*
> (MATTHEW 22:29 – 30, EMPHASIS ADDED)

The word for *eunuch* in Matthew 19:12 refers not just to a castrated male but to any person who chooses not to offer their body sexually to another. After acknowledging that some are celibate due to physical disabilities and others are celibate due to castration, Jesus opens up an entirely new category—those who have renounced marriage *"for the sake of the kingdom of heaven."* That is the very definition of a vowed celibate.

Vowed celibates receive a *charism*, a divine enablement from God given to certain men and women so they might offer a special gift of service to the world.[16] They freely choose to give themselves as an exclusive and lifelong gift to Christ. In doing so, they forgo the temporal sign of marriage on earth so they can participate more fully now in the heavenly reality to which marriage points—eternal marriage to Christ.

Jesus' statement in Matthew 19 makes it clear that few men and women are granted this vocation: "Not everyone can accept this word, but only those to whom it has been given" (Matthew 19:11). Nonetheless, they do exist among the leaders in our churches and ministries. Perhaps you are among that small number. If you are wondering if that may be the case, let me encourage you to visit a monastic community near you to meet men and women who have already made a commitment to vowed celibacy. Listen to their stories and discernment process. It is common, at least in the monastic communities I know best, to require a five- to seven-year discernment process before making a lifetime vow. In fact, one of our former New Life leaders is currently in the midst of her own discernment process in a monastic community.

If you are single but do not feel called to vowed celibacy, there is one more option: dedicated celibacy, the vocation of most single Protestant leaders today.

Dedicated Celibates

Dedicated celibates choose to practice celibacy as long as they remain unmarried as part of their commitment to Christ. I chose to be a dedicated celibate for a nine-year period, between the ages of nineteen and twenty-eight. I wanted to live in undivided devotion and remain undistracted by a relationship in order to grow spiritually and serve

Christ. The desire to marry surfaced when I was twenty-seven. I asked myself, "Who is the most godly woman I know — someone who would follow Jesus even if I did not?" The answer was easy. It was Geri, my good friend and longtime InterVarsity colleague. Over the next year, we dated and the rest is history.

Geri was also a dedicated celibate for eight years in her twenties. She was about to get engaged when she became a Christian. Out of her oneness to Jesus, she went through the painful process of ending the relationship (*Thank God!*). She lived wholeheartedly for Christ, dated occasionally, and served in both vocational ministry and as a high school teacher. When she was twenty-six and preparing to move to Thailand for a two-year ministry commitment, I asked her to consider remaining in the States so we could discern what God might have for our relationship. While Geri was content in her singleness, she was also open to God regarding her future.

We both enjoyed our single years as Christ-followers and ministry leaders. Had we remained single, we would no doubt have encountered new challenges in our thirties, forties, fifties, and beyond. But we have known many single friends over the years who have navigated such complexities well and, in the process, taught us much about dedicated celibacy. Sue is one of those friends.

Sue is a gifted leader and teacher at New Life. She has taught at retreats, provided pastoral care to people in difficult situations, mentored staff, and offered timely wisdom to our community on more occasions than I can remember. Here is how she describes her journey:

> When I became a Christian at age seventeen, I just assumed I would eventually marry. But I also knew that the first call on my life was to love God and others — I was to be a lover. So when I was eighteen, I bought a ring and engraved on it this verse from Song of Songs: "I am my beloved's and my beloved is mine" (6:3). It was a reminder that I belonged first to Christ.
>
> I didn't feel called to celibacy for life. I hoped to eventually meet someone to spend the rest of my life with. I did have one relationship that was serious, but he felt called to serve God in Africa (I did not), and we went our separate ways. So, even though it wasn't initially my plan, I have embraced celibacy.

I am now sixty-four years old and have had a very full life. In my work as a therapist, I have counseled both married couples and singles. I also truly feel that I have many children—not biological children, but people I have poured my life into over the years. I have great joy and satisfaction in that.

I don't feel I have missed anything. In fact, I feel incredibly blessed. Because I am single, I have been free to pursue many things that would otherwise have been impossible. I am also not under any illusions that marriage cures loneliness. Loneliness is part of being human. It is the invitation to open our hearts more deeply to God. However, that doesn't mean we have to live a solitary life.

Even when I lived alone for ten years, I made it a point to frequently invite people over (singles, marrieds, and families). And for the last thirty-four years, I have shared my life with Bonnie, my friend and housemate. Community is a very important part of my life and our lives. I believe the church is a community. We are God's family. There is no reason for any of us to be solitaries. Bonnie and I each have our own lives, but we have a life in common as well.

My word to singles is: *Don't live like you're waiting. Live the most fulfilled, joyful life you can now.*

I love so many things about Sue's story—her understanding of loneliness as part of the human condition, her commitment to hospitality, close friendships, and especially her willingness to embrace a dedicated celibacy she did not initially want. If you met Sue, you'd also see that one of the most beautiful things about her is her intentionality and joy as a single leader. It radiates to all those around her and truly reflects the love of Jesus.

For most singles, however, choosing to live as a single celibate is not an easy choice to make. Emily, a para-church missionary, has worked with university students and trained other workers for the last thirty years. When I asked her to tell me about her intentionality as a dedicated celibate, this was her response:

Intentionality? That is a tough word. I didn't want to be single. This was the hand that was dealt to me. My question was, *Where do I go with this?* I didn't want to sit around waiting. I wanted to get on with my life.

My thirties were tough because I was attending a lot of weddings and wondering what was wrong with me that I was still single. But things changed in my forties. On my fortieth birthday I got out my journal and wrote, "What is good about this?" Then I wrote down the names of people I'd invested in because I was single and available. I had a list of 300 people! My forties were a wonderful time for me. I was making a real difference in people's lives. This got me through some of the hard times.

By the age of fifty-two, I still longed for a partner, a companion in older age, someone to be there. I tried to remain indifferent like Ignatius talks about, holding my desires and longings for marriage with my palms open, not with my hands tightly clenched. Finally, I said, *God I'm not going to pray about it any more. You know what is on my heart. I am done praying about it. From here on, whatever you decide to give me — singleness or marriage — I will receive it as a gift from you. What I really want is you. All I have is you.* Afterward, I cried tears of true contentment and relinquishment.

That's when I realized in a deeper way that my longing for marriage was the outward expression of my inward longing for the Lord. That was a very significant moment for me. God had brought me to a moment of absolute indifference. It truly did not matter to me if I married or not.

Emily's story highlights three truths about the experience of being intentional in choosing dedicated celibacy. First, she was committed to a life of loving union with Jesus, regardless of circumstances. (We will talk more about this in the next chapter.) Second, her intentionality was a process. Surrendering to God's love and will is not a once-and-for-all event. Emily let us into the very human process we all experience in our lives when our will clashes with God's. And finally, this vocation, like the others, carries its own unique kind of suffering, all of which was used by God to form Christ in her.

If you are a single leader, you may well have experienced some or all of these truths in your own life, though perhaps you didn't have the words or framework to see it as a vocation. Or maybe, like Sue and Emily, choosing dedicated celibacy is something you've struggled with. Wherever you find yourself, being intentional about your vocation and allowing God to use it will be a significant step on your journey to becoming an emotionally healthy leader.

A Healthy Singleness Is Your First Ambition

You'll recall from the section on marriage that ambition is "a strong desire to achieve something." The first ambition for single Christian leaders must shift from leading a church, organization, or team to investing in a healthy single life. Similar to married leaders, single leaders are called to lead out of an overflow of love — in this case, the overflow of their love relationship with Jesus and the giving and receiving of love from their close relationships.

This means the first item on your leadership job description as a single leader is to make clear choices to cultivate a healthy singleness. When you awake each day you ask yourself, *What do I need to do today to lead out of a healthy singleness for Christ?* What makes this choice particularly critical is that there is an unwritten rule that single leaders need less time for this than marrieds. Actually, the opposite is true.

Myra, a small group pastor, summarized it well in a letter to her pastor when he asked her, along with other single staff, to stay late to clean up after a retreat while married staff were encouraged to go home to their spouses:

> Please don't take my community for granted. My network of close friends is as critical to me as your spouse is to you. I would like you to take my needs for rest and intimate connection with my network of friends as seriously as you take your commitment to be with your spouse. My close friends are the ones God has given me, and it actually takes more effort, not less, for me to enjoy healthy relationships with them. Why? It's not naturally built in for us because we aren't waiting for one another at home.

Without healthy singleness as her first ambition, it would have been easy for Myra to simply do what her supervisor asked her to do and chalk it up to the price of being a servant leader, even if she privately resented it. But when healthy singleness is your first ambition, you may have to confront situations like this when others are insensitive to the unique challenges of being a single leader. No one else can assert what you need in this regard; you need to graciously but truthfully call others to respect this aspect of your leadership. And you can continue to build on this ambition in three practical ways: investing in excellent self-care, cultivating community, and practicing hospitality.

Devote yourself to excellent self-care. Build into your leadership strong rhythms and boundaries for proper self-care. The biblical principle is: "Watch your life ... closely" (1 Timothy 4:16). Since you are in people-caring work, it is vital that you steward yourself well. Author and educator Parker Palmer says it best:

> I have become clear about at least one thing: self-care is never a selfish act — it is simply good stewardship of the only gift I have, the gift I was put on earth to offer to others. Anytime we can listen to true self and give it the care it requires, we do so not only for ourselves, but for the many others whose lives we touch.[17]

In order to be a good steward of the limited resource that is *you*, it is vital that you discern the kinds of people, places, and activities that bring you joy. Routinely ask yourself, *What restores and replenishes my soul? What fills me with delight?* My friend Hector is a single man who experienced a transformation before my very eyes in this area over a span of ten years. Here is his story:

> So what do I think about being a forty-one-year-old, first-born son of immigrant parents who is still single? While it's not my — or my parents' — preference, I'd still rather be happy, fruitful, and single with Jesus than married and dissatisfied or, worse, miserable. I live robustly and enjoy investing relationally by doing things I love with friends — playing ultimate Frisbee, motorcycling across the country, starting small groups, and even relocating to join a missional business 10,000 miles from New York City. Although I'd still appreciate the opportunity to experience life as a married person, my relationships — with my siblings, nieces, parents, best

buddies, close friends, church family, and colleagues—leave me
a grateful man with my cup overflowing.

One of the things that has impressed me most about Hector over the
years is the broad range of hobbies and delights he invests in as a single
leader—from sports to dancing to motorcycling. In committing to a life
that brings him joy, he not only broke out of his culture's commandment
that work is the most important thing in life but also sidestepped
the misguided view in some Christian circles that pleasure and delight
are somehow suspect if not outright sinful. If you want to devote yourself
to excellent self-care, make pursuing joy and delight an intentional
part of your life and leadership.

Invest in community, cultivating at least one or two companions for
the journey. Whether married or single, being a leader is often a lonely
experience. But that loneliness can be amplified for single leaders, perhaps
especially for those who live alone. As the Son of God, Jesus could
have chosen to conduct his ministry on his own. Instead, he chose to
surround himself with the Twelve. He also developed close friendships
with the family of Mary, Martha, and Lazarus.

Investing in community comes naturally for some single leaders.
For example, Hector prioritizes relationships with five men whom he
refers to as his "five pillars." They are friends he has connected with
at various points of his journey. He prays for them, stays current with
them, knows he can be absolutely transparent with them, and feels free
to contact them at any time for counsel. Sue has been very intentional in
her friendship with Bonnie, her roommate. This has borne rich fruit in
her personal life and leadership. However, for Mark, a forty-five-year-
old associate pastor who recently moved to a new city, developing close
friendships has proved challenging. The following is his story:

> Community is something I desperately need, but being a
> pastor/leader complicates things. When I walk into a room,
> the dynamic changes. People treat me differently. This makes
> it hard to develop authentic relationships. I also find that other
> staff and board members—most of whom are married—
> sometimes don't "get it" when it comes to understanding the
> demands of being a single leader. So I see part of my role as

educating them on how important it is for me to build community outside of work.

Believe it or not, my dog is actually making it possible for me to meet a lot of people and develop new relationships. I have a routine to go to the dog park at set times so I can connect with the people in my neighborhood. I leave the office each day at 4:00 p.m. so I can pick up my dog and see my friends at the dog park by 4:30 p.m.

My dog also keeps me from feeling lonely when I come home to a quiet apartment. Rather than fill the empty space with mindless TV or noise, I am okay with the silence. Being with and caring for my dog reminds me of the goodness of God's creation and how important it is for me to be relating in love to others—even if it starts with my dog.

Mark's story highlights the unique challenges certain leadership contexts present when it comes to building close relationships. But his creativity, initiative, and persistence in pursuing connections within his neighborhood—and being willing to build these relationships from the ground up—offer a model of the simple ways God might lead you to begin making an intentional investment to build community. Deep and authentic relationships won't happen overnight, but you can nurture relationships that, over time, may become close companions for your journey.

Practice hospitality regularly. Invite a wide range of people—male and female, married and single, of all ages—to your home for a meal, or set up times to get together for coffee.

Because Mark lives in a small apartment in a big city, he developed a relationship with a nearby chocolate shop owner. He regularly hosts parties in the chocolate shop for fifteen to twenty people. Each person pays twenty dollars and enjoys a selection of light food and chocolate. Mark invites friends from the dog park, his church, and his apartment building. While it takes time and energy on his part, it has been an excellent means of both self-care and community building. Plus, Mark gets to shine in a hobby—his love of cooking and good food—that is unrelated to his job description as a pastor.

Practicing hospitality will look different for each of us. Sue routinely invites a steady stream of friends and church members to her home. Emily has a number of commitments that are pillars in her life. In addition to hosting a group of women once a week, she participates in semi-annual retreats with a group of married and single women. And every Saturday morning, unless she is traveling, she meets with a good friend for coffee. These commitments have enabled her to welcome a large number of "strangers and sojourners" into her life. In the same way, hospitality is a creative practice easily adapted to our unique needs and circumstances.

Singleness Is Your Loudest Gospel Message

You'll recall from the section on marriage that the perspective of most Christian leaders is that the loudest message we preach to the world comes through our words or, perhaps, the serving of others in Jesus' name. However, when I say that our loudest gospel message is instead our marriage or singleness for Christ, I mean that our vocation points *beyond itself* to something more important — to Jesus. In this sense, singleness, just like marriage, is a sign and a wonder.

Singleness is a sign and a wonder in at least two specific ways. First, as a single leader, you bear witness to the sufficiency and fullness of Jesus through your celibacy. You are not giving your body away. You are not "hooking up." Why? You are married to Christ. Your whole person belongs to him. This serves as the foundation of your life and leadership. Your commitment affirms the reality that Jesus is the bread that satisfies — even amidst the challenges of being a single leader. Every day you choose to maintain that commitment, your singleness stands as a countercultural and prophetic sign of the kingdom of God — to the church and to the world.

Secondly, if you are a single leader who has never been married and had children, you bear witness to the reality of the resurrection in a unique way. In this sense, dedicated celibacy may be a less obvious way of communicating the gospel, but it is no less significant. Author Rodney Clapp puts it this way:

> Christian singles are thus radical witness to the resurrection. They forfeit heirs — the only other possibility of their survival beyond the grave — in the hope that one day all creation

will be renewed. The Christian single makes no sense if the God of Jesus Christ is not living and true.[18]

In other words, our belief in the resurrection of the dead gives us a unique perspective on the shortness and brevity of earthly life. We have numbered our days in light of eternity (Psalm 90:12), knowing that to God a thousand years are like a day. We live in the reality that Jesus is alive, and so we too shall live with him forever, complete as a member of the family of God and the communion of saints.

What does it mean in practical terms for Christian leaders to make singleness the loudest gospel message we preach? It means we expand our definition of leadership success to include being a healthy single leader for Christ. Our aim is to experience God's deep love and delight for us through close friends, community, and the rich gifts encountered in everyday life. Like marrieds, we too must restructure our lives so that the priorities on our weekly to-do list look something like this:

- Spend time alone with God (listing times and spiritual practices for the week)
- Invest in my few close friends and community (listing times and specific actions for the week)
- Practice delight (e.g., hiking, running, art, music, reading clubs, dancing)
- Everything else I need to do in leadership (message prep, staff meetings, board meeting prep, etc.)

I recognize that this notion of leading out of your singleness as a vowed or dedicated celibate may be a new idea for you. Wherever you may be in the ebb-and-flow process of saying yes to God and embracing your singleness for him, I encourage you to continue the journey by accepting an invitation that applies to both marrieds as well as singles.

Begin by Taking a Small Step

You can be sure God wants to use your vocation (as married or single) to make you a more effective leader. He wants to give you the grace of ambition, a passion to be other-centered, strength to prioritize self-care, and clarity about the ways your life and vocation communicate the gospel message. However, the choice to lead out of singleness or marriage *is* a radical one, both within and beyond the church. If you choose to follow through and make changes, you will no doubt encounter resistance, if not outright opposition. And so I encourage you to begin humbly, seeking God's guidance in prayer. Prayer releases the power of the Holy Spirit, making possible what might otherwise appear to be impossible. Ask God:

- To give you a vision of how he can use your married or single vocation to be a sign and wonder that clearly points others to the Lord Jesus Christ.
- To create openness and receptivity in your spouse (if married) or your close friends (if single) as you share this vision to lead out of your marriage/singleness and ask for their companionship and support.
- For power from the Holy Spirit to help you love those closest to you freely, faithfully, fruitfully, and unconditionally.
- For grace to remain deeply connected to the person of Jesus in the process.

If it helps you to have a specific prayer to begin with, I offer the following prayers to help you on your way. I keep the prayer for married couples in my wallet and seek to pray it each day.

A Prayer for Married Couples

Lord, grant me the strength to answer your call
    to be a living sign of your love.
Make my love for _____ be like your love for him/her:
    passionate, permanent, intimate, unconditional, and life-giving.
May I be as present to _____ as you are to him/her,
    so that all the world can see your presence manifested
    in our tender love for one another.
Help us both to stay close to you in the body of Christ.
And continue to nourish our love with your love.
In Jesus' name, amen.[19]

A Prayer for Singles

> Lord, grant me the strength to answer your call
>> to be a living sign of your love.
> Make my love for others today reflect your love for me:
>> loyal, faithful, unconditional, and life giving.
> May I be as present to others as you are to me,
>> so that all the world can see your presence manifested
>> in my tender love for others.
> Help me stay close to you in the body of Christ.
> And continue to nourish my love with your love.
> In Jesus' name, amen.[20]

Leading out of marriage or singleness is inseparable from a life of loving union with Jesus. We cannot bear witness to the Lord Jesus unless we have rearranged our lives to abide deeply in him. This means we must slow down our pace and activities in order to intentionally cultivate our oneness to Jesus. This leads us naturally to the theme of our next chapter — slowing down for loving union.

Understanding Your Assessment of Leading Out of Your Marriage or Singleness

If you took the assessment on page 88 or 89, here are some observations to help you reflect on your responses.

If you scored mostly ones and twos, chances are you have not given much thought to what it might mean — theologically or practically — to lead out of your marriage or singleness. Don't worry. You are not alone. If this chapter has challenged your leadership paradigms, that is a great start. Consider further biblical study to expand your understanding. Research intentional and monastic communities who have thought deeply about marriage and singleness as vocations. Be careful to avoid any abrupt or disruptive changes to your life and leadership. Instead, ask God for one or two practical steps you can take.

If you scored mostly twos and threes, you may be leading out of marriage or singleness to some degree, but still lack a rich theological vision or practical applications of the truths in this chapter. You also may want to consider further biblical study. Talk with people from intentional and monastic communities who have thought deeply about marriage and singleness as vocations. Let God stretch you. Now is your opportunity to make some adjustments to how you live out your singleness or marriage as a leader. Be careful to avoid any abrupt changes. Spend time pondering next steps with God, asking him for clarity on two or three areas he would have you focus on.

If you scored mostly fours and fives, you are blessed. You are leading out of your singleness or marriage. I hope that this chapter has deepened and broadened your perspective around God's vision for you as a leader. What might be an invitation you are hearing from God today? Ask him what your next steps might be in helping others to discern and integrate their marriage or singleness with their leadership.

CHAPTER 4

SLOW DOWN FOR LOVING UNION

L arry is the forty-one-year-old founding pastor of a rapidly growing church. He and his wife, Rebecca, have been married for twenty years and have four children. In his eighteen years leading the church, the congregation has grown from a core group of a hundred to more than four thousand, with thirty-five staff members. Larry is friendly, easygoing, and loved by his team.

Things with the church and his life seemed to be going well until the day he abruptly submitted his resignation to the personnel committee. He said he was burnt out from the last few years, especially after completing a recent capital campaign for a new worship center. It turned out, however, that there was much more to the story.

A recent visitor to the church had encountered Larry with another woman at a hotel in a nearby city. And it was not a random encounter, but a three-year, on-again-off-again affair. Larry seemed to think his resignation would somehow prevent the news from being discovered by the church, but it was too late for that. Later, it was also discovered that Larry had accumulated a sizable financial debt in recent years.

Larry resigned. His marriage ended. The church was left to pick up the pieces.

It's a sadly familiar story, isn't it? But there is another aspect to this story that raises issues every Christian leader needs to grapple with. During the three years that Larry's life was going off the rails, the church was thriving. Attendance increased by seven hundred, many people came to faith in Christ, the giving and the ministry budget increased, and the church's impact on the community expanded. Larry even preached a popular series on biblical marriage and family life for six weeks during that time.

Somehow, the church experienced short-term "success" even when something was terribly wrong at the leadership level. But after Larry's resignation, the church swiftly spiraled downward. People felt betrayed and deceived. Fingers were pointed. Resources and energies once devoted to outreach were redirected to helping people within the church grieve and heal. The budget was slashed by 40 percent. This meant that ministries both locally and internationally were discontinued or radically cut back.

Frustrated church members wanted to know why staff and members of the church board hadn't noticed any early warning signs of Larry's problems. At the end of a quarterly congregational meeting in which this issue was raised, the board chairperson summarized the board's response: "We saw things that concerned us. Larry was always on the move, juggling new projects, speaking at conferences, hiring new staff. It was hard for us to keep up with how quickly the church was changing. None of us probed and asked deeper questions. The reality is, we were so caught up in the excitement over things like the new building campaign and the attendance numbers skyrocketing that we disregarded what we did notice. And we attributed his behavior to the normal stresses that come with growth."

A long pause followed. The room grew painfully quiet.

The board chair quietly acknowledged what many others were thinking: "What makes this whole situation so hard to understand is that some of our most powerful weekend services took place during the three years he was having his affair."

The Danger of Leading without Jesus

If you're a leader in a church, the board chair's statement has to hit you right in the gut. Somehow, it has become part of our default thinking that external markers of success are an indication that all must certainly be well at the leadership level. We wouldn't be successful otherwise, right? But as Larry's story demonstrates, it is possible to build a church, an organization, or a team by relying only on our gifts, talents, and experience. We can serve Christ in our own energy and wisdom. We can expand a ministry or a business without thinking much of Jesus or relying on him in the process. We can boldly preach truths we don't live. And if our efforts prove successful, few people will notice or take issue with the gaps between who we are and what we do.

Jesus warns us about the consequences of engaging in ministry activity without him:

> *"Not everyone who says to me, 'Lord, Lord,' will enter the kingdom of heaven, but only [those] who [do] the will of my Father who is in heaven. Many will say to me on that day, 'Lord, Lord, did we not prophesy in your name and in your name drive out demons and in your name perform many miracles?' Then I will tell them plainly, 'I never knew you. Away from me, you evildoers!'"*
>
> MATTHEW 7:21–23

Jesus confronts the self-deception of those who do wonderful things in his name. They prophesy. They drive out demons. They perform miracles. They are very impressive and successful in really helping people. What could be wrong with that? By all appearances, their efforts have the marks of a vibrant, growing ministry!

But Jesus says one thing is terribly wrong.

"I never knew you," he says.

Wait a minute — how can that be? He knew us in our mothers' wombs. Jesus knows every hair on our heads. He knows us better than we know ourselves. How could Jesus say, "I never knew you"? And, in any event, wouldn't it have made more sense for him to say, "*You* never knew *me*"?

The force of the biblical word used for the verb *know* refers to the intimate, personal knowing of relationship; it is similar to the oneness of Adam and Eve in the garden when they were naked and without shame (Genesis 2:25). We may be sincere in saying, "Lord, Lord," and have what appears to be a successful ministry. We may know a lot about God in our heads. But none of these things matter if we remain *unknown* by Christ. What matters is the genuine fruit that comes only out of a deep and surrendered connection with Jesus.

Bearing fruit requires slowing down enough to give Jesus direct access to every aspect of our lives and our leadership. Just because God has access to everything that is true *about us* does not mean God has access *to us*. Loving union is an act of surrender—giving God complete access—and we can't do that in a hurry. We must be humbly accessible, with the door of our hearts continually open to him. Jesus doesn't force that on us; it is something only we can do.

Imagine accumulating a lifetime of leadership trophies only to have Jesus say to you at the end, "I never knew you." The fact that "many" of us will present our credentials at the final judgment only to be denied by Jesus "should be genuinely frightening to all of us."[1] It is not enough to call Jesus "Lord." It is not enough to be busy racking up impressive ministry achievements. Jesus condemns these outwardly successful followers in the harshest terms and characterizes their efforts not merely as weak or failed but as outright "evildoing."

The key question is: to what extent is the door of our heart open to him? Have we allowed the incessant demands of leadership to so preoccupy us that we don't have time to keep that door open—continuously? Is our abiding in Jesus sporadic? Or are we operating on a kind of spiritual autopilot?

Remember, Jesus doesn't say we can't lead or build a church without him. What he does say is that our efforts are worth nothing unless they flow out of a relationship of loving union with him (John 15:5). In other words, although what we do matters, who we are matters much more.

Because we have so much to do and so much on our minds, we tend to accept it as normal that ...

- Worship leaders or musicians who do not connect to Jesus personally during the week can still lead people into the presence of Jesus during weekend worship services.
- Gifted communicators can teach Scripture and train others without devoting the time needed for God's message to penetrate their own hearts.
- Church administrators can effectively build infrastructure, supervise staff, and manage finances without having a consistent devotional life with God.

It's not that we would intentionally advocate for leaders to conduct themselves in these ways; it's that we don't consider it much of a problem when they do.

I was in my early years as a Christian when I first came to grips with the sad truth that God appeared to use prominent Christian leaders whose relationship with Jesus was either nonexistent or seriously underdeveloped. It was a discovery that left me confused and disoriented. Yet, after decades in ministry, I am no longer so confused. Why? Because I have experienced to some degree what it's like to be one of those leaders. I have prepared and preached sermons without thinking about or spending time with Jesus. I know the experience of doing good things that helped a lot of people while being too busy or caught up in my own whirlwind of leadership worries to be intimately connected to Jesus.

In an exhaustive biblical study, theologian Jonathan Edwards (1703–1758) wrote about how often Scripture describes people who do things *for* God without having a life *with* God. Characters such as Balaam the Old Testament prophet, Judas Iscariot, and Saul were all engaged in what most certainly would have been considered effective work for God by their communities, but without having an authentic connection to him. The only mark of genuine spiritual maturity and ministry effectiveness, Edwards concluded, is the outworking of *agape* — a self-giving love for God and others.[2] That is the one quality of our lives and leadership the devil can never counterfeit. And the source of that agape love can be found only in a life of loving union with God.

As Christian leaders, it's unlikely most of us would take issue with any of this. *Of course we need to experience loving union with God!* Who is going to disagree with that? Here's where the problem comes in. Doing our part to cultivate a relationship of loving union with God requires time — time that, paradoxically, we don't have because we are too busy serving him. And so, intentional or not, we find ourselves bypassing our relationship with God. In the process, we drift into prioritizing leadership over love. In other words, we fail to slow down for loving union with God.

How does this happen? Most of the time, it begins very subtly. Yet the consequences of failing to lead out of loving union are so far-reaching, it is critical to clearly define what loving union is and isn't.

What Is Loving Union?

Loving union is not the de facto equivalent of devotions and quiet time. Nor is it about engaging in a long list of spiritual practices. Or having emotionally intense experiences with God. Loving union is not about managing your schedule better or simply not being busy. It is not so much about having a sustainable pace of life. As important as such things may be, it is possible to engage in them without necessarily experiencing loving union.

So what is loving union, and why does it require so much time?

In his classic book *Prayer*, theologian Hans Urs von Balthasar describes Jesus this way: "Here is a man, sinless, because he has lovingly allowed the Father's will full scope in his life."[3] Think about that simple but profound statement for a moment. Read it a few more times until it really sinks in. What von Balthasar is describing here is loving union — to *lovingly allow God to have full access to your life*. These are Jesus' words to the Christians in Laodicea and to us:

> *"Here I am! I stand at the door and knock. If anyone hears my voice and opens the door, I will come in and eat with that person, and they with me."*
>
> (REVELATION 3:20)

In loving union, we keep that door wide open. We allow the will of God to have full access to every area of our lives, including every aspect of our leadership — from difficult conversations and decision-making to managing our emotional triggers. Cultivating this kind of relationship with God can't be hurried or rushed. We must slow down and build into our lives a structure and rhythm that make this kind of loving surrender routinely possible.

The question we must wrestle with is this: *In what ways does my current pace of life and leadership enhance or diminish my ability to allow God's will and presence full scope in my life?* Any spiritual practices we may choose then become a means to that end, not the end themselves. But make no mistake, remaining surrendered while navigating the intense pressures and demands of leadership is no small task.

Jesus faced overwhelming pressures in his life — pressures that far outstrip anything most of us will ever face. Yet he routinely stepped away from those endless leadership demands to spend significant time with the Father. He slowed down to ensure he was in sync with God — that he was in the Father and the Father was in him, powerfully filling every crevice of his body, mind, and spirit. In routinely stepping away from his active work, he entrusted the outcome of his circumstances, problems, and ministry to the Father. And as a result, every action Jesus took was rooted in a place of deep rest and centeredness out of his relationship with God.[4]

Just as Jesus lived in relaxed, loving union with the Father, he invites us to share in that relationship with him: "If you remain in me and I in you, you will bear much fruit; apart from me you can do nothing" (John 15:5). The Greek verb translated as *remain* can also be translated as *abide, to continue with, to stick with, to make one's home with*. It captures the nonnegotiable requirement of what it means to follow Jesus in loving union. He promises that if we do this, "fruit" will always follow. However, when we refuse to slow down for loving union, the consequences can be significant and long-lasting, rippling out from us and impacting those we lead and beyond.

How Healthy Is Your Experience of Loving Union with God?

Use the list of statements that follow to do a brief assessment of your loving union with God. Next to each statement, write down the number that best describes your response. Use the following scale:

5 = Always true of me
4 = Frequently true of me
3 = Occasionally true of me
2 = Rarely true of me
1 = Never true of me

_____ 1. My highest priority as a leader is to take time each day to remain in loving union with Jesus.

_____ 2. I offer God full access to my interior life as I make decisions, interact with team members, and initiate new plans.

_____ 3. I wait to say yes or no to new opportunities until I have sufficient time to prayerfully and carefully discern God's will.

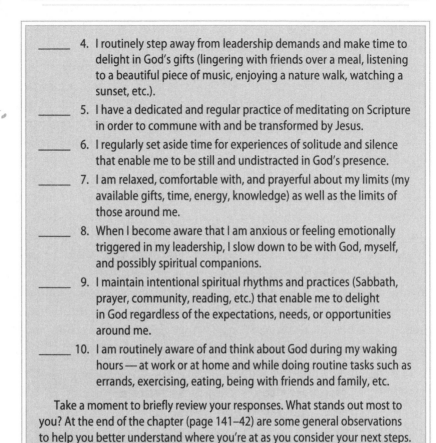

4. I routinely step away from leadership demands and make time to delight in God's gifts (lingering with friends over a meal, listening to a beautiful piece of music, enjoying a nature walk, watching a sunset, etc.).

5. I have a dedicated and regular practice of meditating on Scripture in order to commune with and be transformed by Jesus.

6. I regularly set aside time for experiences of solitude and silence that enable me to be still and undistracted in God's presence.

7. I am relaxed, comfortable with, and prayerful about my limits (my available gifts, time, energy, knowledge) as well as the limits of those around me.

8. When I become aware that I am anxious or feeling emotionally triggered in my leadership, I slow down to be with God, myself, and possibly spiritual companions.

9. I maintain intentional spiritual rhythms and practices (Sabbath, prayer, community, reading, etc.) that enable me to delight in God regardless of the expectations, needs, or opportunities around me.

10. I am routinely aware of and think about God during my waking hours — at work or at home and while doing routine tasks such as errands, exercising, eating, being with friends and family, etc.

Take a moment to briefly review your responses. What stands out most to you? At the end of the chapter (page 141–42) are some general observations to help you better understand where you're at as you consider your next steps.

How Loving Union — and Non-Loving Union — with God Impacts Leadership

Allow me to take a guess at what you might be thinking at this point. Perhaps it's something along these lines: *Pete, all of this sounds good, but I have a really demanding role and a complex situation. I need the bottom line. What does it mean to pursue loving union with God in the midst of the very real demands of leadership?* It's a great question. And perhaps the best way to get at it is to consider a few scenarios that demonstrate the differences in leaders who respond from a place of loving union or non-loving union with God.

Scenario 1. Lucas is a church planter with fifty people in his core group. After almost nine months of preparation, the church has officially launched. More than thirty-five new people visit in the first four weeks. Lucas and his team are filled with excitement and anticipation about what God is doing. The only problem is, Lucas has more to do than is humanly possible.

- *Non-loving union response.* Lucas makes his to-do list faithfully each Sunday night. He knows he can't do it all, so he weighs the pros and cons of each item, trying to identify the activities that have the most potential for impact. Then he sets his priorities, hoping he can cross at least half of them off his list by the end of the week. Lucas prayerfully studies his sermon text for his morning devotions. He works hard, putting in long days (and sometimes sleepless nights). He intercedes for the needs of the church and the people it serves. Fear of the church failing causes him anxiety, but he pushes it away in an effort to focus on the positive. He thinks, *We won't fail because God is faithful, and he's obviously in this. I don't have time for much else right now, but once we reach 100 people in attendance, things should stabilize.*

- *Loving union response.* Lucas is acutely aware of the potentially perilous situation in which he finds himself. The demands on his time are great. His greatest challenge and the highest priorities on his to-do list are to maintain his Sabbath rhythms, to spend time in solitude and silence, and to immerse himself in Scripture aside from times of sermon preparation. He is careful about allowing sufficient time to invite Jesus into every part of his life and leadership. Once a month, he meets with a spiritual director because he knows he needs an anchor in the stormy seas of this first year leading the church. He prioritizes his to-do list on Sunday nights by seeking to discern God's direction and wisdom. He surrenders his anxieties to God and openly shares his fears and vulnerabilities with his spouse, church planting coach, and a close friend. He prays for grace to do God's will in a profound and humble awareness of how easy it would be for him to miss Jesus during this demanding season of planting a church.

Scenario 2. Ruth is the executive director of Emotionally Healthy Spirtualty (EHS), a nonprofit ministry active in the United States and twenty-five countries around the world. She is the organization's only full-time employee, but also leads a small and growing staff team. Ruth left a marketplace career and began to work for EHS at one-third of her previous salary. She reports to a strong, creative, visionary boss (me!) and is responsible to manage a rapidly growing ministry with limited financial resources.

- *Non-loving union response.* During her train ride to work, Ruth reads a page from a free devotional pamphlet she picked up at church. Feeling confident that she has begun her day with God, she doesn't think much more about him during the day unless there is a crisis or problem. In fact, all her waking thoughts are about work since the needs around her are never-ending. Her attitude is: *If I don't put my whole life into this, I am not giving my best for God's work.* She also worries about the ministry's finances and what could happen if it fails to thrive and grow. Gaining the approval of her boss and the ministry board is always on her mind. For Ruth, any failure in the ministry is a personal failure. She has hired the best people with the right skills to serve on her team and doesn't ask questions about their personal lives. The focus of Ruth's work is to add more projects, grow the budget, and expand the work.

- *Loving union response.* During her train ride to work, Ruth spends time praying, reading, and reflecting on Scripture. She endeavors to maintain a sense of connection to God throughout the day, listening to him and inviting him into her efforts to build his ministry, not her own. She feels light and free even though she is earning one-third of her previous salary. Ruth works hard, but sets a boundary around evenings and weekends so she has time to rest and to create a larger life in God. She practices Sabbath and intentionally cultivates her relationships with friends, family, and a few spiritual companions. While she loves her role as the executive director, she feels she can walk away from it at any time. Why? She will tell you, "I know that I am beautiful, lovable, and loved by God and others." She doesn't feel pressure to get things done quickly. In fact, when she begins to feel overloaded, she expresses that to her boss (me) and takes a break. She invites God to help her discern what to do in light of her personal limits as well as those of EHS. In the past, she might have developed a marketing plan and then prayed, *God, here are the steps I'm taking to market EHS. I ask that you bless it.* Now she carefully considers her options and prays, *Lord, what is the best way to maximize our impact with our limited time and resources?* She is profoundly aware that all her actions affect the people who report to her, so she is prayerful in preparing for meetings and careful not to rush through them. "What's most important to me is not what I want, but what is God's best for the members of my team." She sees her staff as people with feelings and concerns, not a means to an end. Her mentoring of them goes beyond skills to do their jobs better and includes expressing interest in their personal lives. She works on her own emotional and spiritual issues, fully aware that, perhaps more than anything else, it is her own transformation that affects her team most.

Scenario 3. Dylan leads the small group ministry in his church where he has been on staff for five years. He recently attended an innovative leadership conference where he heard inspiring stories of other small group ministries that have exploded in growth. Inspired by all the creative ministry strategies he discovered, he returns to the church filled with excitement and fresh vision.

- *Non-loving union response.* Dylan thanks God for the conference and is eager to act on what he's learned. On his first day back at the office, he sets up a meeting with his five key leaders to share his vision and ideas. As he prepares for the meeting, Dylan wants to help the team hit the ground running, so he identifies three practical steps they can implement immediately. He prays, asking God to give his team hearts that are open rather than resistant to change. Dylan is only vaguely aware of an underlying anxiety and disregards the adrenaline running through his body. He knows the lead pastor will be thrilled if they can make significant progress connecting new people in the church through new groups. He charges into the meeting with great enthusiasm, eager to envision and mobilize his team to help take small groups and the church to the next level.

- *Loving union response.* Before Dylan sets up a meeting with his five key leaders, he takes an afternoon alone with God to pray and process his excitement from the conference. He is fully aware of the anxiety and adrenaline rush he feels. Dylan asks himself questions like these: *Where is my excitement coming from, and what might God be communicating to me through it? Am I excited because implementing these new ideas will help my ministry to grow — which means the lead pastor and church board will see the great job I am doing? Or is it truly because it could help so many people?* He then sets up a meeting to talk with Fran, a wise colleague, so he can share his excitement with her over lunch. He asks her for feedback and any insights she might have. Next, he meets with the lead pastor to get additional feedback. After taking three weeks for still more reading, reflection, and prayer, Dylan calls the meeting with his five key leaders. He shares his experience from the conference and describes the ideas and strategies that excite him most. He listens to everyone's feedback, concerns, and questions. During the meeting, Dylan listens for God through his team and through his own thoughts and emotions. The team prays together for wisdom and discernment and then agrees on three specific action steps.

It is important to note that the loving union responses in all three scenarios are not a leadership strategy, not a more effective way of *doing*. Instead they are the natural outgrowth of loving union with God, a different way of *being*. These kinds of responses are possible only when we intentionally allow Jesus' will and presence to have full access in every area of our lives.

Both Lucas, the church planter, and Ruth, the executive director, have more to do than is humanly possible. That is one of the greatest challenges most of us routinely face. Their approach to decision making, setting priorities, and how they define success is grounded not in circumstances or outcomes, but in their loving union with God. As a result, they enjoy a unique, God-given freedom and joy in their roles despite the pressures they face. As a result of slowing down to be with God, Dylan, the small group ministry leader, wisely and sensitively is able to bring his team on a new journey. His commitment to remain in loving union empowers him, and his team, to more fully discern God's plans for their ministry.

The consequences of not slowing down for loving union may not always seem evident at first. We can justify skimming on time with God and rushing through leadership tasks, thinking, *Okay, maybe I got a little ahead of myself, but at least we seem farther down the road than before. No harm done.* But left unchecked, this approach to leadership eventually creates an illusion of healthy growth and progress that will eventually bear bad fruit.

You Know You're Not Experiencing Loving Union When You ...

- Can't shake the pressure you feel from having too much to do in too little time.
- Are always rushing.
- Routinely fire off quick opinions and judgments.
- Are often fearful about the future.
- Are overly concerned with what others think.
- Are defensive and easily offended.
- Are routinely preoccupied and distracted.
- Consistently ignore the stress, anxiety, and tightness of your body.[5]
- Feel unenthusiastic or threatened by the success of others.
- Routinely spend more time talking than listening.

The Consequences of Not Slowing Down

The apostle Paul reminds us that the desire to be a leader is a "noble" task (1 Timothy 3:1). It is fine, good, praiseworthy, and excellent to give our lives in service to others for Jesus' sake. The church and the world desperately need leaders, but we will only make things worse if we don't lead God's way. When we fail to slow down for loving union, sooner or later we will reap the consequences — and they are serious, both for us and for those we aim to serve. In nearly thirty years of ministry, I have reaped all of the consequences I'm about to describe. While I can say I learned a lot as a result, it was a painful and costly education. My hope is that you can learn from my mistakes, avoid these pitfalls, and chart a different course than so many of us who have gone before you.

You Can't Do God's Work Your Way without Paying a Steep Price

Moses, along with his brother and executive pastor, Aaron, worked and waited for almost forty years to enter the Promised Land. Having started with 603,550 men[6] to manage—not to mention all the women and children—Moses' and Aaron's patience was repeatedly tested to the limit by a seemingly endless barrage of complaints. When the people cry about their lack of food and water and accuse Moses of bringing them out into the desert to die, Moses is livid. At this point, he is also exhausted and has little capacity to manage his anger and resentment. Imagine the scene as he loses his cool:

> The LORD said to Moses, "Take the staff, and you and your brother Aaron gather the assembly together. **Speak to that rock before their eyes** and it will pour out its water. You will bring water out of the rock for the community so they and their livestock can drink." So Moses took the staff from the LORD's presence, just as he commanded him. He and Aaron gathered the assembly together in front of the rock and Moses said to them, "Listen, you rebels, must we bring you water out of this rock?" **Then Moses raised his arm and struck the rock twice with his staff.** Water gushed out, and the community and their livestock drank. But the LORD said to Moses and Aaron, "Because you did not trust in me enough to honor me as holy in the sight of the Israelites, you will not bring this community into the land I give them."
>
> NUMBERS 20:7–12, EMPHASIS ADDED

There is no doubt that Moses and Aaron are serving the people. Only now, after decades of faithful leadership, Moses strays from loving union with God and takes matters into his own hands. He lashes out and rebukes the people, calling them "rebels." Rather than honoring and obeying God, he relies on an old strategy of striking the rock because, hey, why not, it worked once before (Exodus 17:6).

And, miraculously enough, sufficient water bursts forth again to satisfy the thirst of nearly 3 million people—and their animals! The people's needs get met, but Moses and Aaron pay a stiff price. God names their underlying offense rebellion and unbelief[7] and prohibits them from leading the people into the Promised Land.[8]

I've "struck the rock" out of frustration and anger at God's round-about ways more often than I care to admit.[9] I also know the experience of opening a staff meeting in prayer and asking for direction, only to then proceed in making my own plans without God. I have relied on what worked in the past—and what appeared to be working for other leaders and ministries—without a prayerful process of discerning God's will for our particular situation. Why? It was quicker and easier. And, like so many other leaders I know, I have missed out on the joy and contentment of the "promised land" that would have come had I been willing to do God's will, God's way, in God's timing.

So when was the last time you took matters into your own hands and "struck the rock" in your leadership? What "promised land" might you be sacrificing right now? Whatever the particulars of your situation, I can promise that one of the first things to go will be Jesus' joy and peace. Leadership will become hard. The people you serve will feel like a burden, and you will find yourself wishing you could be somewhere else. You will begin to feel like you are wandering in a desert asking, *Where is God? What happened?* You might eventually realize where you got off course and attempt to go back and do it all over again. But then you may wonder, "What will be the cost of that?"

You Can't Live at Warp Speed without Warping Your Soul

When I challenge leaders to rearrange their lives in order to pursue loving union, one of the most common responses I get is, "Pete, I just don't have that kind of time." If that's your response as well, then chances are good that you're moving too fast. And even if you somehow manage to keep from dropping any of the balls you're juggling, the speed at which you're living and leading is exacting a hidden toll. Warp speed will blind you to the damage you are doing to your soul—every time. An important, yet often overlooked, New Testament story illustrates the dangers of rushing to have a powerful ministry without slowing down for loving union with Jesus.

When the seven sons of Sceva observe the apostle Paul's extraordinary miracles and the explosive growth of the Ephesian church, they want a piece of the action. They long for Paul's powerful ministry and success. Here's the story:

> *Some Jews who went around driving out evil spirits tried to invoke the name of the Lord Jesus over those who were demon-possessed. They would say, "In the name of the Jesus whom Paul preaches, I command you to come out." Seven sons of Sceva, a Jewish chief priest, were doing this. One day the evil spirit answered them,* **"Jesus I know, and Paul I know about, but who are you?"** *Then the man who had the evil spirit jumped on them and overpowered them all. He gave them such a beating that they ran out of the house naked and bleeding.*   Acts 19:13 – 16, EMPHASIS ADDED

If we give them the benefit of the doubt, we could say that the seven sons of Sceva were trying to do a good thing — they wanted to participate in advancing the kingdom. However, chances are good their motives were mixed at best. In an effort to capture some of the prestige that was bestowed on those who released God's power over evil spirits, they took a spiritual shortcut. They skipped over making a long-term investment in a life of loving union — the source of Paul's miracles — and rushed headlong into spiritual realities they did not understand and were woefully ill equipped to deal with. As a result, they barely escaped with their lives.

Whenever we find ourselves wanting the ministry impact *of* Jesus while simultaneously resisting spending time *with* Jesus, we are positioning ourselves for a beating and some variation on being run "out of the house naked and bleeding." The seven sons of Sceva tried to speak and act on truths that were not rooted in their lives. They did not have sufficient strength in their life *with* God to support the level of spiritual warfare in which they were engaged. The integrity gaps in their walk with God exposed them to danger and harm.

I have never been beat up by evil spirits or run out of the house naked and bleeding. But I do know the empty feeling of speaking truths to others that I had not digested myself. I have borrowed insights or ideas because they worked for someone else. I was impressed by how powerful the words sounded when a particular person said them. *Why wouldn't they also be powerful for me?* The problem was I didn't have time to allow God's words spoken through them to actually become God's words to me. I thought, *There is just too much to do now. God, you know the pressure I'm under. I'll get to it later. Just help me help my people now.* So what happened? Nothing. My words rang hollow. Little power. Little effect. Little life change.

Every time we do what the sons of Sceva did, we buy into an illusion. We present ourselves as something or someone we are not. We don't take the time to give Jesus access to our motivations and fears. Then our souls shrivel and warp as we stray further and further from what is true.

You Can't Skim without Paying a Long-Term Price

Jesus spent over 90 percent of his life — thirty of his thirty-three years — in obscurity. In those hidden years, he forged a life of loving union with the Father. The observable greatness of his three-year ministry is built on the foundation of the investment Jesus made in those unseen years.[10] And Jesus continued to make this investment in his relationship with the Father throughout his three-year ministry, regardless of the ministry pressures he faced. From his first days in Capernaum, waking up early in the morning to pray (Mark 1:35), to his final hours in Gethsemane (Matthew 26:36–46), Jesus set aside time to be with the Father.

If it was necessary for Jesus to have this kind of foundation and ongoing relationship with the Father, we'd have to be delusional to think we could skim on investing in our hidden life in God without experiencing long-term consequences. Jesus models contentment under pressure, calmness in the face of betrayal, and power to forgive at his crucifixion — all of which is the fruit of a long history of oneness with his Father. I am convinced that a significant reason so many Christian leaders lack the qualities Jesus modeled is because we skim in our relationship with God. Instead of contentment and calm, our leadership is marked by discontent and anxiety. Ryan's story is typical.

Ryan has been the lead pastor of First Assembly for the last eleven years. He faithfully has his quiet time each morning, reading through the Bible once a year. He follows this half hour of reading with ten to fifteen minutes of intercession for his family, the church, and the world. Ryan works six days a week (sometimes seven in the case of emergencies) and takes three weeks each summer for vacation. In addition to preparing sermons and leading the Sunday service, Ryan faithfully visits the sick, teaches midweek Bible study, oversees volunteers who coordinate different ministries, and serves as the police chaplain for his town.

When he began, weekend church attendance averaged about 200 people. Good things are happening at First Assembly. People consistently come to Christ. The church is unified. A number of healthy relationships provide a great sense of safety and stability to the larger church family. The students' and children's ministries are strong. And the church is active serving the city in a number of practical ways.

However, Ryan feels like a failure. He is discontented and unhappy. After eleven years of investing blood, sweat, and tears, weekend church attendance remains static, with only a slight gain over the 200 he started out with. He thinks, *I'm not a very good leader. If I were, we would have more people by now.*

At the annual denominational meetings, it is always the achievements of the larger churches that are celebrated. As much as he knows there is more to church leadership than attendance numbers, he feels he is measured by how many people he has. It gnaws at his gut and he frequently feels anxious.

Ryan loves pastoring people one on one. He knows he needs to learn some new skills for leadership to release people's gifts. Nonetheless, his larger, more far-reaching problem is not external. It is internal. Although his practice of morning quiet time is well intentioned, it is narrow. By limiting his quiet time to Scripture reading for sermon preparation and intercession for his church and family means he has few spiritual practices that allow Jesus access to his interior life. He does not practice solitude or silence or spend time simply meeting Jesus in Scripture. Ryan is skimming.

Ryan needs a wider range of spiritual practices to position himself for a deep, beneath-the-surface transformation of his life in Christ. He needs an overhaul of the way he follows and immerses himself in the love of Jesus. This will enable him to redefine success as being faithful to what God has given him to do in his church and to resist the internal pressure he feels that is causing so much *dis*-ease and anxiety. If Ryan summons the courage to take this journey, he will very likely experience the three classic elements of conversion: a revelatory insight into who he is and who God is, a radical turning to Jesus, and a deep transformation of his life.[11]

It's a conversion I hope you might experience as well. In asking you to make the necessary changes to slow down for loving union with God, I am not asking you to add one more item to your already over-burdened schedule. I am asking you to make a U-turn and rearrange your life around an entirely new way of being a leader. In fact, what I am asking you to do is nothing short of a groundbreaking, culture-defying act of rebellion against the contemporary Western way of doing leadership.

Take Your First Steps to Slow Down for Loving Union

Investing in a life of loving union is a topic worthy of an entire book, and many books have been written on various aspects of what it means to do this. My goal here is to offer a few ideas to help you take the first steps on your journey to slow down for loving union with Jesus. As you begin, know that this is a lifelong process, just as any intimate relationship is, that will evolve and blossom more fully over time.

Find Your "Desert" with God

Throughout Scripture and the history of the church, the desert has been a place of spiritual preparation, purification, and transformation. Moses spent forty years in the desert before God called him to lead his people out of Egypt. The prophet Elijah lived in the desert and, as a result, stood firm as God's prophet in one of the lowest moments of Israel's history. John the Baptist spent much of his adult life in the desert. Out of that place in God, he called a nation to repentance and discerned Jesus as the Messiah. Paul spent three years in the Arabian Desert receiving God's revelation before going to Jerusalem to begin his apostolic ministry. Jesus intentionally moved back and forth from active ministry with people to a desert place of being alone with the Father. In order to slow down for loving union, we need to develop a similar rhythm of finding our "desert" with God.

In their own pursuit of loving union with God, the Desert Fathers and Mothers of the third to the fifth centuries lived as monks or hermits in the deserts of Syria, Palestine, and Egypt. One such monk was

Anthony the Great of Egypt (AD 251 – 356). After receiving an excellent education and upbringing from his Christian parents in Egypt, Anthony began living in solitude outside his village before eventually retreating to the desert to live for twenty years. Author Henri Nouwen writes, "He renounced possessions to learn detachment; he renounced speech in order to learn compassion; he renounced activity in order to learn prayer. In the desert, Anthony both discovered God and did intense battle with the devil."[12]

When Anthony emerged from his solitude after twenty years, people recognized in him the qualities of an authentic and healthy man—he was whole in body, mind, and soul. Thousands sought him out for counsel, and God used him mightily. Later in life, he retreated again, this time to an "inner mountain" in the wilderness where he lived alone for the rest of his life. Here is how one author described him: "It was not his physical dimension that distinguished him from the rest, but the stability of character and purity of the soul. His soul being free of confusion, he held his outer senses also undisturbed … he was never troubled, his soul being calm, and he never looked gloomy, his mind being joyous."[13]

Obviously, as Christian leaders, we can't spend vast amounts of time alone in a desert. But the desert provides a rich metaphor for finding a space—a park bench, a library, a bedroom, a chair facing a window, a retreat center—where we can disengage from people and activities to be alone with God. Each of us needs to identify and protect a desert space with God even if we live in a congested urban environment. In the desert—that solitary, undistracted place—we position ourselves to open the door of our hearts as best we can so that Jesus' presence and his will have full access to every area of our life. We slow down to make this kind of loving surrender possible.

Here is a little story from Anthony's life that I have pondered for years:

> Abba Anthony received a letter from emperor Constantine to visit him in Constantinople. He wondered if he should go and asked Abba Paul who said, "If you go, you will be called Anthony, but if you stay here [in the desert], you will be called Abba Anthony."[14]

Anthony ultimately declined the invitation to go to Constantinople to minister to the king. Why? It would have pulled him away from what God had for him in the desert. He was called to grow into an "Abba," a father of the faith, who would have an impact on those he served in relative obscurity. Had he abandoned the desert and a lifestyle of slowing down for loving union with God, the title *Abba* would not have applied to him. Anthony was careful and discerning, as we need to be, about the delicate balance the Father had for him as a leader. God has different callings for each of us as well in terms of the balance of our *activity for* God and *our being with* him.

In the Protestant tradition especially, we are so steeped in the achievement values of our contemporary Western milieu that we assume an intense level of ministry activity is normal. We believe that if a door of opportunity has opened for us, then walking boldly through it must be God's will. But that is hardly the case. In fact, this tendency to blindly seize more and more opportunities for God has destroyed many a leader whose good intentions lacked a strong foundation in and with God. In order to establish this kind of foundation, we need to embrace the gift of our human limits.

Perhaps the most powerful limit Geri and I embraced was the ancient practice called a Rule of Life. Ultimately, this is what gave us a framework to strip nonessentials from our life and make room for a larger, more expansive life in God.

Establish a Rule of Life

The term Rule of Life has its linguistic roots in an ancient Greek word that means "trellis." A trellis is a support structure that enables plants such as grapevine to get off the ground, grow upward, and become fruitful. It's a beautiful image of what a Rule of Life is and how it functions—it is a support structure that helps us to grow up and abide in Christ. This in turn enables our lives to thrive spiritually and our leadership to be abundantly fruitful.[15]

Most of us have some kind of plan for developing our spiritual lives. This may include, for example, reading the Bible completely every year, spending thirty minutes every morning with God, participating in a small group, taking an annual overnight retreat. However,

very few of us have the kind of support structure we need. Slowing down sufficiently for the will and presence of God to fill our lives and our leadership requires a thoughtful and integrated plan.

A formal Rule of Life organizes our unique combination of spiritual practices into a structure that enables us to pay attention to God in everything we do. While an infinite number of variations exist for developing a Rule of Life, I have used the following framework for several years (see next page). It includes the four primary categories of Benedictine spiritual life: prayer, rest, relationships, and work. Although this four-part framework remains the same, I update the particulars in each category once or twice a year.

Each category is not just a way of thinking about things I need to do, but a means of receiving and giving the love of God. The love of God itself is located at the center because, unless I am receiving and relying on God's love all through the day, I have nothing of lasting value to give. Keeping the four areas in balance prevents me from adding activities or commitments in one area that would prohibit me from maintaining my commitments in another. For example, I won't make a work commitment that would knock off balance my rhythms of rest, prayer, and relationships.

I actually keep this diagram before me every time I consider taking on a new work commitment. For example, it recently helped me say no to an opportunity to speak at a large international conference, something I would really like to have done. When I looked at my existing commitments to prayer, rest, and relationships, it was clear there was no way I would have adequate time to prepare for the event, travel across the globe, expend the energy to speak to a large gathering, recover from the exertion and jet lag, and still faithfully attend to my responsibilities

Prayer

- Weekly Sabbath
- Daily Offices (3 to 4 times per day)
- Lecto Divina
- Day alone with God (1 to 2 times per month)
- Journal regularly
- Solitude and silence
- Daily Examen
- Read Desert/Church Fathers
- 4-to-5-day monastic retreat (yearly)

Rest

- Exercise 5 to 6 times per week
- Well-planned vacations
- Two-thirds to all day off on Fridays
- Read broadly/library visits
- 3-to-4-month sabbaticals every 7 years
- Seasons of therapy
- Go to beach, be in nature, hike, bike
- Limit social media
- Limit speaking

Love of God
(Receive and Give)

Relationships

- Attentive to fun with Geri
- Engage with Eva, Maria, Christy, and Faith
- Stay in good communication with siblings
- Regular mentoring with spiritual director
- Be present to NLF/EHS staff
- Participate in NLF small group
- Spend time with friends
- Join in extended family events
- Vacation/holidays with Geri's family

Work

- Personal development
- Mentor senior NLF staff
- Preach/teach NLF
- Resource NLF/NLCDC next phase
- Equip staff in the five M's/values
- Blog/Facebook/Twitter
- Develop, plan, train EHS trainers
- Oversee finances at home
- Limit writing
- Pray/process before saying yes

at home and at New Life. In order to pursue this opportunity, my only option was to eliminate one or more of the tasks within the "work" box. Because none of the work responsibilities were things I was willing or able to cut, the choice was easy. I declined the speaking opportunity.

There are two common temptations that undercut leaders when it comes to following through on developing a Rule of Life. The first is to do nothing—to feel paralyzed and think, *I could never do this! It's too limiting and overwhelming.* The second is to do everything—to make too many changes all at once and then flame out after a month because they've crafted a Rule of Life that, while ideal, is impossible to follow in their current circumstances and spiritual condition.

Let me caution you against giving in to the all-or-nothing temptations — or to taking a shortcut by trying to adopt my Rule of Life (or anyone else's) as your own. I have been adding and deleting items on my Rule of Life for more than thirteen years. If you are just beginning, don't try to tackle more Rule of Life than you can handle. Make a Rule of Life that fits who you are at this phase of your journey. It's important to start small and simple. Figure out how much structure you need in light of your personality and season of life — a lot or a little — and then build on it.

The best way to begin crafting a Rule of Life is to first do some prep work. Before filling out a sheet with commitments for prayer, rest, relationships, and work, take some time to work through the following questions:

- **What do you currently do that nurtures your spirit and fills you with delight?** Consider people and places as well as activities. Write down everything you can think of. Your list may include gardening, walking the dog, being in nature, talking with close friends, cooking, painting, jumping out of airplanes, or any number of other possibilities. List them all. If you don't currently do much that nurtures your spirit, spend some time identifying some things you'd like to try.

- **What people, places, and activities do you need to avoid because they deplete you or make it difficult for you to remain anchored in Christ?** This includes anything that negatively impacts your spirit — violent movies, hurrying, going beyond your limits, etc. Again, write down everything that comes to mind.

- **What "have to's" impact your rhythms in this season of life?** For example, this might include caring for aging parents, raising a young child or a child with special needs, dealing with health concerns, or navigating a demanding season at work, etc.

Once you have a good idea of the things that nurture you, deplete you, and are nonnegotiable on your schedule, you have a baseline for

considering what you want to include in the four Rule of Life categories — prayer, rest, relationships, and work. (You may find it helpful
to use the Rule of Life worksheet provided in appendix 2, page 311.)
Because almost every leader I meet has a "work" box that is much fuller
than their other three boxes, I encourage you to begin with the others
and fill in the work box last.

As you consider each category, listen first to your heart's desires.
What is it you want most in this area of your life? God often speaks to
us through our desires, so don't overlook them or diminish their importance. Make sure your rule includes some joy, play, and fun. Take baby
steps. Don't make your rule impossible to follow.

When you consider the prayer and rest categories, I encourage you
to begin by choosing one or two of what I consider to be the top five
practices that enable us to be more intentional about slowing down for
loving union: silence, Scripture meditation, the Daily Office, the prayer
of Examen, and Sabbath-keeping.

Silence. In silence we are still before the Lord in wordless prayer. I
seek to be silent in God's presence for twenty minutes a day. When I
do it, I am calmer and less anxious when I am active. If twenty minutes
seems too much, consider starting with two to five minutes and work
your way up from there.

Scripture Meditation. We slowly and prayerfully spend time in small
portions of Scripture, seeking to hear God's voice and to know God's
thoughts and heart. In my own practice, I meditate each day on a passage from one of the Gospels so I might know Jesus better. I also regularly carry with me a verse or two that I am meditating on during the
week outside of my time alone with God.

The Daily Office. This is an ancient practice of using prayer to mark
the times of the day, for example, morning prayer and evening prayer.
The purpose of the Daily Office is to create a rhythm that enables us
to stop our activity at set times during the day in order to be present
with God.[16] Stopping three to four times a day for brief times of prayer
creates a meaningful rhythm for my days.

The Prayer of Examen. This is a tool that helps us to reflect on the
day in order to attend to the movements of God's Spirit within us,

identify God's presence, and discern God's will. In its simplest form, it includes five steps:

1. Be grateful for God's blessings.
2. Review the day with openness and gratitude, looking for times when God has been present and times you may have ignored him.
3. Pay attention to your emotions in order to listen to God.
4. Express sorrow for sin and ask for God's forgiving love.
5. Pray for the grace to be more available to God who loves you.[17]

It's step three that I especially encourage leaders to pay attention to. One of the ways God speaks to us is through our deepest feelings and yearnings, what Ignatius of Loyola (1491 – 1556) called "consolation" and "desolation." Consolations are those experiences that fill us with joy, life, energy, and peace. Desolations are those that drain us and feel like death. Consolations connect us more deeply with God, ourselves, and others. Desolations disconnect us. As you replay the activities of your day, ask yourself:

- Where am I experiencing feelings of joy and peace? Where am I sensing connection with God (consolation)?
- Where am I experiencing sadness, apathy, and a sense of life draining out of me? Where am I sensing disconnection from God (desolation)?

I recommend practicing the Examen once or twice a day until it becomes something you do almost unconsciously throughout the day. It serves as the cornerstone for my discernment of God's will every day in small matters, such as how much to say in a staff meeting, or larger matters, such as bringing on a new team member.

Sabbath-Keeping. Sabbath is a twenty-four-hour period in which we cease all work in order to rest and delight in God's gifts. It is so transformative and indispensable to being an emotionally healthy leader that the entire next chapter is devoted to this one practice.

As you begin to craft and follow your Rule of Life, surround yourself with grace. I can guarantee you that sometimes you're going to have trouble maintaining your commitments. Unexpected and unavoidable things come into our lives. It takes experimentation and a willingness to keep trying to discern the form *your* rule should take. Also, remember that the point and purpose of every spiritual practice is to cultivate a life of loving union with Jesus. I have missed the point more than once, doggedly engaging in a spiritual practice while at the same time keeping the door of my heart shut to him. Endeavor to keep your heart open, soft, and responsive.

Rest in the Journey of Being an Imperfect Leader

Making the necessary changes to slow down your life for loving union with Jesus is a countercultural, prophetic stance. We are not living in a desert or a monastic community with built-in structure and supports. You can expect starts and stops, successes and failures as you find your way and figure out what works best in light of your unique personality, responsibilities, limits, and family dynamics.

What is critical is that you take the long view. Inhale, exhale, and *relax*. We don't suddenly slam on the brakes of life to slow down and get it all at once. Whenever I feel discouraged in my own progress, I remember what one Trappist monk said to me as he reflected on his sixty years of life dedicated to prayer, "I am only a beginner."

Understanding Your Loving Union Assessment

If you took the loving union assessment on page 121–22, here are some observations to help you reflect on your responses.

If you scored mostly ones and twos, you are likely doing too much in your own power, perhaps more than God has asked you to do. You may be doing a number of leadership tasks without any thought of Jesus. Because you are overloaded and distracted, your prayer may feel like more of a duty than a delight. The fact that you took the assessment and are reading these words is a grace from God. God is bringing this to your awareness for a reason. Consider the invitation God may be extending to you to slow down. Ask God what he is saying to you through this assessment. Identify a wise mentor or friend who can support you as you take your next steps.

If you scored mostly twos and threes, you are making progress but likely are still out of balance, with insufficient *being with* God to sustain your *doing for* God. You understand that Christian leadership is about enjoying communion with God as well as serving God. Ask yourself: *Am I moving in* the direction of more loving union with God or less? What adjustments might God be inviting me to make in this season? Consider which of the practices described in "Take Your First Steps to Slow Down for Loving Union" (pages 133 – 41) might be most helpful to you at this point.

If you scored mostly fours and fives, you are in a good place of rest and centeredness in your relationship with God. Your *doing for* God is fed and sustained by your *being with* God in a rhythm that works for your present leadership responsibilities. Let me encourage you to take time to craft a Rule of Life (if you haven't already done so), putting on paper how you are living your life with Jesus. Then, after taking time to get greater clarity on the principles God has given you, offer them to your coworkers and/or to those looking to you for leadership. At the same time, ask yourself what might be one additional invitation God is extending to you to deepen your relationship with him from this chapter.

CHAPTER 5

PRACTICE SABBATH DELIGHT

A few years ago, I'd had it "up to here" with pastors and Christian leaders. In a fit of frustration, I called my friend Bob. In addition to having a fancy plaque on his wall that says, "PhD," Bob is a clinical psychologist with thirty-five years of experience in counseling troubled leaders. I hoped he might help me sort out the aggravations I had with my own professional tribe.

"Bob, I need your help," I said. I was in no mood to mince words. "I don't understand what's wrong here. Pastors and leaders agree with me every time I speak to them about slowing down for God, about Sabbath, about our need to sit at the feet of Jesus. Not only do they agree, they often say it is one of the most impactful truths they get out of my talks. Some of them even turn right around and preach it to their congregations. But very few of them actually do anything about it."

My voice lowered as my frustration gave way to discouragement. "They start out and make a few very minor changes," I lamented, "but before you know it, they're right back to where they started. I feel like I'm wasting my time."

I thought Bob's response would be sympathetic. Instead, he laughed. I wasn't laughing.

"What's so funny?" I asked, not even trying to hide my irritation (and wondering if I'd made a mistake calling him).

"Oh, Pete," he said, "they *can't* stop. Christian leaders aren't any different than the international lawyers, CEOs, and marketplace leaders I see in my office every day."

"What are you talking about?" I said, cutting him off. "These folks are pastors and church leaders! They know Christ."

"No, Pete," he said, "you don't get it."

Bob was calm.

I was not.

Then Bob dropped the bombshell. "They can't stop. If they stop, they'll die. They're terrified. They're frightened to death of what they'll see inside themselves if they slow down. And you want them to immerse themselves in things like solitude, Sabbath, and silent reflection?" He chuckled again. "Do you have any idea how foreign this is for *any* leader — Christian or not? Something so much deeper is driving them; they just have no idea what it is."

It was the penetrating truth of this statement that stunned me: *If they stop, they'll die. They're terrified.*

"The terror of stopping reveals the depth of their emptiness," Bob continued matter-of-factly. "Pete, you're inviting them into practices that might well obliterate their entire sense of self — the self that's rooted in their work performance. Can't you see the magnitude of that?"

"Not really," I replied, deciding he had given me more than enough to think about for one day.

One part of me despaired as I thought about how hard it would be for Christian leaders to experience transformation in this area of their lives. But another part of me was elated. Bob had effectively put in place a missing piece of the puzzle about why Sabbath was nearly impossible for so many leaders to practice, and why it had been such a struggle for me. Fear and shame were lurking beneath the surface of our lives.

Later in the chapter, we'll talk more about this issue, along with other crucial reasons why Sabbath remains such a challenge for leaders today. But before we do that, it's important to have a clear understanding and definition of what Sabbath is.

What Is the Sabbath?

Biblical Sabbath is a twenty-four-hour block of time in which we stop work, enjoy rest, practice delight, and contemplate God. The traditional Jewish Sabbath begins at sundown on Friday and ends at sundown Saturday. In most Christian traditions, Sabbath has been observed on Sunday. The apostle Paul considered one day for Sabbath as good as another (Romans 14:1 – 17). So the particular day of the week doesn't matter. What matters is to set aside a twenty-four-hour period and protect it.

The fact that Sabbath happens weekly means that it has a rhythm, one that stands in stark contrast to the typical rhythm of the world around us. That secular rhythm looks something like this:

"SECULAR" RHYTHM:

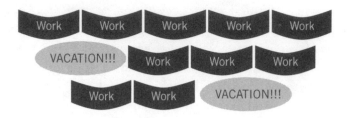

In contrast, God's rhythm looks like this:

"SACRED" RHYTHM:

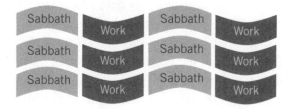

God's Sabbath rhythm is a reflection of the rhythm that undergirds all of creation. In the cycle of a day, there is light and dark, sunrise and sunset, tides coming in and going out. Over the course of months, there are cycles of the moon, the seasons and their attendant cycles of growth and dormancy, as well as the great movements of the galaxies. As author Wayne Muller says so well, "To remember the Sabbath is not a burdensome requirement ... but rather a remembrance of a law that is firmly embedded in the fabric of nature. It is a reminder of how things really are, the rhythmic dance to which we unavoidably belong."[1] All work — paid and unpaid — is good, but it needs to be boundaried by the practice of Sabbath.

The problem with too many leaders is that we allow our work to trespass on every other area of life, disrupting the balanced rhythm of work and rest God created for our good.

When Geri and I began our journey into emotionally healthy spirituality in 1996, one of the things I gained was a new perspective on the importance of having a Sabbath rhythm. So I read a few books, occasionally mentioned Sabbath in sermons, and experimented with taking a day of rest each week. But I wasn't quite sure how Sabbath really differed from a day off. *What was, and was not, permissible? How could I set aside a full day for rest with four small children to care for? What about the inevitable pastoral crises that routinely impinge on a day?* Eventually, the incessant demands of life, leadership, and pastoral work crushed my Sabbath experiment. I returned to taking a regular day off on Mondays and, from time to time over the next seven years, I made several unsuccessful attempts to restart a consistent Sabbath practice.

It was only after the life-changing experience of our second sabbatical in 2003–2004 that I felt compelled to figure out this "Sabbath thing" once and for all — not only for myself but also for the sake of our church. I set aside time to study Sabbath, doing a biblical word study on every occurrence of *Sabbath* from Genesis to Revelation. I read most available Christian books on Sabbath and looked closely at the rich 3,500-year Jewish origins and traditions of Sabbath.

Out of this intensive study, I identified the four foundational characteristics you read in the opening line of this section that define Sabbath as a twenty-four-hour block of time in which we *stop* work, enjoy *rest*, practice *delight*, and *contemplate* God. These four characteristics have since served me well in distinguishing a routine day off from a biblical Sabbath. From a secular perspective, the purpose of a day off is to replenish our energies and make us more effective the other six days of the week. Such a day off may produce positive results but is, in the words of pastor Eugene Peterson, "a bastard Sabbath."[2] So let's take a closer look at these four foundational characteristics of Sabbath.[3]

Stop. Sabbath is first and foremost a day when we cease all work—paid and unpaid. On the Sabbath we embrace our limits. We let go of the illusion that we are indispensable to the running of the world. We recognize we will never finish all our goals and projects, and that God is on the throne, managing quite well in ruling the universe without our help.

My Sabbath begins Friday night at 6:00 p.m. and ends on Saturday night at 6:00 p.m. When I stop my work for Sabbath, I step back from anything to do with my role as pastor of New Life Fellowship Church as well as any writing or speaking prep. I purposefully do not answer e-mails, return phone calls, finish sermons, write, or complete undone leadership tasks. I avoid Twitter and Facebook since social media is connected to my work. I also step back from my unpaid work, such as paying bills, doing laundry, running errands, grocery shopping, and cleaning up around the house.

Rest. Once we stop, we accept God's invitation to rest. God rested after his work of creation. Every seventh day, we are to do the same (Genesis 2:1–4). We engage in activities that restore and replenish us—from napping, hiking, reading, and eating good food to enjoying hobbies and playing sports. The key is to rest from both paid and unpaid work.

Resting from unpaid work, however, requires advance planning. If I am to have any hope of enjoying a Sabbath rest, I need to set aside time during the week to attend to the routine tasks of life I won't do on Sabbath—paying bills, cleaning or fixing something around the house, doing laundry, and balancing the checkbook, etc.

What do I do for rest? I nap, go out on a date with Geri, spend time with our daughters, read a novel, watch a great movie, go for a long hike, swim, visit friends and family, or take a train to enjoy the arts in Manhattan. I may even mow our small lawn as a nice diversion from my work.

Delight. After finishing his work in creation, God pronounced it "very good" (Genesis 1:31). This was not an anemic afterthought—*Oh, well, it's nice to be done with that*—but a joyful recognition and celebration of accomplishment. As part of observing Sabbath, God invites us to join in the celebration, to enjoy and delight in his creation and all the gifts he offers us in it. These innumerable gifts come to us in many forms, including people, places, and things.

As part of preparing to practice the Sabbath, one of the most important questions to consider is, "What gives me joy and delight?" This will differ for each of us, but part of the Sabbath invitation is to enjoy and delight in creation and her gifts. Geri and I both delight in the beauty and grandeur of nature — the ocean, lakes, beaches, mountains, and star-filled skies. Geri is a "foodie," so tasting, smelling, and savoring the gift of food is a high priority for us. I delight in libraries and bookstores. Geri loves cooking a fresh meal. Through any and every means possible, on Sabbath we seek to feast on the miracle of life with our senses.

Contemplate. Pondering the love of God is the central focus of our Sabbaths. What makes a Sabbath a biblical Sabbath is that it is "holy to the Lord." We are not taking time off from God; we are drawing closer to him. Sabbath is an invitation to see the invisible in the visible — to recognize the hidden ways God's goodness is at work in our lives. It does not mean we necessarily spend the entire day in prayer or studying Scripture, though those activities may be part of a Sabbath day. Instead, contemplation means we are acutely focused on those aspects of God's love that come to us through so many gifts from his hand. As British poet and priest Gerard Manley Hopkins writes, "The world is charged with the grandeur of God." Scripture affirms that all creation declares his glory (see Psalm 19:1). On Sabbath, we intentionally look for his grandeur in everything from people, food, and art to babies, sports, hobbies, and music. In this sense, contemplation is an extension of delight — we are intentional about looking for the evidence of God's love in all of the things he has given us to enjoy.

Before I routinely observed the Sabbath, I often returned from vacations or days off feeling somehow farther away from God. Now my Sabbath days are times I experience his presence and love in very tangible ways that I might otherwise associate with my "work" as a pastor. For example, when I experience a sense of God's pleasure and approval on Sabbath, I know it has nothing to do with my work-related accomplishments. This in itself is a gift that has helped me to separate my relationship with God (my *being* with God) from my work as a leader (my *doing* for God).

I hope these four characteristics will provide a helpful framework as you begin to consider what it might mean for you to practice a meaningful observance of Sabbath, but if you ever find yourself getting too caught up in the details and logistics — which is easy to do — I encourage you to take a step back. Refocus your attention on the larger significance of Sabbath — the opportunity to experience a foretaste of eternity. As Rabbi Abraham Joshua Heschel wrote:

> Unless one learns how to relish the taste of Sabbath while still in this world, unless one is initiated in the appreciation of eternal life, one will be unable to enjoy the taste of eternity in the world to come.... The essence of the world to come is Sabbath eternal, and the seventh day in time is an example of eternity.[4]

On Sabbath, we practice eternity in time. We look forward to that day at the end of our earthly lives when we will perfectly stop, rest, delight, and contemplate the glory of God. For a brief moment in time, we reorient ourselves away from this world in all its brokenness and anticipate the world to come — how things on earth are meant to be. In a very real sense, the practice of Sabbath joins heaven and earth, equipping us not merely to rest from our work but also to work from our rest.

How Healthy Is Your Practice of Sabbath Delight?

Use the list of statements that follow to do a brief assessment of your practice of Sabbath. Next to each statement, write down the number that best describes your response. Use the following scale:

5 = Always true of me
4 = Frequently true of me
3 = Occasionally true of me
2 = Rarely true of me
1 = Never true of me

_____ 1. I regularly practice Sabbath by setting aside a twenty-four-hour period in which I stop my work and rest.

_____ 2. Sabbath provides a healthy boundary and limit around my paid and unpaid work.

_____ 3. I take time on my weekly Sabbath to delight in God's innumerable gifts (e.g., people, beauty, hobbies, mountains, food, music, etc.).

_____ 4. I view Sabbath as a day to practice eternity and taste the ultimate Sabbath rest when I will see Jesus face-to-face.

_____ 5. I practice Sabbath as a prophetic, countercultural act that resists the culture's value that defines me by what I do rather than who I am (i.e., God's beloved son/daughter).

_____ 6. I am comfortable letting go of my responsibilities on Sabbath, fully trusting God to run the world and build his kingdom without me.

_____ 7. I find my identity primarily in God's love rather than in my work or my role as a leader.

_____ 8. I often receive unexpected insights and discernment during Sabbath.

_____ 9. I apply my Sabbath guidelines of stop, rest, delight, and contemplate to extended vacations and holidays.

_____ 10. I intentionally prepare and plan for Sabbath so that I have the time and space to focus on God's love coming to me through the many gifts from his hand.

Take a moment to briefly review your responses. What stands out most to you? At the end of the chapter (page 172) are some general observations to help you better understand where you're at as you consider your next steps.

Why Sabbath Is Such a Challenge Today

Sabbath was a revolutionary concept when God introduced it 3,500 years ago, and it remains a countercultural concept to this day, though perhaps for different reasons. In my work with pastors and Christian leaders, I've observed three primary challenges that make Sabbath observance especially difficult.

We Are Afraid of What We Might Find Inside Us

Remember my conversation with Bob and his comment about why so many leaders can't seem to slow down? "They can't stop," he said. "If they stop, they'll die. They're terrified. They're frightened to death of what they'll see inside themselves if they slow down.... Something so much deeper is driving them, but they just have no idea what it is."

What is that "something"? What lies behind the resistance — for some, even terror — when leaders consider slowing down for Sabbath? After observing and talking with pastors around the world for many years, I believe the answer is *shame.*

Shame is the intensely painful feeling or experience of being fundamentally flawed, defective, unworthy, and "deficient in some vital way as a human being."[5] So we work harder, and then work even harder. *Maybe, if I get over this next hill at work, then I'll feel better about myself and how things are going to step back and relax. But for now I can't stop.*

It's important to distinguish shame from guilt. Guilt is about something I *do.* For example, "I ran a red light." It is one mistake I made, not a reflection of my entire person. Shame, on the other hand, is about who I *am.* "I didn't just make a mistake when I ran that red light, I *am* a mistake." When we fall short as a leader, we think things like, *I'm such an idiot. I'm awful and worthless! I'm such a fraud — this wouldn't have happened if I were a decent leader.* Shame testifies not to wrong *doing* but to flawed *being.*[6]

Sabbath can be terrifying because doing nothing productive leaves us feeling vulnerable. We may feel emotional exposure and nakedness before God or others. Overworking hides these feelings of inadequacy or worthlessness not just from others but also from ourselves. As long as we keep busy, we can outrun that internal voice that says things like:

I am never good enough.

I am never safe enough.

I am never perfect enough.

I am never extraordinary enough.

I am never successful enough.

Do you recognize that voice?

Far too many Christian leaders and pastors use workaholism to run from these shaming messages. I count myself among them, though at this point I would consider myself more of a recovering workaholic. For a quick-take assessment on your own tendencies to work too much, consider how many of these qualities might be true of you:

Do you get more excited about your work than about family or anything else?

Do you take work with you to bed? On weekends? On vacation?

Is work the activity you like to do best and talk about most?

Do you work more than forty hours a week?

Have your family or friends given up expecting you on time?

Do you take on extra work because you are concerned that it won't otherwise get done?

Do you underestimate how long a project will take and then rush to complete it?

Do you get impatient with people who have other priorities besides work?

Have your long hours hurt your family or other relationships?[7]

How did you do? If you answered yes to even a few questions, workaholism may be something you'll need to wrestle with in order to have a Sabbath. And you need to know that you'll be dealing with something more substantial than just busyness or learning a few new skills and techniques. If you've been in the habit of overworking for months or years, the need to overwork may actually be hardwired into your body.

Did you know that a consistent pattern of overworking can impact the neurochemistry of your brain?[8] When we are constantly in an intense and demanding environment, our brains release hormones and chemicals to help us meet the challenges we face. Over time, the body becomes accustomed to these hormones and chemicals to the point that we develop a kind of dependency on them. In some cases, business executives in intense environments have actually developed clinical adrenaline addiction.

So what does all this have to do with Sabbath? It means that when we attempt to make a significant lifestyle change, say from working 24/7 to maintaining a balanced work and Sabbath rhythm, our bodies can experience a type of withdrawal. And if you decide to take up the challenge of being serious about the Sabbath, the battle may be physical as well as emotional and spiritual.

We Associate Sabbath with Legalism or a Dead Past

Confusion around Sabbath goes back as far as Sabbath itself, and ever since, Jews and then Christians alike have struggled to define the rules that should govern its practice. In the fourth century, Constantine, the first Christian Roman emperor, dealt with Sabbath by legally mandating a day of rest for everyone. In the early years of the American colonies, so-called "blue laws" restricted various activities and commerce in order to accommodate the Christian Sabbath. The earliest Sunday-closing laws date back to 1610. They included not simply the closing of businesses but also mandatory church attendance. And even more than 180 years later, the laws were strictly enforced:

- George Washington, the newly elected president of the United States, when traveling from Connecticut to New York, was stopped for violating Connecticut's law forbidding travel on Sunday.
- In the 1800s, in Arkansas, James Armstrong was fined $25.00 for digging potatoes in his field.
- John Meeks was fined $22.50 for shooting squirrels on Sunday.[9]

The Talmud, a central text of mainstream Judaism and the basis for all codes of Jewish law, identifies thirty-nine categories of activity prohibited on the Sabbath. Among them are sowing, reaping, weaving, building, baking, and lighting a fire. The application of these prohibitions evolved over centuries. In many Orthodox or Hasidic communities today, it is forbidden on Sabbath to turn electric devices on or off, to drive a car, or to walk more than a certain distance beyond one's home. Lights and hot plates are often set on automatic timers. In one New York City hospital where a high percentage of doctors and patients are Orthodox Jews, elevators are programmed to stop on each floor of the hospital so riders don't have to work on Sabbath by pushing an elevator button.

For some Christian leaders, such outdated rules and impositions make Sabbath observance seem like a pointless legalism. But for many others, including me in my first twenty-seven years as a Christian, there is simply a lack of understanding about the larger purpose of Sabbath and the rich biblical material affirming the necessity of having safeguards to protect it.

We Have a Distorted View of Our Core Identity

When meeting someone for the first time we usually ask, "What do you do?" We ask because, in our time and culture, identity is defined in large part by occupation or job title. And if you've ever been unemployed or a full-time stay-at-home parent, you know how awkward it can be not to have one. It is how we typically define ourselves and how we understand our place in the world. We also classify and value people based on what they do. Tell me which of these two would be more esteemed among a group of young pastors: a thirty-eight-year-old leader who has built a large and growing international ministry or a sixty-eight-year-old retired pastor who faithfully served a 75-member rural church for over thirty years?

Part of who we are *is* what we do. God is a worker, and we are workers. But that is not the deepest truth about who we are. We are first of all human *beings*. But when things get switched around and our role or title becomes the foundation of our identity, we are reduced to human *doings*. And when that happens, ceasing work or productive activity becomes extremely difficult. Consider Elliot's story.

Elliot, a Sunday school superintendent at New Life, approached me one Sunday after hearing me teach about the Sabbath. He told me how his upbringing had made Sabbath especially challenging for him: "Whenever my sister and two younger brothers and I heard my mom's footsteps coming down the stairs, we jumped up to make it look like we were doing something, anything—dusting, arranging things, cleaning up. It was understood that you don't just sit around and do nothing! And God forbid we weren't outside in time to help her carry in the bags when she arrived home from the grocery store. Even though it's now thirty years later, I still feel guilty when I'm not being productive in some way."

I relate to Elliot's story. The clear message in my family growing up was, *You are what you accomplish*.[10] Our identity and value were closely tied to our ability to produce and to achieve. From earning good grades and playing sports as children to getting good jobs and raising good children as adults, the expectation was that we work hard. Resting was something done in order to recuperate so we could get right back to work. The idea of using rest for anything related to pure enjoyment was inconceivable.

Sadly, I've discovered that this distorted concept of identity and rest in families like mine and Elliot's is not that unusual. From Asia to Latin America, from North America to Africa, from the Middle East to Europe and Oceania, the bias of families and cultures is to define and value one another not by who we are, but by what we do. That kind of pressure is not easy to resist.

What then will motivate us to reimagine, reprioritize, and rearrange our lives around Sabbath? The answer lies, I believe, in capturing a greater biblical vision of Sabbath as a beautiful diamond whose many facets reflect the light and beauty of life on earth in relationship with the living God.

The Sabbath Is a Beautiful Diamond

Facets are the polished, flat surfaces that reflect a diamond's brilliance, fire, and sparkle. Each facet shows a unique aspect of the diamond's quality and beauty.[11] A standard round brilliant diamond, for example, may have up to fifty-eight facets!

Sabbath is a priceless diamond with many facets, each reflecting God's presence with us and his love for us. And just as facets reflect unique aspects of a diamond, Sabbath becomes increasingly brilliant the more we explore and practice it. That's when we find ourselves standing in the radiance of Sabbath's lovely facets, in wonder and awe at the brilliance of God to which Sabbath points.

For millennia, the Jewish people have treasured this beautiful diamond called Sabbath. Francine Klagsbrun, best-selling author of *Jewish Days*, describes it well:

> Before I fully understood the holiness of the Day, before I truly appreciated its beauty, before I could interpret its rituals, I knew the Sabbath was a "miracle." That was how my father always spoke of it, from the time I was a child and well into his hundredth year of life.... A miracle indeed. No such day existed in the universe until it appeared full-blown in the Hebrew Bible. Other ancient peoples had certain "evil days"... But none had a fixed day in every week of every month of every year in which all work stopped and all creatures rested — yes, even the animals.[12]

I love how Klagsbrun describes the miracle of Sabbath as she gazes on one small facet of its brilliance—the uniqueness of God's declaration of a fixed day as holy and set apart.

In light of 3,500 years of Jewish history, my twelve years of faithfully studying and practicing Sabbath is something like a puff of smoke. Nonetheless, I have been able to glimpse a few facets of this seemingly inexhaustibly beautiful diamond, four of which have made significant contributions to my understanding and experience of the miracle of Sabbath:

- Sabbath as a core spiritual formation discipline
- Sabbath as resistance to principalities and powers
- Sabbath as play
- Sabbath as a place of revelation

I hope and pray that each facet will motivate and encourage you to take your next steps in reordering your life to practice Sabbath delight and to say a weekly, twenty-four-hour *no* to the relentless pressures around you.

Sabbath as a Core Spiritual Formation Discipline

Almost every spiritual discipline has value, but some practices constitute the *core* of maturing in Christ. These practices don't *save* us, but they are indispensable for growth. Think of it this way. We are not saved by reading the Bible. We are not saved by prayer. We are not saved by worship. We are saved by trusting in Jesus Christ alone, who died for our sins and rose from the dead. But if we are not routinely reading Scripture, praying, or encountering God in worship, it is unlikely we are growing much spiritually. Keeping the Sabbath is a *core* spiritual discipline—an essential delivery mechanism for God's grace and goodness in our lives. It provides a God-ordained way to slow us down for meaningful connection with God, ourselves, and those we care about.

I believe part of the reason we find ourselves disenchanted with spiritual disciplines like Sabbath keeping is because our practice has degenerated into one of two extremes—legalism or licentiousness.

Legalism can be defined as relying on our own obedience to gain acceptance from God. In the New Testament, we observe legalism among the Jewish religious leaders who objected so vehemently to Jesus breaking the law by healing on the Sabbath. Later, the apostle Paul clearly warned against any type of legalism in the church: "Therefore do not let anyone judge you by what you eat or drink, or with regard to a religious festival, a New Moon celebration or a Sabbath day. These are a shadow of the things that were to come; the reality, however, is found in Christ" (Colossians 2:16–17).

Licentiousness, on the other hand, is an abuse of God's grace by completely disregarding his commands. In connection with spiritual disciplines, this extreme leads people to dismiss such practices as Sabbath as irrelevant and unnecessary. A contemporary example of this would be people skipping weekly worship services because there are just so many other good things to do on the weekends. God isn't keeping score of our church attendance, right?

In the first twenty-five years of my Christian life, I was definitely in the camp of the licentious when it came to Sabbath. The fog cleared for me when I finally grasped that Sabbath is a core discipline for spiritual formation that is just as important as prayer, Bible Study, worship, and giving.[13] Even more, Sabbath is God's good gift to his people. Jesus said, "The Sabbath was made for people, not people for the Sabbath" (Mark 2:27 NET).

Instead of thinking of the Sabbath as an imposition, we need to embrace it as an essential delivery mechanism for God's love. Why would anyone want to miss out on something like that? As leaders, it reminds us that life is about more than work; life is about God. When balanced by a Sabbath rhythm, work takes its proper place as a good, but not a god.

Sabbath as Resistance to Principalities and Powers[14]

"Principalities and powers" are among what the apostle Paul described as "powers of this dark world" and "spiritual forces of evil" (Ephesians 6:12). They represent a wide range of malign influences that could take almost any form. Theologian Walter Wink described them as "both heavenly and earthly, divine and human, spiritual and political, invisible and visible."[15] They can be found in educational, economic, and political systems that dehumanize and destroy people. They are powerful forces behind such things as unbridled ambition, lust, racism, sexism, and worship of money. And these same demonic powers seek to keep us enslaved to our work and prevent us from Sabbath delight.

When we practice Sabbath, we resist principalities and powers. Consider the rationale God gives for practicing Sabbath:

> *Observe the Sabbath day by keeping it holy. … Remember that you were slaves in Egypt and that the LORD your God brought you out of there with a mighty hand and an outstretched arm.*
>
> (DEUTERONOMY 5:12, 15)

The key phrase in this command is: *Remember that you were slaves in Egypt and that the Lord your God brought you out of there.* As slaves in Egypt for over 400 years, the Israelites worked seven days a week, 365 days a year. Their parents, grandparents, great grandparents, and great-great grandparents existed for only one reason—to work. They never stopped. They never rested. They never delighted.

As a power set in opposition to God, Pharaoh was what the apostle Paul might have called a "spiritual force of evil." He was considered a god and worshiped as such. Behind his demonic rule were principalities and powers that enslaved God's people, defining their very existence as nonpersons whose only purpose was to work and produce. But now Pharaoh's oppression over God's people had been broken. And they were given a new identity. Their worth and value is no longer based on what *they do*; it is based on *who they are*—sons and daughters upon whom the living God has set his love and grace.

Sadly, many of us remain under a harsh and controlling taskmaster, a "Pharaoh" who now lives inside our heads, telling us we can't stop or rest. The culture shackles us in chains, telling us our only value is in what we achieve or produce, that we are losers unless we accomplish more—whatever it may cost us. We are doing well only if things are "bigger and better." We compare ourselves to other leaders who seem to produce more bricks more quickly, and we wonder, *What's my problem?*

In offering us the gift of Sabbath, God invites us to resist the principalities and powers and side with him. Author and scholar Walter Brueggemann wrote, "Sabbath becomes a decisive, concrete, visible way of opting for and aligning with the God of rest."[16] And what a delightful invitation it is! God invites us to revel, to dance and sing like the ancient Israelites when they were delivered from Egyptian slavery. Through this weekly practice, we defy every influence that defines us either by our leadership role or our productivity. We publicly proclaim to the world that we are not slaves, but free men and women purchased by the blood of Jesus.

When we practice Sabbath as leaders, we not only resist the principalities and powers for our own lives, we also model resistance to those we lead, to the larger church, to the world, and even to the powers and principalities themselves.

To this day, the Jewish people consider Sabbath keeping a central feature of their identity as God's chosen people. And it's remarkable to see how Sabbath still functions as a form of resistance. I especially love the example of B&H Photo.

Located on 9th Avenue in New York City, B&H Photo is the largest non-chain photo and video equipment store in the United States and the second largest in the world—only Yodobashi Camera in downtown Tokyo is bigger. The owners, along with many of their employees, are Hasidic Jews who dress just as their eighteenth-century ancestors did in Eastern Europe. On any given day, 8,000 to 9,000 people pass through the front door. Yet 70 percent of their business is online, serviced by a 200,000-square-foot warehouse located nearby in Brooklyn.

Even in a competitive marketplace, B&H won't conduct business on the Sabbath or on about a half-dozen Jewish holidays during the year. They close their doors at 1 p.m. on Fridays and keep them closed all day Saturday, the biggest shopping day of the week. During Sabbath, customers can peruse the B&H website, but they can't make an online order.

Recently a customer asked the B&H director of communications how they could close not just the retail store but also the website on Black Friday, the day after Thanksgiving and the busiest shopping day of the year. The director simply replied, "We respond to a higher authority."[17]

Author and Holocaust survivor Elie Wiesel also attests to this aspect of Sabbath as resistance when he describes how Sabbath observance persisted even in the horrors of Nazi concentration camps:

> I remember a Lithuanian preacher, a *maggid*, who wandered among us every Friday night, accosting everyone, with the hint of a smile: "Brother Jew—don't forget, it's Shabbat." He wanted to remind us that Shabbat still reigned over time and the world despite the smoke and stench.[18]

Both that Lithuanian preacher and the workers at B&H grasp an important biblical principle: God is sovereign over every principality and power in the world. God is King of kings and Lord of lords.

When we practice Sabbath delight, we proclaim that Jesus Christ defeated every spiritual force of evil at the cross (Colossians 2:15). We affirm that human beings have infinite value and worth apart from their productivity, and that God's love is the most important reality in the universe.

Sabbath as Play

On a recent visit to the Holy Land, my friend Christine was sitting with friends at an outdoor cafe in Jerusalem one Friday afternoon when a group of teenage boys ran by singing and shouting. At first she thought something might be wrong because they were making such a loud racket. When she asked the waiter what was going on, he said, "They're very happy that it will soon be the Sabbath."

"Happy about the Sabbath?" she asked, uncertain if she'd heard him right.

"Yes," he said, "they are welcoming the Sabbath with their songs and shouting."

In telling me the story, Christine likened the boys' enthusiasm to the excitement teenagers in the States might have about spending a day at Disney World—a day of play in the Magic Kingdom of play!

Wow! Can you imagine looking forward to Sabbath with that kind of joy and delight?

It was the great German theologian Jürgen Moltmann who first introduced me to the notion of Sabbath as play. In his book *Theology of Play*, he asks, "Why did God create the universe if he is a free and all sufficient being?" His answer, rooted in the book of Proverbs, is that we observe God "playing" when he made the world. Wisdom, who was from all eternity before the world began (Proverbs 8:23, 25), played in the Father's presence when the world was created: "I was filled with delight day after day, rejoicing always in his presence, rejoicing in his whole world and delighting in [hu]mankind" (8:30–31). It is God's "good will and pleasure to create. Hence the creation is God's play, a play of his groundless and inscrutable wisdom. It is the realm in which God displays his glory."[19]

God informs Job that when he created the world, "the morning stars sang together and all the angels shouted for joy" (Job 38:7), indicating we are the fruit of God's love and delight. God enjoys being God.

There is a playful extravagance built into God's creation — an over-abundance of seeds is produced that will never germinate, leaves on trees turn brilliant colors in autumn whether or not anyone sees them, incredible species of fish swim hidden from human sight in the deeps of the ocean, and every flower remains beautiful even when no one is looking. All of it is there to be enjoyed.[20] One theologian adds that if you are unsure if God is playful, just look at some of his creatures, such as the platypus, ostrich, and giraffe. The very sight of them makes us smile and laugh like children.[21]

Moltmann's point is that, as creatures made in the image of God, we are to reflect God by playing. Moltmann imagines play as engaging in a variety of games that tap into the joy of God. He writes:

> Like the creation, man's games are an expression of free-dom … for playing relates to the joy of the creator with his creation and the pleasure of the player with his game. Like creation, games combine sincerity and mirth, suspense and relaxation. The player is wholly absorbed in his game and takes it seriously, yet at the same time he transcends himself and his game, for it is after all only a game.[22]

This kind of play points to the joy at the end of history when we will see Jesus face-to-face and all sin and death is wiped away. In a very real sense, play offers us a foretaste of eternity. "We are increasingly playing with the future in order to get to know it," Moltmann says.[23]

Most pastors and leaders, myself included, are not great at play. Sometimes I think we are more serious about life than God is! Play has been difficult for me to learn. My family did not play; we worked. All the churches I attended in my life were play-deficient, often associating lighthearted pleasures with silliness or foolishness. There was simply too much work to do for God! So learning to play on Sabbath has been a significant part of my discipleship to become a healthier Christ-follower and leader.

Play is important because it is an indicator that we really do believe life is more than work. It balances our tendency to be too serious and too focused on results. When we are playing, we accomplish no pragmatic purpose.[24] We are more relaxed, less uptight, more trusting in God's sovereignty, and more alert to integrate playfulness into the other six days.

Sabbath Wisdom from a Seventeen-Year-Old

Peter and Renee Hoffman were part of New Life Fellowship Church for almost seven years before they moved to Michigan. Two things made them incredibly unique for New York City. First, they lived in a three-bedroom, rented apartment with twelve children. (Fortunately, not all of them lived at home at the same time.) And they faithfully practiced Sabbath as a family and had been doing so for ten years before coming to our church.

The following is an excerpt from a high school paper written by their seventeen-year-old daughter, Abbey:

> Every Saturday night at 6:30, my whole house is dark except for one small candle on the kitchen table. It casts a warm glow on the faces of those seated around: my parents, six younger siblings, and commonly one or two guests. Covers are pulled off of enormous platters of food and the aromas fill the air like a cool breeze on a summer night.... This is how my family welcomes the Sabbath, a weekly ritual that we have had for about ten years. It begins at 6:00 p.m. on Saturday and lasts until 6:00 p.m. on Sunday.

It is so easy to get caught up in the mixed messages around us, and we need time to slow down as a family and keep in mind what our lives are really about. The ritual of Sabbath-keeping is a radical statement that we are *not* God, and we trust him to hold the world together, even if we stop for one day each week. We turn off all phones and computers and refrain from watching TV. We replace them with activities that will build us up spiritually and bring us closer together as a family. This includes anything from playing guitar and singing worship songs, to taking walks in the park and appreciating the beauty of the autumn leaves, to playing games and being silly. On Sunday mornings we wake up early, rain or shine, and pile into our fifteen-passenger van to make it to church by 9:00 a.m. Attending church serves as a reminder that we are part of a larger body of believers who are seeking a common goal.

Sabbath is my favorite day of the week. If God chooses to give me a family someday, I would continue with this ritual. The Sabbath brings peace, love, and order to our home and family, and the benefits carry even further.

Wow, did you catch all of that insight and wisdom? The Hoffman Sabbath described by Abbey captures all three of the Sabbath facets we've covered so far — Sabbath as an essential spiritual formation discipline, as resistance to principalities and powers, and as play.

Sabbath as a Place of Revelation

We receive revelation from God through several forms, including Scripture, prayer, wise mentors, creation, and closed doors. And most Christians will acknowledge that there are some revelations of God that come only through things like the crucible of suffering and the storms of life. Few, however, realize that a similar principle applies to Sabbath. There are some things God can deposit into our souls only when we unplug completely from work and rest.

On Sabbath, something of God's holiness and goodness is revealed, not simply in the way he works but in the way he rests. This means that when we fail to receive God's gift of Sabbath, we miss out on something of God — something we can't get any other way. Allow me to illustrate this with a simple biblical example.

God commanded the ancient Israelites to let the land remain fallow for a full year every seventh year, calling it a sabbatical rest for the land. Why? So he could replenish depleted nutrients in the soil. To work the soil year after year without this rest would have left the soil infertile. The soil of our souls is not all that different. Work requires something of us; it depletes our energies, our wisdom, our reserves. If we don't allow the soil of our souls to rest, we do violence to ourselves. As human beings, we were created for a balanced rhythm of work and rest. Over time, fatigue and exertion make it more difficult for us to live and lead from the fruits of the Spirit. But on the Sabbath, God uses rest, delight, and play to replenish depleted spiritual nutrients such as love, joy, peace, patience, and kindness. We receive his love and he replenishes us — as persons and as leaders — so we can bear fruit.

Once we stop and rest, we also discover that God is speaking — a lot. There are things he wants to reveal to us that we will never be able to hear, much less attend to, unless we are in a place of rest. For example, goals we might think are important suddenly seem less important or perhaps even distractions from what God might be inviting us to do. We realize life is broader and richer than our leadership goals and concerns. As we practice entrusting God with our work (and all its attendant problems and worries) for twenty-four hours, we begin to find it easier to entrust the outcome of our work to him the other days of the week as well.

Geri and I are continually amazed how often God uses Sabbath to deepen in us crucially important truths that we believe. Here are two recent examples:

- **God is not in a rush.** He often moves more slowly than the timetable I have for my goals. In fact, I often discover he has different goals! During the other six days, I strategize, recruit, and envision others to expand God's kingdom. My mind is filled with exciting ideas and plans. On Sabbath, I stop my work and taste God's contentment in his unhurried, deliberate plan to save a world that I think desperately needs all of him *now*!

- **God's primary work for me as a leader is to trust in Jesus (John 6:28–29).** During the other six days, I do the best I can to bring my gifts and talents to bear on building God's church in the world. I seek to trust him as I do that. On Sabbath, I trust only in Jesus and receive his love. I am reminded that Jesus is the head of the church and that he runs the world better than I do. He really is in charge. I am not in control of things. In fact, when I sleep, God is working; and when I awake, I join him in his work (Psalm 121, 127).

So much revelation awaits us on Sabbath if we would just stop to receive it. Most of us are good at speaking. We are not equally good at listening. When we practice Sabbath, we become better listeners, finding that God is speaking to us, and we have been too busy to hear.

As you read about four facets on the beautiful diamond that is Sabbath, did you find yourself longing to experience these things and wishing you weren't missing out? You don't have to miss out! It is never too late to embrace the beauty and joy of Sabbath rest.

Create a Container for Your Sabbath

It takes creativity and perseverance as well as trial and error to make the transition from merely having a day off to observing a "Sabbath to the Lord our God." Anyone who's tried to take Sabbath seriously realizes pretty quickly that Sabbath-keeping requires significant thought and advance planning. It also requires defining and maintaining boundaries on how you use your Sabbath time.

My friend Todd Deatherage is cofounder of a nonprofit devoted to fostering peace and understanding among peoples in the Holy Land. As part of his work, he makes many trips to the Holy Land every year. I was fascinated when Todd described his experiences of Sabbath (*Shabbat*) in Jerusalem with a Jewish family:

> Beginning about ten years ago, a rabbi friend invited me into his home again and again to experience *Shabbat* with his family. *Shabbat* always begins with a beautiful meal shared with family and friends. Prayers and blessings are said, and a relaxed evening of conversation follows — sometimes for three to four hours. The care and intentionality given to choosing the place settings, preparing special foods, and gathering of friends and family always made it feel to me more like a full-blown holiday celebration than a weekly meal. Imagine doing Thanksgiving once a week, and you'll have an idea of what *Shabbat* is like.

The rabbi and his family taught me how their adherence to a rigid set of guidelines about what they can and cannot do on Sabbath served as a container that allowed them to enter into the Sabbath's rest. For them, *Shabbat* is very different from the other six days of the week. Everything that distracts—and there are many distractions in our technological and information-saturated age—is put aside in favor of things like prayer, study, long walks, naps, hikes, shared meals, and meaningful conversation. There would be no time or space for such things without the protection of firm limits on the day.

When I think of setting Sabbath boundaries or limits in the way Todd describes—as creating a protective container—it changes my perspective from one of legalism (a long list of dutiful thou-shalt-nots) to one of anticipation. This is a day in which I set aside my labors in expectation of something better. I not only look back with gratitude on what God has done, I also look forward to what he is going to do.

Sabbath observance can be rich and beautiful, but we have to be willing to create the protective container—the boundaries—that make it possible. In order to enter into it, we have to submit ourselves to concrete guidelines that distinguish Sabbath from business as usual the other six days of the week. For some, this may include turning off all social media, phones, and computers. For others, it may be a zero tolerance for any talk about work. Perhaps the Sabbath might start and end with a meal, the lighting of a candle, and prayer. The key is to take the four principles of Sabbath—stop, rest, delight, and contemplate God—and build your protective container accordingly. Here are some guidelines to consider as you anticipate and begin to create your own Sabbath container.

Read up on the Sabbath. There are a number of excellent books on Sabbath from both Christian and Jewish perspectives. An excellent place to start is with Wayne Muller's *Sabbath: Finding Rest, Renewal and Delight in Our Busy Lives* and Abraham Joshua Heschel's *The Sabbath: Its Meaning for Modern Man*. Read them slowly and prayerfully.

Identify a twenty-four-hour block of time. Most pastors take Monday as a day off. If that is the case with you, you might start with that day and transition it into a Sabbath. However, I often recommend that pastors and church leaders who work on Sundays try to keep the hours of a traditional Jewish Sabbath—from 6:00 p.m. Friday night through 6:00 p.m. Saturday night. However, if you routinely perform a lot of weddings or have other nonnegotiable Saturday commitments, Monday may be a better Sabbath for you long term. The key is to land on one consistent Sabbath day (rather than hopping around on different days). A consistent Sabbath day is essential for creating a meaningful and balanced rhythm of work and rest in your weeks. Although I do occasionally switch my Sabbath in order to accommodate a conference or unexpected events, I try to make these rare exceptions.

Make a list of what brings you delight. As simple as this sounds, you may actually find it difficult to do, especially if it's been a while since you experienced anything that brought you delight. So set aside some time to reflect on the places, activities, and people that energize you. Also consider things you haven't done that you would like to pursue. For example, particular sports, games with friends, eating out, movies, outdoor activities, ballroom dancing, reading (for enjoyment, not work), museums or other cultural institutions and events, etc. The key question here is, *What can I do that would bring me delight because it feels like play?*

Prepare in advance. Preparation requires rearranging how you do life the other six days of the week so you can actually stop and enjoy a full twenty-four-hour Sabbath. Identify the unpaid work you usually attend to on your day off and make time to do it during the week. If you fail to prepare, you will no doubt end up doing unpaid work during your Sabbath. On the day your Sabbath begins (or the night before), begin your transition to Sabbath three or four hours before. Use your transition time to take care of any last-minute tasks, for example, grocery shopping, paying bills, mowing the lawn, or making a final phone call to set up something work related for next week.

Define your protective "container"—and then experiment. This is where you identify the rules and limits of what you will and will not do on Sabbath. Here you are seeking to respond to questions such as, *What will make this Sabbath day different from business as usual on the other six days of the week?* And, *What do I need to do (or not do) to protect my ability to rest on this day?* Go ahead and begin by making a "will" and "will not" list. For example:

On Sabbath, I will ...

• Mark the official start of Sabbath by lighting a candle and giving thanks.

• Spend intentional time listening to God in Scripture, prayer, and silence.

• Expose myself to the beautiful works of God's creation, either outdoors in nature or through art (music, drama, visual art, etc.).

On Sabbath, I will not ...

• Look at Twitter or Facebook or read any work-related e-mails.

• Talk about or engage in any work-related tasks (unless there is a true emergency).

• Try to catch up on household chores or errands that have been left undone.

There is no such thing as a definitive list that applies to everyone. Your Sabbath container may look very different from that of your supervisor, your colleagues, or your friends. That's not only okay but necessary, since all of us are in different seasons of life and have unique concerns that impact our ability to fully experience Sabbath.

Once you create your container, practice these Sabbath boundaries for at least four to six weeks. You can count on it being both disruptive and challenging in the beginning, so give yourself some time, and I promise it will get easier as you go. After several weeks, make some adjustments, adding or deleting items from your "will" and "will not" lists. After about six months, you should have a pretty good idea of the kind of Sabbath that works for you.

Find support. If you know people who observe a regular Sabbath, talk with them. What do they do? What have they learned? What are pitfalls they recommend you avoid? If you don't know anyone who practices Sabbath, find a friend or colleague and invite them to begin observing Sabbath with you so you can learn from each other and process your experiences together. If you are single, finding support is particularly important. Many singles are intentional about joining with others on Sabbath for meals, organizing or attending social events, participating in a book club, joining a church activity, hosting a meal themselves, or developing a hobby like dance, hiking, or cooking. Also, if taking a Sabbath has significant implications for your job, be sure to talk to anyone who would be impacted by your decision — your supervisor, colleagues, or those who report to you. Taking a Sabbath should not become a source of contention among those you work with, so include them in your process and thinking. As much as possible, you want to seek their understanding and support.

Once you develop your own Sabbath rhythms and container, then you can begin to lead out of your Sabbath.

What Does It Mean to Lead Out of Your Sabbath?

As someone who has been in leadership for nearly three decades, I can tell you that Sabbath is without a doubt the most important day of the week for my leadership. It is also the one day of the week I most believe — and live out — a fundamental truth of the gospel. How? *I do nothing productive, and yet I am utterly loved.* Allow me to tell you a story that illustrates what I mean.

When Geri was recently away overnight on our Sabbath, I took the opportunity to devote our regular Sabbath time together to spending one-on-one time with each of our four daughters. My Sabbath evening began by watching a movie with Maria. The following morning, I traveled from Queens to Manhattan for breakfast with Christy, went for a one-mile walk, and then enjoyed lunch and the afternoon with Eva. I returned home and spent time in a leisurely conversation with Faith. I remember saying to myself at the end of that Sabbath, "I am the most blessed man alive!"

Sabbath has taught me what is most important — God, love, delight, joy, Geri, our daughters, friends, extended family. As a result, I am a very different kind of leader than I would be without the Sabbath as the foundation of my weekly work. I am better able to let go. I am more attentive to God's voice. And I am (most of the time) more relaxed.

As it has changed me in these ways, Sabbath has positively impacted those around me, not just my family but also those I lead. Because I have slowly learned the truth that Sabbath is about working from rest (as much as it is resting from work), I've found it much easier to give rest to those I lead. Here is the biblical principle:

"Observe the Sabbath day by keeping it holy.... On it you shall not do any work, neither you, nor your son or daughter, nor your male or female servant ... so that your male and female servants may rest, as you do. DEUTERONOMY 5:12, 14, EMPHASIS ADDED

Although the staff members and volunteers we work with are certainly not our servants, they are under our authority and subject to our influence. This means it falls within the legitimate scope of our responsibility to encourage the boundaries that make Sabbath possible for them.

As you consider what it might mean for you to lead out of your Sabbath, here are a few things to keep in mind:

Lead by example. Talk about your Sabbath experiences, both successes and failures. Practicing Sabbath delight is a prophetic act and a powerful teaching tool. People need a variety of models. And while yours may be only one, it probably will be the first and most influential one for those you lead.

Provide support resources that address questions and challenges. At New Life, we have trained our board members, staff, and key leaders about Sabbath. Teaching about Sabbath is part of our membership process and our core spiritual formation course. We also routinely provide a variety of books, sermons, articles, and podcasts as well other resources.[25]

When you first begin to introduce Sabbath as a value, people will have a lot of questions, especially as they begin to practice Sabbath-keeping. If you begin with your team or staff, carve out time to process those questions in weekly meetings. When you teach Sabbath-keeping to a congregation, be prepared for the many unique challenges people will have to overcome — from caring for small children or elderly parents to emergencies to jobs that require constant changes in their schedule. You can't solve all their problems, but you can be ready to provide resources and support and to answer frequently asked questions.

Engage your team by asking them about their Sabbath experience. Part of supporting the value of Sabbath is demonstrating interest in it. I routinely ask our volunteers and team, our coworkers and our friends specific questions about their Sabbath rhythms and pace of life. It communicates that I care about them as whole persons and not simply about what they do in their role at work.

In part 2, we'll take a closer look at how the practice of Sabbath has significant implications for developing a healthy culture and building a healthy team. However, before you can really lead out of your Sabbath and give the gift of Sabbath to others, you have to begin practicing it yourself.

What Will You Do with Sabbath?

A friend of mine, Sam Lam, a managing partner of Linkage, chairs a unique leadership program called the "Linkage 20 Conversations @ Harvard." His goal is to help his students, who are already top executives from around the world, maximize their productivity and output by learning directly from other dynamic leaders. Most of them tend to be ambitious, hard-driving, Type-A achievers. Sam says that, whether his students are Christians or not, nearly all of them could be described as Sabbath abusers because they consistently violate their limits. (He confesses that he is a Sabbath abuser in remission.)

However, for Sam the core issue for these leaders is not, *How many hours do you work in a week?* The real question is, *What do you do with Sabbath?* He writes:

> If you do not keep the Sabbath, God will keep it for you. For many years, I thought it was idolatry and other sins the people of Israel committed that resulted in their seventy years of captivity in Babylon. Then, one day, I came across a Scripture that changed my view about Sabbath. It reads, "This is exactly the message of GOD that Jeremiah had preached: the desolate land put to an extended Sabbath rest, a seventy-year Sabbath rest making up for all the unkept Sabbaths" (2 Chronicles 36:21 MSG). In other words, failure to keep the Sabbath required a kind of compensation — the loss had to be accounted for. I took that to mean that a similar principle applies to us today. If we do not keep the Sabbath, we are incurring a deficit and God himself will stop us, through a crisis, a health issue, an emergency, or anything that gets our attention.

While I am not sure I want to build an entire theology of Sabbath based on Sam's exegesis, I have repeatedly witnessed the truth of his words. God often does stop us when we repeatedly violate our limits and disregard our need for rest. If you refuse the gift of Sabbath, sooner or later, one way or another, you will find yourself flat on your back — emotionally, physically, and/or spiritually. Perhaps you find yourself in this condition right now. In this place of vulnerability, God will begin to restore you, and he will offer you again the gift of Sabbath. He has done this for me more than once. He loves you and me that much.

Understanding Your Sabbath Assessment

If you took the Sabbath assessment on pages 149–50, here are some observations to help you reflect on your responses.

If you scored mostly ones and twos, you probably are working more than God intends, perhaps without even a consistent day off. Your body, mind, and spirit were built for a rhythm of work and Sabbath, which is something you desperately need. I encourage you to carefully ponder the Scriptures cited in this chapter around Sabbath and to prayerfully consider their implications for your leadership, your personal life, and your team. You may want to begin with a 12-hour Sabbath and expand from there.

If you scored mostly twos and threes, you have likely begun the journey toward a healthy leadership rhythm of balancing work and Sabbath. You have the ability to let go and set boundaries around work, understand your identity is not built on your work, and enjoy God's gifts. With this foundation, you have what you need to experience a rich and powerful Sabbath that will inform the other six days of the week. I encourage you to think through — theologically and practically — the nature of Sabbath. You may also want to talk with a friend or use a journal to explore the roots of any obstacles or resistance you feel to practicing Sabbath.

If you scored mostly fours and fives, you are wonderfully positioned to deepen your experience and enjoyment of the riches God offers in Sabbath. You are ready to more clearly articulate the theological underpinnings and the practical nuances around Sabbath to those who serve with you — and perhaps to a larger group as well. I encourage you to invest the necessary time and energy to equip yourself more fully so you can break new ground in helping others practice Sabbath delight as a core spiritual formation discipline.

Part 2

The Outer Life

I considered starting this book with the four chapters that follow on the outer life of a leader. Why? Because most of us in leadership look for practical material and new ideas we can implement immediately. I discovered, however, that when we start with outer life practices without addressing our inner lives, the positive changes we make are unsustainable.

In part 1, I introduced the image of a Manhattan skyscraper where concrete or steel columns (called "piles") are hammered into the ground until they penetrate solid rock. This image effectively communicates the key point of the first half of this book — to be an emotionally healthy leader we must drive certain practices deep into our inner life if we are to build well. I defined these inner life issues as: face your shadow, lead out of your marriage or singleness, slow down for loving union, and practice Sabbath delight.

As we move into part 2 about the outer life of the leader, I want to shift from the image of a skyscraper to the ancient imagery of a large fruit-bearing tree. It captures more clearly the inseparable organic connection between the roots (our inner life) and the branches producing fruit (our outer life).

A tree with a shallow root system may still look beautiful on the outside, but it is incapable of supplying the water and nutrients for long-term upward growth of an entire tree. This becomes a significant problem when our ministries and organizations grow larger and faster than the depth of our roots can sustain. Deep and wide roots anchor a tree, allowing it to draw up plentiful water and nutrients from a larger and deeper area of soil. In many cases, the root systems of our spiritual lives are inadequate for the challenges of shaping and leading a growing church, organization, or team (part 1).

At the same time, it seems logical that a deeper inner life should lead to good organizational practices. Sadly, however, it often does not. There is a disconnect when we fail to apply our spirituality with Jesus to such leadership tasks as planning, team building, boundaries, endings, and new beginnings. Too often, we rely instead on unmodified business practices to navigate these tasks, grafting secular branches onto our spiritual root system. This tends to bear the wrong kind of fruit. While we are called to redeem the best of what we can learn from the

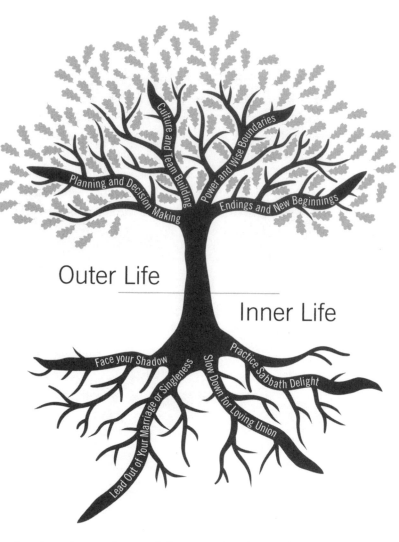

Outer Life

Inner Life

Culture and Team Building

Power and Wise Boundaries

Planning and Decision Making

Endings and New Beginnings

Face your Shadow

Practice Sabbath Delight

Lead Out of Your Marriage or Singleness

Slow Down for Loving Union

marketplace, it must be carefully pruned so that it "fits" into the inherently spiritual life of our teams and ministries. The life from our root system with Jesus must flow upward and outward into every aspect of our outer leadership tasks if we are to bear good fruit.

In the chapters that follow, we'll examine specific ways the nutrients and water from the roots of the tree actually inform the critical areas (or branches) of leadership. I have chosen to focus on four critical tasks in the outer life of a leader:

- Planning and Decision Making
- Culture and Team Building
- Power and Wise Boundaries
- Endings and New Beginnings

These four tasks are foundational to the life of every leader yet are too often overlooked. Integrating my inner life with these four outer life tasks was nothing short of exhilarating and life-giving—both for me personally and for our church. God gave us a joy, a grace to patiently wait for his will to unfold, and a clarity for going forward that was liberating. That is my prayer and hope for you as you read these pages.

So let's begin now with the first outer task we confront every day as leaders—planning and decision making.

CHAPTER 6

PLANNING AND DECISION MAKING

Two years after planting New Life in 1987, Geri and I were on an airplane en route to a Christian conference. I had some news to share, and I had been waiting for just the right moment to share it. This was that moment.

"Oh, Geri, by the way, we'll be launching an afternoon Spanish service in five months. Everything is already in motion. It's going to be great!"

Silence.

I scrambled mentally, rehearsing our history to reassure myself about the decision.

Everything we had done up to this point—attending seminary, studying in Costa Rica, working in a Spanish-speaking church for a year, and then launching New Life in a largely Spanish-speaking community—had brought us to this place. And now God had led a couple, recently arrived from Colombia, to join our leadership team.

As far as I was concerned, there was no doubt that launching a Spanish-speaking service was God's will. We could reach people for Christ and expand our impact in the community. *How could that not be God's will?* Having a second congregation also opened a door for more people from our core group to use their gifts in ministry. *A win-win! Of course this is the right thing to do!*

"What are you talking about?" Geri finally said in a clearly annoyed tone. "You haven't fully established the church in English and you're ready to expand into another language? We don't even have a solid leadership base yet! Who is going to preach there anyway? You?"

I was ready.

"No," I said calmly, "there is this couple who have pastored in Colombia. They are arriving next week. They come highly recommended. I won't have to do much except maybe preach once or twice a month."

"You have got to be kidding me," Geri muttered as she turned away from me and stared out the window into the clouds.

In the back of my mind I was thinking, *She is probably right, but if we don't launch this soon, I'm going to lose the Spanish I worked so hard to learn, and all that investment of time, energy, and money will have been for nothing.*

The armrest-width space between us widened into a silent abyss.

While Geri continued to stare down the passing clouds, I asked God to give her faith and vision. Then I broke the silence.

"Don't worry, Geri," I said, trying to sound both calm and confident, "I talked it over with our advisory board, and they're all excited about it."

Geri sighed. "Pete, you're not ready. You haven't thought it through, but I know you are going to do it anyway. And there isn't anything I can say to stop you."

She was right.

The ministry to our Spanish-speaking community grew rapidly the first year. But the couple from Colombia didn't work out, and we quickly replaced them with another pastor. Three years later, that pastor took 200 people from the congregation and started another church. That church would split three more times before eventually closing its doors ten years later.

The Spanish-speaking congregation that was left at New Life after the split eventually stabilized and became its own thriving congregation alongside the English-speaking congregation. But this whole chaotic and painful episode would take nine long years and a lot of needless misunderstanding and hurt to work itself out.

When Geri and I had that airplane conversation, I was still many years away from understanding the four crucial roots (described in chapters 2 – 5) that ground a leader's inner life with God. Without that anchor, my leadership was weak and fragmented, especially when it came to planning and decision making. Our leadership structure — everything above the surface — was beginning to reveal my shallow root system. And the implications were evident at New Life. There were strained relationships, exhausted volunteers, and ongoing conflicts. People began to drop out, ministries struggled, and I felt a constant and rising pressure to cover it all with a veneer of ministry excellence, which only made things worse and harder to manage.

I knew we had problems, but for years I believed that if I could simply identify the right planning and decision-making process, we would then make good decisions. That, it turned out, was both naïve and misguided. It wasn't until we developed our root system (i.e., our inner lives described in chapters 2 – 5) that we began to make progress in overcoming our poor planning and decision making. Our life with Jesus began to flow upward and outward in new and powerful ways. The dramatic difference from our old standard to our new emotionally healthy planning and decision making was suddenly crystal clear.

How Healthy Is Your Practice of Planning and Decision Making?

Use the list of statements that follow to do a brief assessment of your planning and decision making. Next to each statement, write down the number that best describes your response. Use the following scale:

5 = Always true of me
4 = Frequently true of me
3 = Occasionally true of me
2 = Rarely true of me
1 = Never true of me

_____ 1. My planning and my decision-making process consistently demonstrate my belief that discernment of and doing God's will are among my most important tasks as a leader.

_____ 2. I am aware of how my shadow might tempt me to say yes to more opportunities than God intends, or to say no to doors God has opened (e.g., out of fear of failure).

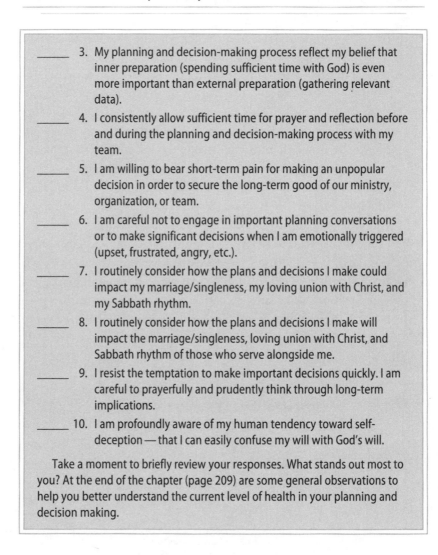

_____ 3. My planning and decision-making process reflect my belief that inner preparation (spending sufficient time with God) is even more important than external preparation (gathering relevant data).

_____ 4. I consistently allow sufficient time for prayer and reflection before and during the planning and decision-making process with my team.

_____ 5. I am willing to bear short-term pain for making an unpopular decision in order to secure the long-term good of our ministry, organization, or team.

_____ 6. I am careful not to engage in important planning conversations or to make significant decisions when I am emotionally triggered (upset, frustrated, angry, etc.).

_____ 7. I routinely consider how the plans and decisions I make could impact my marriage/singleness, my loving union with Christ, and my Sabbath rhythm.

_____ 8. I routinely consider how the plans and decisions I make will impact the marriage/singleness, loving union with Christ, and Sabbath rhythm of those who serve alongside me.

_____ 9. I resist the temptation to make important decisions quickly. I am careful to prayerfully and prudently think through long-term implications.

_____ 10. I am profoundly aware of my human tendency toward self-deception — that I can easily confuse my will with God's will.

Take a moment to briefly review your responses. What stands out most to you? At the end of the chapter (page 209) are some general observations to help you better understand the current level of health in your planning and decision making.

Characteristics of Standard Planning and Decision Making

I love strategizing, casting vision, and dreaming up creative solutions to problems. However, in the process of doing these things, I have often made a lot of wrong assumptions. See if you can relate to any of these.

I assumed . . .

- If we opened and closed our meetings in prayer, God would guide all our decisions.

- It was always God's will that our church be in a season of bearing fruit (and rarely, if ever, in a season of pruning).
- If an initiative was strategic and impactful, it was therefore God's will.
- It was always God's will for us to overcome the limits we faced.
- Each member of our team routinely paid attention to what was happening inside them as well as using Scripture and wise counsel to discern God's will in planning and decision making.
- Each member of our team arrived at meetings in an undistracted state, having anchored themselves in loving union and prayer ahead of time.
- Numerical growth and increased levels of participation in serving through our ministry programs was evidence of authentic growth in Christ.
- God overlooked any mixed motives we might have as long as our plans and decisions overall were headed in the right direction.

Sadly, every assumption is wrong. Even worse, these and other faulty assumptions remain in the standard planning and decision-making practice of many Christian leaders and the teams they lead. When we default to assumptions like these, we are succumbing to one or more of three common temptations: we define success too narrowly, we make plans and take action without God, and we go beyond God's limits.

We Define Success Too Narrowly

In churches, we tend to define success by such things as attendance, finances (giving, meeting or exceeding budget, etc.), decisions for Christ, baptisms, numbers participating in small groups or other ministry programs, etc. If we work for a nonprofit or in the marketplace, we might measure increased market share, program expansion, or numbers of people served. When the numbers are up, we're successful; when the numbers are down, we're not.

Numbers can be valid as a measure of fruitfulness for God, but using numbers to define success is not without its dangers. I know this from experience.

In the early days of launching New Life, we were offered a $5,000 grant if we would participate in a community outreach strategy. It involved hand addressing 10,000 envelopes in which we inserted a professionally produced flyer to invite people to our Easter service. This strategy had worked brilliantly for a number of churches, and we were told it would help New Life grow as well. I cast the vision and our little core group worked feverishly, writing names and addresses on every envelope over a two-week period. Easter came. An additional fifty people attended along with our regular twenty-five. Most were out-of-town guests and friends of our core group. Two people visited from the community. Neither returned. The little momentum we had built stalled.

What happened?

Looking back, I chalk a lot of it up to my immaturity and lack of leadership experience. Ten thousand letters in English didn't go far in a community where people spoke multiple languages and where 70,000 people lived on one square block in high-rise apartments! And word may have gotten out that we had other problems as well, such as cars getting broken into while people attended services. But perhaps the biggest reason our efforts failed was due to something more insidious—a narrow view of success.

The models of success I'd been exposed to in books, the media, and at numerous Christian leadership conferences were based mostly on large, rapidly growing churches in middle- to upper-class suburban contexts or mega-churches in South Korea, Latin America, and Africa. I was also strongly influenced by what I'd read about the history of the Great Awakenings in the United States and revivals led by people like John Wesley (1703–1791) in England, Charles Finney (1791–1875) in New York, and William J. Seymour (1870–1922) at Azusa Street in Los Angeles.

I learned a lot from all of these sources, but my efforts to apply what I learned were focused primarily on externals—things like ministry expansion, mobilizing people to serve with their gifts, strategizing to add more people to our church, multiplying small groups, and pursuing excellence in worship and preaching so people would keep coming back. These externals were important. The problem was that the portion of our time and energy devoted to thinking about external issues far exceeded the amount of time and energy we devoted to internal measures of transformation, such as the depth of people's personal relationship with God, the quality of marriages and singleness, the level of emotional maturity, and the integrity of our relationships as a community. At the leadership level, we also minimized the importance of beneath-the-surface transformation in our own lives as the source of power from which we would reach the world. It wasn't that we didn't believe in it. I preached it from the pulpit as much as any good pastor. But in the flurry of ministry activity, we simply didn't have the time or energy available to make it possible. We were too preoccupied by our busyness and overloaded calendars.

If I'd had a broader definition of success, it might have slowed us down enough to enter a more prayerful discernment process about that $5,000 offer and the promise of numerical growth. At the time, I didn't know how to discern God's definition of success or his will for us in our particular context, so I just accepted the standard model that was based largely on externals. And I didn't learn from these mistakes for many years. Why? Because the issue went deeper than my lack of experience — I was locked into and blinded by a narrow definition of success.

We Make Plans and Take Action without God

It would seem that God's leaders have been making plans without him since the beginning of recorded history. Consider ...

Abraham and Sarah waited eleven years for God to provide their promised son. When God failed to meet their timeline, they grew impatient and decided Abraham would sleep with Hagar, the family's Egyptian maidservant. Ishmael was born, and we all know that only trouble and heartbreak followed (Genesis 16:1–4).

Moses impulsively killed an Egyptian in a misguided effort to secure justice for his people. His rash decision cost him forty years in the desert, relationships with his adoptive family, and very nearly his life (Exodus 2:11–23).

The ancient Israelites wanted to be like other nations who were led by kings. Instead of having an invisible God as their leader, they demanded a human king to protect them from their enemies. "We want a king over us. Then we will be like all the other nations" (1 Samuel 8:19–20). The prophet Samuel tried to dissuade them, but the people refused.

Tensions, conflicts, and idolatries followed, ultimately resulting in a divided kingdom (1 Kings 12).

Solomon planned, developed strategic partnerships, and negotiated deals to build a bigger and better kingdom for God on the earth. To the average citizen, his accomplishments were no doubt an obvious success and evidence of God's approval and blessing. But God deemed Solomon's efforts worthless self-aggrandizements—Solomon was making his plans without God.[1]

The list goes on—from King Saul's decision to remain on his throne and kill David, to the prophet Jonah running away from God's command to go to Nineveh, to Judas Iscariot's decision to turn Jesus over to the religious authorities, to the apostle Peter's refusal to eat with the Gentiles in Galatia. Making plans for God without listening to him has been standard practice for thousands of years.

British author and television commentator Malcolm Muggeridge once claimed that if Jesus were alive today, the devil would no doubt have added a fourth item to the list of temptations he posed to Christ in the wilderness. He speculated that the fourth temptation might have looked something like this:

> One day a Roman tycoon named Lucius Gradus hears Jesus preaching in Galilee and is very impressed. "This Jesus has star potential. He could be a superstar!"
>
> He instructs his representatives to "puff Jesus," and then bring him to Rome. He tells them to bring the John the Baptist guy with him, along with some talk show teachers from the Athens philosophy school.
>
> Lucius Gradus continues: "I'll put him on the map and launch him off to a tremendous career as a worldwide evangelist. I'll spread his teaching throughout the civilized world and beyond. He'd be crazy to turn it down! Instead of a ragtag lot following him from Galilee, everyone will know him."
>
> "In fact, there will be no commercials, just one highly respected public relations sponsor—Lucifer, Inc. No more than: 'This program comes to you courtesy of Lucifer, Inc.' at the beginning and end of the program."[2]

Muggeridge wrote these words in the 1960s. How much more true do they ring today, saturated as we are in social media and digital technologies? And who among us would challenge his logic or counsel Jesus to say no to such an offer? I might have worked hard to get Lucifer out of the credits, but I doubt I would have outright declined such an obviously God-ordained offer on Jesus' behalf, especially in the early years of my ministry. Why? Because my team and I defined success as reaching people for Christ; anything that met that baseline qualification was automatically deemed God's will. And Muggeridge's fictional opportunity passes that test with flying colors, making it easy to make plans without God.

It is biblical and wonderful to make plans to expand God's kingdom. The questions we must continually ask, however, are these: *Where does this opportunity or plan fit within the larger plan of what God is doing in the world? How do we sense God is inviting us to do this work?* Our perspective is limited. His thoughts and ways are far higher and different than ours (Isaiah 55:8–9). The only way we can know his plans is to listen carefully to his voice.

We Go Beyond God's Limits

As Christian leaders, we have a whole host of limits — human limits, personal limits, team limits, and ministry or organizational limits. We are limited in time, energy, and gifts. We have limits related to our resources and facilities. Our responsibilities to our families put a limit on how much time we can devote to other things. As human beings, we are creatures who must routinely face up to any host of limits, some mild and some extreme.

It was with this in mind that theologian Reinhold Niebuhr described the very nature of sin as "the desire to overcome our limitations and finitude because of anxiety about our creaturely existence."[3] And Christian leaders today continue to do this — all the time. For some reason, we find it impossibly difficult to wait, listen, and honor our limits. It is perhaps one of the greatest and yet most subtle ways we rebel against God. Take it from me, I have "been there, done that" on more than one occasion. Allow me to share one of the more "spectacular" examples.

Due to our close proximity to Manhattan, New Life has attracted many talented Christian actors and actresses over the years. When some of them offered to use their gifts on behalf of the church, it seemed only natural for the church to incorporate a theatrical production as part of our upcoming Christmas outreach to the community. We assumed that since God had clearly given us an opportunity to reach people for Christ in this way, then it surely was his will. At least, that was clearly what I thought — until we did *Godspell*.

It was 1993, just six years after the church had launched. Because of all the buzz about the production, we attracted crowds five to six times the size of our congregation over four nights. The performances were brilliant. People came to Christ. We were the talk of the community. By all appearances, *Godspell* and our Christmas outreach were a huge success.

But "success" isn't exactly the word everyone involved in the production itself would have used to describe it. Words like "chaos" and "confusion" might have been used in polite company. Looking back on it now, I'd say it was an unmitigated behind-the-scenes disaster. We didn't have sufficiently mature leadership to manage the complex relational dynamics involved in putting together such an elaborate production. Numerous personality clashes and conflicts required countless meetings and phone calls to clean up. The rehearsals aimed at achieving excellence (or perhaps it was more like perfection) exhausted actors, crew, and support staff, virtually all of whom were volunteers. Spouses complained, families were stressed, Christmas holidays with extended family were canceled.

We also lacked sufficient infrastructure to support the scope of the outreach we had planned — and outreach was ostensibly the purpose of the whole production! So, even though we carefully collected contact information from visitors who attended the four services, the list of names simply collected dust after the holidays. No one had the energy to follow up with people.

Was God against our desire to use our Christmas services to extend the message of his love to the community? No, I don't think so. But it's hard to imagine how we could have been within his will when we so blatantly defied our limitations in the way we went about it.

Going beyond our limits is one of the most significant challenges and temptations we face as leaders.[4] It takes maturity to decline a great opportunity for growth and to embrace a modest plan. If we are one hundred people, why not become two hundred? If we are three hundred, why not become five hundred? It is easy to have fantasies for ourselves that our real lives cannot support. But attempting to do more than God intends is a formula for both failure and burnout.

Limits touch the core of our relationship with God. Without explanation, God set a clear limit for Adam and Eve — they were "not [to] eat from the tree of the knowledge of good and evil, for when you eat from it you will certainly die" (Genesis 2:17). They were to trust the goodness of God and his hard-to-understand ways. Theologian Robert Barron describes the heart of Adam and Eve's rebellion as the refusal to stop and accept God's rhythm.[5] It's not all that different from my refusal to surrender to the limits God has for me and for those I lead. It has always been my greatest leadership temptation and struggle. And I am not alone.

Too many of us fall into the sin of presumption. Presumption is a failure to observe the limits of what is permitted or appropriate. It also carries with it a whiff of arrogance. It's a sin the psalmist seemed particularly sensitive to and eager to avoid: "Keep back your servant also from presumptuous sins; let them not have dominion over me! Then I shall be blameless, and innocent of great transgression" (Psalm 19:13 ESV). Because of this, I see limits as a guardrail, protecting me from straying outside of God's will and keeping me on his path that will slowly unfold later.

Let's pause for a moment. As you reflect on the three characteristics we've just covered — defining success too narrowly, making plans without God, and going beyond God's limits — which represents the greatest temptation for you? Why do you think that might be true? And if these characteristics represent standard planning and decision making among Christian leaders today, then what might it look like to engage in emotionally healthy planning and decision making?

I'm glad you asked.

Characteristics of Emotionally Healthy Planning and Decision Making

Emotionally healthy planning and decision making begins with an assumption (though it's not a faulty one like the others). The assumption is this: as fallen human beings, we have a tendency to develop hardened hearts. In the twelfth century, Abbot Bernard of Clairvaux wrote this warning to one of his monk-disciples, Eugene III, who had recently been made the pope:

> I am afraid that you will despair of an end to the many demands that are made upon you and become calloused ... It would be much wiser to remove yourself from these demands even for a while than to allow yourself to be distracted by them and led, little by little, where you certainly do not want to go. Where? To a hard heart. Do not go on to ask what that is; if you have not been terrified by it, it is yours already.[6]

In other words, says Abbot Bernard, if you're not concerned that your heart might become hard, it already is. A hardened heart is a big problem for a leader in any context, but it will utterly derail any hope of being able to clearly hear and do the will of God. We cannot engage in plans and decisions that honor God until we prepare our hearts and are intentional about keeping them soft and responsive to his leading.

Over the years, I've come to rely on four characteristics of emotionally healthy planning and decision making that I believe must become ever more deeply rooted in the soil of our hearts. These four characteristics emerged from our leadership work at New Life as well as our work with churches and leaders around the world.

Let's begin with the foundation from which all the others follow—defining success as radically doing God's will.

EMOTIONALLY HEALTHY PLANNING AND DECISION MAKING
1. **We define success as radically doing God's will.**
2. We create a space for heart preparation.
3. We pray for prudence.
4. We look for God in our limits.

We Define Success As Radically Doing God's Will

From the time I became a Christian, I believed intellectually that listening for God's will was vitally important. This belief deepened when Geri and I began our journey into emotionally healthy spirituality in 1996 and I realized then how much of God's will I had missed or outright ignored up to that point. But it wasn't until our four-month contemplative sabbatical in 2003–2004 that my approach to planning and decision making was utterly transformed. That is when the four inner-life issues described in part 1 began taking root in the soil of my soul. As a result, my definition of success so broadened and deepened that my approach to discerning God's will experienced an extreme makeover.

What happened? I slowed down my life so I could spend much more time *being* with God, integrating regular times of solitude and silence, observing a weekly Sabbath, praying the Daily Office, and crafting an intentional Rule of Life. Listening for and surrendering to God's will became the focus of my life—both personally and in leadership. I realized that New Life had one objective: to become what God had called us to become, and to do what God had called us to do—regardless of where any of that might lead us. That would be the sole marker of our success. It meant that all the previous markers—increased attendance, bigger and better programs, more serving—had to take a backseat to this one. I was no longer willing to "succeed" at the expense of hearing and listening to the will of God.

Have you ever considered that your ministry, organization, or team may be growing and yet actually failing?

Before answering that question, think with me for a moment about some of God's faithful and, hence, most successful leaders. Jesus said of John the Baptist, "Among those born of women there is no one greater than John" (Luke 7:28). Yet, if we were to create a bar chart on the size of John's ministry over time, it would demonstrate a peak followed by a steady and precipitous decline (not to mention a dead stop after his beheading). The prophet Jeremiah served God with passion and obedience, but was mostly written off or ridiculed by an unresponsive remnant—definitely not what anyone considered success. For the prophet Amos, success was leaving his more spiritually fruitful home in the southern kingdom of Judah in order to preach to the northern kingdom of Israel whose people never responded to his message. Jesus left a revival in Capernaum where large numbers of people were responding in order to start all over again in other cities (Mark 1:39–40).

It's hard to see how any of the names on this list would be considered successful in most leadership circles today. And yet the Bible makes it clear that God approved of their ministries. The implications are that we may well be growing our ministries but nevertheless failing. Why? Because God's standard of success isn't limited to growth. Success is first and foremost doing what God has asked us to do, doing it his way, and in his timing.

Years ago, when I was first wrestling with redefining success, I imagined what it might be like to come before God's throne at the end of my earthly life and say, "Here, God, is what I have done for you. New Life now has 10,000 people." Then he would respond, "Pete, I love you, but that was not what I gave you to do. That task was for a pastor in another part of the city."

Consider the wide range and diverse responsibilities God entrusts to Christian leaders today. You may be a CEO of a Fortune-500 company, a staff member in a para-church organization working with homeless teens, a pastor in a hostile urban environment, a marketplace leader in Central Europe, an elder at a rapidly growing church in Africa, or a bi-vocational pastor in a sparsely populated rural area. How could there possibly be one cookie-cutter definition of success in so many diverse circumstances? And yet, that is the standard we too often apply when we use *only* external markers to define and measure success.

What you need to remember is that it is your unique situation, and God's will for you in it, that will define what God considers success — both for you personally and for the church, ministry, or team you lead. The challenge every leader and team must face is undertaking the slow and painstaking discernment work to identify precisely what that is for you at any given point in time.

Embracing God's definition of success for New Life over the years was initially difficult for me to accept. It slowed me down, and I suddenly felt like I didn't look as good as the leaders of other, larger ministries to which I compared myself. But as time went on and we leaned into God's wisdom for our context at New Life, there were three markers of success we felt God had clearly given us. This is how we defined success:

Success is when people are transformed deep beneath the surface of their lives. At New Life, our commitment to radically doing God's will led us to prioritize emotionally healthy spirituality as the key way we would reach the world for Christ. This meant we had to figure out ways to measure success not simply by numerical growth, but in terms of spiritual transformation. Here are several examples of the measures we set:

- Each leader at New Life will develop his or her relationship with God by spending ten to thirty minutes in prayer and Scripture reading in the morning, and a few additional minutes of prayer and reflection in the afternoon/evening.
- Our staff, board, and key leaders will slow down their lives by practicing Sabbath for twenty-four hours each week.
- Our staff, board, and key leaders will pray the Examen at least once a day in order to discern and follow God's will in their lives.[7]
- Every member of our pastoral and administrative staff team will consistently integrate emotionally healthy skills into their ministries and relationships.
- Each member at New Life will develop a personal Rule of Life that enables them to receive and give the love of God. They will share this at their membership interview.
- Eighty-five percent of our members will connect in a small group and/or ministry (i.e., a smaller community) as part of their spiritual formation.
- Every child/teenager will participate in a discipleship small group with an appointed leader.
- Fifty percent of married couples will go through training to view their relationship as a living sign of God's passionate love for the world.

Some of these are fairly easy to measure, but others have proved more difficult. Yet, even when the measurement is fairly straightforward, it is vitally important to humbly acknowledge our limits in "measuring" a person's transformation into the image of Jesus. Think of it this way. Just as the conditions required for the growth vary among the 800,000 plants in the world, every Christian is unique and in need of a tailored, personal approach for spiritual growth. Every plant needs a different combination of resources — light, temperature, fertilizer, pH, etc. Legumes, such as soybeans and clover, have bacteria in their roots and make their own nitrogen. They need a particular type of fertilizer without nitrogen. Some plants, such as grasses, need full sun. Others, such as impatiens, need full shade. Mastering a working knowledge of the unique combinations for all 800,000 plants is the work of a lifetime. And knowing the many unique pathways God uses to help his people grow into maturity is also a lifework. One size does not fit all.[8]

Geri and I recently engaged in a process of defining the measurements of growth with our marriage ministry leadership team. We hammered, chipped, and chiseled away at our definition of spiritual formation in marriage until everyone in the room was comfortable and agreed on every word. We stayed with it, for as long as it took, because it is such a critical piece of our ministry's direction and planning.

At the same time, we recognize our limits in measuring a person's transformation in Christ. We are dealing with people, not widgets. So it is important we approach every measurement task with humility and gentleness. We all share some common elements in our formation in Christ, such as Scripture, prayer, and community (just like virtually all plants need sun and water), and we do define our markers for success. Yet the particulars of how that works out will differ from person to person. So we seek to cultivate a humble caution whenever we teach and apply various measures of spiritual growth and maturity.

Success is bridging racial, cultural, economic, and gender barriers. From the beginning, New Life has been called to be a multiracial, international church that bridges a host of "divides" — racial, cultural, economic, and gender — as a prophetic witness to the power of the gospel. Our commitment is to model this on all levels and in every ministry of our church. It informs our hiring, our programming, our worship, our small groups, our outreach, our finances, our preaching, and our definition of what constitutes ministry excellence.

What might that look like in practice?

Each level of leadership — elders, staff, ministry leaders, etc. — reflects our diversity. That means there are deep cultural and racial differences that could divide us from one another. In an attempt to bridge these divides, we regularly take the time to listen to each other's stories as part of doing life together. This radical doing of God's will has led us into conversations and situations that have been both painful and time consuming. It's not easy to hold all the tensions, for example, of listening to a Chinese American church member talk about his experiences and attitudes toward Latinos and African Americans, and then listening to a Latino or African American member talk about her experiences and attitudes toward Chinese Americans. But this is part of what it means to bridge the divides, and so we do it. We talk openly and regularly about the tension points of reconciliation at New Life—at staff meetings, in sermons, small groups, and at equipping events. This definition of success has affected the way we worship, the places we live, the way we raise our children, our day-to-day friendships, and the way we discuss difficult political issues.

Success is serving our community and the world. We are called to be a church *of* the poor and marginalized, and not simply a church *for* the poor and marginalized. So we offer, for example, clean showers to the homeless population in our neighborhood. That commitment means our building experiences a lot of wear and tear. Our location near a crowded crossroads in Queens means it can take thirty to forty minutes to find a parking space on Sundays. A large hotel one block from New Life recently was converted to a homeless shelter with over two hundred families representing almost seven hundred people. This added enormous stress to the schools and social service agencies in our neighborhood. As a result, we expanded existing ministries, such as our food pantry, and launched a number of new ministries, such as a mentoring program and after-school services. Serving our community as a measure of success also means we have a strong commitment to mobilize those in our congregation who are blessed with greater resources, education, or skills so they can be involved in such practical ministries as outreach to the homeless, at-risk youth, or the medically uninsured.

Before moving on to the three remaining markers of success, I encourage you to pause and reflect for a moment. What might change in your context if you were to define success not by the numbers but as radically doing God's will? What are the markers of success to which God is calling you and your team? What fears or anxieties are you aware of as you even consider such questions? Believe me, I understand how disorienting these questions might be. But I also know how rewarding and freeing it is to live and lead from the center of God's definition of success. If you are willing to take some risks and live with the tensions, I promise you won't regret it.

We Create a Space for Heart Preparation

In emotionally healthy planning and decision making, we don't simply open meetings with prayer and then leap headlong into our agenda. We begin by creating a space for heart preparation. We intentionally step back from the distractions and pressures that surround us so we can discern and follow God's will. This preparation takes place on two levels—personal heart prepara-tion and team heart preparation.

> **EMOTIONALLY HEALTHY PLANNING AND DECISION MAKING**
> 1. We define success as radically doing God's will.
> 2. **We create a space for heart preparation.**
> 3. We pray for prudence.
> 4. We look for God in our limits.

Personal Heart Preparation

Before entering a meeting room, our first priority as leaders is to prepare our heart with God. How much time is needed for this? That depends on the level of the decision or plans being made and how much internal noise might be cluttering your inner life at the moment. The simple principle we follow at New Life is: the weightier the decision, the more time is required for preparation. Jesus models this kind of heart preparation for us. Before choosing the Twelve, he stayed up all night:

> *One of those days Jesus went out to a mountainside to pray,* and *spent the night praying to God. When morning came, he called his disciples to him and chose twelve of them, whom he also designated apostles.*   LUKE 6:12–13, EMPHASIS ADDED

In order to discern the Father's priorities in the midst of voices clam-oring for him to stay in Capernaum, Jesus rose early in the morning for solitude:

> *At daybreak, Jesus went out to a solitary place. The people were looking for him and when they came to where he was, they tried to*

keep him from leaving them. But he said, "I must proclaim the good news of the kingdom of God to the other towns also, because that is why I was sent."   Luke 4:42–43, emphasis added

Jesus consistently engaged and then withdrew from people and the demands of ministry in order to pray alone:

Yet the news about him spread all the more, so that crowds of people came to hear him and to be healed of their sicknesses. **But Jesus often withdrew to lonely places and prayed.**

Luke 5:15, emphasis added

Perhaps most instructive of all is Jesus' struggle to surrender to the will of his Father in Gethsemane. This is one of the most significant planning and decision-making texts in all of Scripture. Three times, Jesus prays the same thing:

"My Father, if it is possible, may this cup be taken from me. Yet not as I will, but as you will."   Matthew 26:39

Jesus, the leader, did not fall mindlessly into obedience. He learned it — and so must we:

During the days of Jesus' life on earth, he offered up prayers and petitions with fervent cries and tears to the one who could save him from death, and he was heard because of his reverent submission. Son though he was, he learned obedience from what he suffered.

Hebrews 5:7–8

All true obedience is a learned, struggled-for, and prayed-for obedience. If it took falling with his face to the ground and great struggle for the Son of God to submit himself to the will of the Father, how can we expect that it will require any less of us?

My goal in preparing my heart for planning and decision making is to remain in a state Ignatius of Loyola referred to as *indifference*. By indifference, he does not mean apathy or disinterest. He simply means we must become indifferent to anything but the will of God. Ignatius taught that the degree to which we are open to any outcome or answer from God is the degree to which we are ready to really hear what God has to say. If we are clutching or overly attached to one outcome versus another, we won't hear God clearly. Our spiritual ears will be deafened by the racket of our disordered loves, fears, and attachments. In such a state, it is almost a forgone conclusion that we will confuse our will with God's will.

Ignatius considered this state of *indifference* to be spiritual freedom. If we are truly free, he argued, we wouldn't worry about whether we are healthy or sick, rich or poor. It shouldn't even matter whether we have a long life or a short one.[9] We place our life in God's hands and trust him for the outcome. Admittedly, no one *wants* to be sick or die young, but his point is that what we do, where we go, or who we see are determined by God's leadings, not our external circumstances. What is more important than all these things is choosing to love and obey God out of the love he offers us and the world.

Arriving at this place of interior indifference and trusting that God's will is good — no matter the outcome — is no small task. We are attached to all kinds of secondary things — titles, positions, honors, places, persons, security, and the opinions of others. When these attachments are excessive, they become disordered attachments, or disordered loves, that push God out of the center of our life and become core to our identity.[10]

What this means for me is that I pray *for* indifference so I can pray the prayer *of* indifference. Every day, I pray for the grace to honestly say, *Father, I am indifferent to every outcome except your will. I want nothing more or less than your desire for what I do.* And I pray for both daily. If I fail to engage in this necessary heart preparation — praying the prayer *for* indifference and the prayer *of* indifference — I run the risk of missing God's voice.

I also prepare my heart with a Benedictine monastic practice called *statio*, especially when I have a day with multiple meetings. The practice of *statio* acknowledges the significance of transition, or "between times." Author Joan Chittister describes *statio* well: "The practice of *statio* is meant to center us and make us conscious of what we're about to do and make us present to God who is present to us. *Statio* is the desire to do consciously what I might otherwise do mechanically. *Statio* is the virtue of presence."[11]

Like so many leaders, when I spend a day going from one meeting straight into another, I can easily find myself dragging the issues and problems from one meeting into the next. In order to be fully present for the next meeting, I need to bring closure to the one before. If I fail to do this, I won't be able to hear God's leading above my own internal noise. And so I practice *statio*. I take a few minutes alone for silence between meetings. Knowing that God can speak to me through my body, I begin by paying attention to whether or not my body feels tense or anxious. If it proves impossible to get alone for a few minutes, I may begin the meeting with two to three minutes of silence, read a portion of a psalm, or light a candle to remind those of us in the room that Jesus is the light we seek. I am doing these things to center myself in Jesus, but hopefully the team is also helped in the process!

Team Heart Preparation

In order to make good decisions, we begin our meetings — whether it is a weekly team meeting or a full-day planning meeting — by creating the necessary space for the team to center their hearts before God.

If I am leading the meeting, I'll begin with two to three minutes of silence, or perhaps we might pray the Daily Office together. I may read a devotional reflection to center us in Christ. The purpose of these opening moments is to create an environment free of striving or manipulating outcomes so we can seek God's will together. We are silent or in prayer in order to be still before the Lord and wait patiently for him (Psalm 37:7).

When our staff team goes off-site for one of our three planning retreats in the year (typically September, January, and June), we devote a portion of our retreat time to allow team members to meet God personally before we gather to make plans. We might provide a biblical text for meditation or offer a guided time of silence with reflection questions. We like to begin every important planning retreat with a "being" experience before tackling the "doing" component of these longer meetings. For example, we began a recent staff retreat by reading about Jesus' rhythms of solitude and ministry, followed by a discussion of a poem by Judy Brown. We read the poem twice aloud, asking people to underline and take notes on what spoke to them.

Fire

> What makes a fire burn
> is space between the logs,
> a breathing space.
> Too much of a good thing,
> too many logs
> packed in too tight
> can douse the flames
> almost as surely
> as a pail of water would.
>
> So building fires
> requires attention
> to the spaces in between,
> as much as the wood.
>
> When we are able to build
> open spaces
> in the same way
> we have learned
> to pile on the logs,
> then we can come to see how
> it is fuel, and absence of the fuel
> together, that make fire possible.
>
> We only need lay a log
> lightly from time to time.
> A fire
> grows
> simply because the space is there,
> with openings
> in which the flame
> that knows just how it wants to burn
> can find its way.[12]

Judy Brown

Afterward, we took about ten minutes for discussion. We asked the group: *What words or phrases call out to you from this poem?*

We then gave everyone about twenty-five minutes on their own for guided personal reflection using these questions:

- When in your ministry or life in the past year have you piled on too many logs?
- When has *too much of a good thing* not been a good thing?
- What does it look like for you to create sufficient spaces in this season of your life?
- What fire(s) from God might emerge if you allow more space between the logs?

The team then met for an additional twenty-five minutes in groups of three:

- How did you experience God in your personal time?
- In light of what you experienced, what do you need from God right now (for example, discipline, courage, faith, strength, prudence)?
- Conclude by praying for one another.

Giving the team this two-hour block of time to connect with God prepared us to enter more effectively into the planning part of the retreat. It bonded us around a common longing—our need for rhythms, to *be* with Jesus as the source from which we *do* for him. It also established a sense of team as we shared together. All of this enabled us to make better decisions. For example, on that retreat it became obvious that the church calendar for the coming season was much too full. We were able to step back and make a few minor but significant adjustments. If we hadn't invested in the *being* exercise first, we could easily have just run ahead without realizing we were "piling too many logs" onto our own fires in the process.

We Pray for Prudence

Prudence is one of the most important character qualities or virtues for effective leaders. Without it, it is impossible to make good plans and decisions. The word *prudence* is used to characterize people who have the foresight to take everything into account. Prudent people think ahead, giving careful thought to the long-term implications of their decisions. It's how they exercise good judgment, which is one of the great themes of the book of Proverbs. Here are just a few examples:

> EMOTIONALLY HEALTHY PLANNING AND DECISION MAKING
> 1. We define success as radically doing God's will.
> 2. We create a space for heart preparation.
> **3. We pray for prudence.**
> 4. We look for God in our limits.

> *The wisdom of the **prudent** is to give thought to their ways.*
> PROVERBS 14:8A, EMPHASIS ADDED

> *Only simpletons believe everything they're told! The **prudent** carefully consider their steps.*
> PROVERBS 14:15 NLT, EMPHASIS ADDED

> *It is not good to have zeal without knowledge, nor to be hasty and miss the way.*   PROVERBS 19:2 NIV 1984

> *The plans of the **diligent** lead to profit as surely as haste leads to poverty.*   PROVERBS 21:5, EMPHASIS ADDED

> *The **prudent** see danger and take refuge, but the simple keep going and pay the penalty.*   PROVERBS 22:3, EMPHASIS ADDED

> *Put your outdoor work in order and get your fields ready; after that, build your house.*   PROVERBS 24:27

Prudence has been called the "executive virtue," meaning it enables us to think clearly and not be swept up by our impulses or emotions. Prudence remembers past experiences, our own and others, and draws out any applicable lessons and principles. It partners with humility and willingly seeks counsel from others with more experience. Prudence is cautious and careful to provide for the future. Prudence asks, "Feelings aside, what is best in the long run?"[13] It carefully considers all relevant factors, possibilities, difficulties, and outcomes. Perhaps most important is that prudence refuses to rush — it is willing to wait on God for as long as it takes and to give the decision-making process the time it needs.[14]

The Bible often contrasts those who are prudent with the *simple*, or *foolish*. Such individuals are naïve and easily influenced by those around them. They don't want to do the hard work of thinking things through and asking hard questions. Their decisions are often rushed, impulsive, and focused on short-term, quick-fix solutions.

So call me simple and foolish, because all of these things characterized my decisions in the early years of ministry. In fact, I used to joke that I had a PhD in mistakes. How many times did I appoint volunteers and staff too quickly without asking hard questions? How often did I add a new ministry without thinking through the support it would need? How many times did I say yes to a commitment without looking at my calendar? I often said yes to expansive moves for our church without taking into account the impact they might have on our team's families, rhythms, and Sabbaths. We often seemed to be cleaning up an old mess while, at the same time, launching something new that would create an additional set of problems. Asking God for prudence was not even on my prayer list. But I long ago learned my lesson, and asking God for prudence has become a constant refrain as I seek to do God's will.

Praying for prudence and seeking to practice it to the best of our ability has served us well in our ongoing discernment process. It continues to make an immeasurable contribution to our joy as leaders, especially when joined with a radical commitment to do God's will. The following story is one recent example.

We were in the final year of a significant four-and-a-half-year leadership transition. I had been mentoring and co-pastoring with Rich for fourteen months so I could step down from being lead pastor of New Life and Rich could step into the role with strength. (We'll talk more about this succession process in chapter 9.) He was doing well and finding his own voice. The transition was going smoothly. As one of his first leadership initiative moves, he reignited our long-term vision for becoming a multisite congregation. Over the next few weeks, more and more space was allotted for this in our one-on-one conversations. People from around the country had been encouraging us to go multisite for years, and two pastors from other cities were interested in possibly serving as multisite pastors. My initial thought was that this was a fantastic idea.

When the idea was presented to the leadership team and staff, it created a palpable sense of anticipation and momentum. New Life was growing rapidly and the staff was excited about the possibilities of even greater growth and impact. One day, however, Redd, a member of our executive team, approached the rest of the leadership team with a recommendation.

"This is such a big decision," he said, "we really need to discern this in an intentional way. I think we need to take two to three hours for a group discernment process." We all agreed and set a date to do so a couple weeks later.

We had prepared ourselves in part by reading a book about communal discernment, *Pursuing God's Will Together: A Discernment Practice for Leadership Groups* by Ruth Haley Barton.[15] Redd simplified a few of the principles for our context, and then we began. First, we prayed for indifference — that each of us would be willing to let go of our attachments to any particular outcome. Then we did a roll call to assess how open each of us was to whatever God might say. Redd asked, "How many in this room are now indifferent about the outcome?" We started with a simple yes-or-no question, but in subsequent discernment meetings have used a one-to-ten continuum, with one meaning we are entrenched in and committed to a particular outcome, and ten meaning we are totally open to following through on whatever God might want.

At the end of our three-hour process, it was clear to everyone that six months was much too soon to launch additional sites, and that there were a number of things we needed to tend to before launching. Perhaps most significantly, we needed to complete the succession process. And there were two key hires that needed to be made. We also needed to strengthen our leadership development strategy on all levels.

The prudence of a slowed-down decision-making process also gave Rich time to become aware of the role his shadow might be playing in this decision. Although he wasn't completely aware of it at the time, after our discernment process and additional reflection, he was able to describe it clearly:

> It was difficult to admit at first, but it became clearer and clearer to me as our discernment meeting unfolded. A big part

of me wanted to prove to myself and those around me that I could take New Life to the next level. I couldn't help but realize that so many other pastors my age are aggressively planting multisite campuses and new congregations and having great success in adding to their numbers. With the limitations of our current facilities, I concluded that we are not keeping up. Yes, I know that is ugly, but it is true. I'm so grateful Redd organized this process. I am not sure where I would have been without it.

Scripture teaches that "a person's wisdom yields patience" (Proverbs 19:11). Prudent people are patient. Rich demonstrated self-awareness and prudence in being able to withstand the external and internal pressures that would have caused him to launch campuses too quickly. This not only saved him and his family a lot of anguish, but the church as well.

We learn prudence from other people's mistakes.[16] We learn from our own failures.[17] We learn from wise counsel.[18] But the most important way we grow in this indispensable virtue is to continually ask God for this gift.

There remains one final characteristic of emotionally healthy planning and decision making that we must talk about—finding God *in* our limits.

We Look for God in Our Limits

Our limits may well be the last place we look for God. We want to conquer limits, plan around limits, deny limits, fight limits, and break through limits. In standard leadership practice, we might even consider it a mark of courage or stepping out in faith to rebel against limits. But when we fail to look for God *in* our limits, we often bypass him.

At an Emotionally Healthy Leadership Conference for pastors and leaders a few years ago, we failed to set a limit on the number of attendees. Our administrative team had recommended we close

> EMOTIONALLY HEALTHY PLANNING AND DECISION MAKING
>
> 1. We define success as radically doing God's will.
> 2. We create a space for heart preparation.
> 3. We pray for prudence.
> 4. **We look for God in our limits.**

registration at 325 people. I said no, thinking of all the benefits a full house might bring—additional impact, increased revenue, the excitement of a packed room. In the end, we finally did close registration, but not until there were already far more people coming than our staff, volunteers, systems, and building could absorb. As a result, everyone worked excessively long days and nights in the weeks leading up to the conference. I increased my caffeine intake from two to six cups of coffee a day. And at the conference itself, the staff and teachers gave far in excess of the time and energy we had from God to give. By the time the conference ended, our team was beyond exhausted. Adrenaline carried me through the conference, but I found myself flat on my back for ten days afterward. I did not have the flu or a cold, but I could not function or even move without pain. I finally went to my doctor and asked what was wrong. He swiftly diagnosed the problem: "Pete, you're exhausted. Your body wants to rest. Go home and sleep."

What happened? I violated God's gift of limits, ignoring the many signals my body had been giving me all along that I was off my center in God. I rebelled *against* God right in the midst of my work *for* God. And I had even written a book about how not to do this very thing![19]

Why did I blow by all our limits? Because I saw a big opportunity for expanded impact. What did I not see? That God could be present in—and make an impact in—the little and the small.

New Life, like every church, is constrained by limits. Our building, our under-resourced neighborhood, and our humble people—are just a few. But if I look for God in these limitations, instead of trying to get around them, I begin to see something different. Our very limitations become our greatest means of introducing others to Jesus. Remember the words of the apostle Paul? God's power is made perfect in our *weaknesses*, not in our strengths (2 Corinthians 12:9).

God reveals himself to us, and to the world, through limits in unique and powerful ways—if we have eyes to see. Consider these examples from Scripture:

- Moses was limited by the fact that he was slow of speech. He shares his concerns with God, who then says, "Who gave human beings their mouths? ... Is it not I, the LORD? Now go: I will help you speak and will teach you what to say" (Exodus 4:10–12). God makes it clear that he is present in and through Moses' limitations. Moses then leads three million people for the next forty years in the power of God.

- Jeremiah was limited by a melancholy disposition. He cursed the day he was born and wanted to die. Yet God was present in and through the limits of his temperament, giving him insights about the heart of God that still touch millions of God's people to this day.

- John the Baptist was limited by his simple, semi-monastic life in the desert. But God was present in that limitation, granting John an ability to see something nobody else in his day could see clearly — the extraordinary revelation of Jesus as the Lamb of God.

- Abraham was limited by having only one son with Sarah. He suffered under that limitation, yet he met God in extraordinary ways through his journey of faith. He became the father of us all (Romans 4:17), and his story provides us revelations of who God is — all of which came out of his limits.

- Gideon was limited by the size of his army — just 300 Israelites going up against 135,000 Midianites. But God was with him in that limit, and Gideon's army won a battle he could not have won with his own resources. Thus, his story has testified for thousands of years about the power of God and the importance of humble obedience.

- The twelve disciples were limited in feeding 5,000 men (15,000 – 20,000 people) with only five barley loaves and two fish. Jesus fed the multitudes through them and revealed himself as the Bread of Life.

And if you need a more contemporary example, consider Craig Groeschel, founder and senior pastor of LifeChurch.tv, a multisite church with twenty-three locations in seven states. He says they never would have launched LifeChurch.tv had they not leaned into their limits — which, at the time, was a lack of finances that kept them from building a larger facility.

Limits are often simply God's gifts in disguise. This makes them one of the most counterintuitive, difficult truths in Scripture to embrace. It flies in the face of our natural tendency to want to play god and run the world. But it remains a steady truth, and one I have consistently experienced in at least two ways in my own leadership.

My time limits are a gift. Thanks to Geri, we have led an intensive small group in the basement of our home almost every year during the twenty-six years I was senior pastor. But I wasn't always 100 percent on board. I often thought, *How many senior pastors are spending this amount of time with a group of fifteen people over a year, a few of whom aren't even that responsive?* With so many apparent "bigger" things on my to-do list, it would have been easy to step away from hosting and participating in a group. It limited the time and energy I had to invest in higher impact efforts to grow our church—at least, it seemed that way. Yet God has consistently used Geri to keep me grounded in the little and the important throughout our ministry. Out of this quiet but consistent investment over the years have come a steady stream of leaders who have served the church and expanded its reach far beyond what I could have imagined. And virtually all of the published small group resources and books we have written were shaped and refined in the crucible of our basement over those years.

Our location limits are a gift. I have often grumbled and complained when I compared our location to that of other churches. For example, it's hard to hire staff from outside our church because many don't want to move to Queens, New York. In my early days, I was actually jealous of other leaders and churches whose congregations were populated by CEOs and people with management/business experience and resources. Nevertheless, out of the limits of Queens, God has raised up a gifted staff team to serve an amazing array of diverse people who have emigrated from all over the world to live in our little corner of New York City. So many people at New Life have a depth of faith, a hunger and thirst for the kingdom of God, and unique gifts to serve that I cannot imagine a more blessed place to be. What is perhaps even more amazing is that so many Christian leaders from around the world travel to Queens to meet *them*!

We see only a small part of God's plan at any point in time. His ways are not our ways. But what he does in and through our limitations is more than we could ever accomplish in our own strength.

We've covered a lot of ground about emotionally healthy planning and decision making. Take a few minutes to reflect on the four characteristics: defining success as radically doing God's will, creating a space for heart preparation, praying for prudence, and looking for God *in* our limits. When you consider the challenges you face in your own leadership, which one speaks to you the most? What fears or concerns do you have when you imagine implementing this in your leadership? What are the short-term costs of stopping, turning, and doing something different? What might be the long-term implications if you don't? If you are willing to take the risks and live with some temporary disorientation, I can promise you that God is waiting for you there.

> EMOTIONALLY HEALTHY PLANNING
> AND DECISION MAKING
>
> 1. We define success as radically doing God's will.
> 2. We create a space for heart preparation.
> 3. We pray for prudence.
> 4. We look for God in our limits.

Ask the Four Questions

I began this chapter with a story about announcing a bad decision on an airplane. Knowing what you now know about emotionally healthy decision making, consider what was wrong with my process when I informed Geri we were launching a new Spanish-speaking congregation:

- I was unaware of my own shadow. My decision to rush ahead flowed from my own unconscious need to feel significant and validated as a leader. I was unaware of how this distorted my ability to hear God's voice. I was also selfishly motivated by an unwarranted fear of losing my Spanish language skills.
- I was not leading out of my marriage, nor was I thinking about how this new congregation might impact my relationship with Geri or our family. I foolishly made a big decision with significant implications without first talking it through with Geri.
- I assumed that, because it was God's will, the demands of adding a new congregation would not affect my loving union with Jesus.

I was wrong. It contributed to greater pressure in my week that spilled over to further limit my time with God.

- At the time of that conversation, I was not practicing Sabbath. Monday was my day off. Although I continued to take Mondays off, I was increasingly distracted and preoccupied on that day by a host of additional problems and responsibilities connected to the addition of the Spanish-speaking ministry.

As we close this chapter, I invite you to avoid my mistakes by using the four inner life roots from part 1 to reflect on your own experiences and to begin a transition to (or to deepen your existing practice of) emotionally healthy planning and decision making.

- **Face your shadow.** How might my shadow, or that of others on my team, be impacting my decisions and plans? What are my greatest fears? In light of the decisions before me, am I setting aside enough time for personal heart preparation to minimize any influence my shadow might have on my decisions and plans? How much heart preparation time do the members of my team need? What wise counsel do I need to minimize my shadow's influence on my decisions?
- **Lead out of your marriage or singleness.** How will this decision or plan impact my ability to lead out of my marriage or singleness? What changes might we need to make as a team in order to take into account our need for healthy, vibrant marriages or singleness? Are we embracing the God-given limits of our particular marriage and single situations?
- **Slow down for loving union.** How might this decision or plan impact my ability to remain in loving union with Jesus? On a scale of one to ten, what is the level of anxiety of our team as we consider this decision? Have we prayed for prudence and gathered all the important facts? Have I (we) done the slow, diligent work needed to listen for God's whisperings about his definition of success for us? What temptations do I/we need to be careful to avoid?
- **Practice Sabbath delight.** How will this decision affect our work-Sabbath rhythms? Have we thought through the details of how these plans will affect the rest of our work so that it does not

spill over into our Sabbath delight? Am I, and is our team, making these plans and decision from a place of rest? What difference will this decision make ten, fifty, or a hundred years from now? What difference will this decision make after we have entered our eternal Sabbath and see Jesus face-to-face?[20]

Prayerfully engaging these four issues will help you to be more watchful and prudent in your decision making, protecting you from confusing your will with God's will. I like to say that working through all four of these is how I "watch for the canaries."

Watch for the Canaries

Long ago, before coal or gold miners had high-tech equipment to measure carbon dioxide levels in the air, dangerous gases would accumulate in the mines and lead to devastating explosions. So miners learned to use a low-tech solution — they carried canaries (who are highly sensitive to poisonous gasses) as a barometer of the air quality in the mines. The canaries would chirp and sing all day long. But when the carbon monoxide levels rose too high, the canaries stopped singing. If they remained in the mines, they would begin to have trouble breathing, swoon, and eventually die. When the singing stopped, that was the signal that gas levels were too high and miners must quickly leave the mine to avoid being caught in an explosion.

Who or what are your decision-making canaries — those small indications that something may not be right? How do you identify within yourself when you are making decisions or plans that are not from God? And who are people God has placed in your life who love you enough to tell you when the danger level is rising and you may be at risk of an explosive event in your planning and decision making? If you don't have anyone right now, ask God to give you one or two people. And prepare to experience a newfound joy and deep contentment as you add "emotionally healthy" to your planning and decision-making process.

Next, in chapter 7, we'll explore how intentionally changing the way we make plans and decisions changes the culture of our organization and the way we build teams.

Understanding Your Planning and Decision-Making Assessment

If you took the assessment on pages 179–80, here are some observations to help you better understand the condition of your planning and decision-making process right now.

If you scored mostly ones and twos, chances are good that your relationship with Christ is compartmentalized from your planning and decision-making process. You are in the early stages of learning how to be both prayerful in seeking God's will and prudent in gathering information and making wise decisions. You can take your first steps by continuing to deepen the roots that ground your inner life with God (part 1) and slowly building a healthy support system to influence the way you lead. Then slowly build on that, integrating one or two principles from this chapter.

If you scored mostly twos and threes, you are probably operating with only a partial understanding and practice of emotionally healthy planning and decision making. This means you are likely reaping a mix of leadership chaos and good fruit. Receive your assessment score as God's invitation to integrate more fully your spiritual root system in good organizational or team practices. Prayerfully ask God for wisdom on which principles from this chapter are most important for you to begin implementing now.

If you scored mostly fours and fives, you are most likely doing well integrating both prayerfulness and prudence in your planning and decision making. You can expect to experience further growth and greater freedom in your process of discerning God's will. Expect surprises from God as he takes you and your team on an exciting journey. Expect transformative moments from him along the way. And allow the ideas described in this chapter to stimulate you to create new ways to lead your team in a more healthy and dynamic planning and decision-making process.

CHAPTER 7

CULTURE AND TEAM BUILDING

A llow me to share with you a story about a lamb and a tiger.

Once upon a time in the Friendly Forest there lived a lamb who loved to graze and frolic about. One day a tiger came to the forest and said to the animals, "I would like to live among you." They were delighted. Unlike some of the other forests, they had no tiger in their woods. The lamb, however, had some apprehensions, which, being a lamb, she sheepishly expressed to her friends. But, said they, "Do not worry, we will talk to the tiger and explain that one of the conditions for living in this forest is that you must also let other animals live in the forest."

So the lamb went about her life as usual. But it was not long before the tiger began to growl and make threatening gestures and menacing motions. Each time the frightened lamb went to her friends and said, "It is very uncomfortable for me here in the forest." But her friends reassured her, "Do not worry; that's just the way tigers behave...." They pointed out that no harm had really befallen her and that perhaps she was just too sensitive.

So the lamb again tried to put the tiger out of her mind.... But every now and then, usually when she was least prepared, the tiger would give her another start.

Finally the lamb could not take it anymore. She decided that, much as she loved the forest and her friends ... the cost was too great. So she went to the other animals in the woods and said good-bye.

Her friends would not hear of it.... "Surely this whole thing can be worked out.... There is probably just some misunderstanding that can easily be resolved if we all sit down together and communicate."...

Though one of the less subtle animals in the forest ... was overheard to remark, "I never heard of anything so ridiculous. If you want a lamb and a tiger to live in the same forest, you don't try to make them communicate. You cage the bloody tiger."[1]

It's a great story, isn't it? And actually, it's not so much a story about a lamb and a tiger as it is a story about the lamb's friends, the leaders of the Friendly Forest. The tiger is a tiger—and tigers don't change into lambs or any other kind of benign forest creature. More meetings and "communication" would not solve the problem. What was needed more than anything else in the Friendly Forest was healthy, differentiated leadership—leaders who know their values and aren't swayed by disagreements and pressure from others.[2] The leaders needed the courage to "cage the tiger" out of love for their community. No amount of negotiation would change the nature of the tiger. They needed to stand firm in a decision to protect their community and be willing to tolerate the discomfort from criticism (sure to come from the tiger and others) as well as the inevitable accusations. *What happened to you? You've become so unloving and controlling since you became a leader. Who made you the judge and jury?*

The leaders in the Friendly Forest also needed to define the values of their culture, limiting the tiger's power lest he emerge as the unofficial leader of the community. In minimizing the severity of the threat ("probably just some misunderstanding") and refusing to deal with the issue directly (under the guise of being reasonable), they not only left their community open to dreadful harm but also missed an opportunity to clearly define the boundaries of acceptable and unacceptable behavior. And, assuming they were a Christian community (the forest was "friendly," after all), they also failed to discern that this intense conflict might contain within it a gift from God that would enable them to grow and mature together into Christlikeness.

What Is Culture and Team Building?

Creating an emotionally healthy culture and building a healthy team are among the primary tasks for every leader, whether that leader is a senior pastor, a para-church ministry department head, a nonprofit or a marketplace executive, a church board member, or a small group leader. And the task for *Christian* leaders is even more demanding because the kind of culture and teams we create are to be radically different than those of the world.

So what precisely are these things called *team building* and *culture* that we are responsible for developing and stewarding well?

Team building is fairly easy to define; it involves mobilizing a group of people with diverse skills who are committed to a shared vision and common goals. *Culture*, however, is somewhat more challenging to describe. Why? Because it consists primarily of unspoken rules about "the way we do things around here."

Culture is that imprecise something, the invisible presence or personality of a place that can be difficult to describe without actually experiencing it. It is often more readily felt than articulated. Perhaps the simplest and best definitions I've come across describe culture as "the sum-total of the learned patterns of thought and behavior" of any given group;[3] and "culture is what human beings make of the world."[4]

Multinational companies such as Google, Apple, and IBM have very distinct cultures. Ethnic communities, political groups, and countries have cultures. Denominations and para-church organizations have cultures. Every church, ministry, task force, and team has a certain style that constitutes the spirit or ethos of that particular community.

Culture includes such things as our vision, values, and strategy (seeker-targeted, multisite, purpose-driven, etc.), common practices and style (we have a choir and they wear robes, we sit silently before services, we dress informally, etc.), and even our language and use of space. How we exercise authority, conduct relationships, handle conflict, position ourselves in the community (or marketplace), and define personal and/or spiritual growth are all expressions of the culture in which we lead. And as Christian leaders, we must be intentional about taking the chaos of what people bring to the organization (from their very different backgrounds and families of origin) and shaping it into a new culture that seeks to operate as the family of Jesus.

How Healthy Is Your Practice of Culture and Team Building?

Use the list of statements that follow to briefly assess your leadership practice when it comes to culture and team building. Next to each statement, write down the number that best describes your response. Use the following scale:

5 = Always true of me
4 = Frequently true of me
3 = Occasionally true of me
2 = Rarely true of me
1 = Never true of me

_____ 1. I invest in key people from my team, both in their transformation in Christ and in their skill or professional development.

_____ 2. I directly and promptly address "elephants in the room" (tensions, lateness, hostile body language, sarcasm, unkind remarks, silence, etc.).

_____ 3. I consider healthy rhythms and loving union with Jesus of team members as the indispensable foundation for building a healthy culture and team. Our schedule and agenda reflect these values.

_____ 4. I explore and ask questions when people are highly reactive, or triggered, rather than ignore them.

_____ 5. I negotiate differences and clarify expectations when there is frustration and conflict.

_____ 6. I communicate in ways that are clear, honest, respectful, and timely.

_____ 7. I am intentional to set aside time and space in team meetings to instill particular values (e.g., Scripture, expressing appreciations, sharing new insights on leadership).

_____ 8. I dedicate the necessary time to explore the root causes of inappropriate behavior, seeing it as a spiritual formation opportunity.

_____ 9. People experience me as willing to take the time to "tune in" to them.

_____ 10. I ask specific questions about the quality of people's marriage or singleness because it is a key factor to build a healthy culture and teams.

Take a moment to briefly review your responses. What stands out most to you? At the end of the chapter (page 237) are some general observations to help you better understand the current level of health in your leadership of culture and team building.

Characteristics of Emotionally Healthy Culture and Team Building

When it comes to culture and team building, I have spent too many years operating like the leaders of the Friendly Forest. They were unaware of their responsibility to build a healthy culture and team. So was I. They were conflict averse. Me too. They were shortsighted, not thinking about the long-term implications of their decisions. I did that as well—a lot.

I didn't give much thought to the kind of culture I wanted to create, nor did I invest the necessary energy to help it become a living reality. We didn't talk about culture on our team—not because we didn't want to, but because we didn't know there was such a thing. Of course, we took appropriate action when someone's behavior was clearly inappropriate (committing immorality, yelling at someone during a meeting, making a racist remark, etc.), but otherwise, our focus was on achieving our goals. Team chemistry was important but only as a means to maximize our effectiveness.

Yet creating an emotionally healthy culture and team is one of the most powerful opportunities we have to impact people's lives and our long-term mission. This applies equally to pastors, teachers, ministry leaders, board members, executives in the marketplace, and mission workers.

Over the years, I've identified four core characteristics for emotionally healthy culture and team building. When an organizational culture and team are healthy, these things are true:

- Work performance and personal spiritual formation are inseparable.
- The elephants in the room are acknowledged and confronted.
- Time and energy are invested in the team's personal spiritual development.
- The quality of people's marriages and singleness is foundational.

Each of the four characteristics were birthed out of many painful mistakes and years of trial and error at New Life. Each required that I move from indifference to intentionality and thoughtfulness. In the process, I felt compelled to regularly ask God for the courage to reshape our culture in specific ways and to have difficult conversations that I preferred to avoid.

Let's take a closer look at these characteristics, beginning with the foundation from which all the others follow — the necessity of making work performance and spiritual formation inseparable.

Work Performance and Personal Spiritual Formation Are Inseparable

How the members of our team perform on the job is important. We invite them to serve — as volunteers or paid staff — in order to accomplish a task, and we need them to do that task well. In emotionally healthy cultures and teams, such role expectations are openly talked about and agreed upon. We speak respectfully, honestly, and clearly to one another in evaluating how we are doing. But that is not enough.

How the people on our team care for their inner lives also is important. The question is, "How important?" In an emotionally healthy culture or team,

> EMOTIONALLY HEALTHY CULTURE AND TEAM BUILDING
>
> 1. **Work and personal formation are inseparable.**
> 2. Elephants in the room are acknowledged and confronted.
> 3. Time and energy are invested.
> 4. The quality of people's marriages and singleness is foundational.

the answer is, "Very important." In fact, the health and growth of a person's inner life is inseparable from work performance. Unfortunately, while most of us are clear about certain boundaries that can't be crossed (immorality, stealing, lying, contentious behavior, etc.), our expectations of people's spiritual maturity remains superficial and unclear. Consider how the following leaders describe their approach to some problematic team members:

- *Jacob? Well, I just have to be careful what I say around him. He is very sensitive to criticism. If I raise any questions about the way he oversees the children's ministry program, I'm afraid he'll quit. Then I'll have an even bigger problem because I won't be able to find anybody else who's willing to run it as a volunteer.*

- *Mia is young, immature, and sometimes brash. I used to try to bring it to her attention when she said something inappropriate, but now I tend to let it go. Yes, she tends to lose volunteers because (as she alleges) they lack commitment. But I'm sure she'll eventually become more patient and less abrasive. Regardless, I just don't have the time to get into it all with her. Besides, she does amazing work with our website and social media, so I figure it all somehow balances out.*

- *Owen is a great guy and faithful small group leader, but he doesn't do conflict. I have to be sure to watch his body language and tone for clues about whether or not something is bothering him. He won't tell me even if I ask him point-blank, so I have to read between the lines with him. I've gotten pretty good at it, so things are okay most of the time.*

- *Claire's car looks like a tornado swept through it. Fast-food bags, receipts, toiletries, file folders, and music scores are scattered all across the front and back seats—and her office doesn't look much different. On top of being a last-minute kind of person, she's also a little overwhelmed by life right now, but she always somehow manages to get the job done at the end. She's a great worship leader, so I'm willing to put up with the chaos that always seems to follow in her wake.*

So, do you have any Jacobs, Mias, Owens, or Claires on your team? Someone whose raw edges routinely complicate or cause problems you have to either tolerate or spend excessive time cleaning up after?

I know I certainly did. And like most pastors and leaders, I didn't have time to help these dear folks address the myriad of unresolved family-of-origin dynamics or lack of self-awareness that impacted our team—especially since, in the early years of my ministry, I hadn't yet traveled that path myself. The best I could do was offer a few suggestions:

"Try to be less sensitive."

"There's a great book on resolving conflicts you might want to read."

"I encourage you to assert yourself. You have great things to say."

You can imagine how helpful such suggestions were in dealing with the problems. Nothing I had to offer at that point could help these problematic team members break through their layers of emotional immaturity and lack of awareness. And that was a big problem.

Minimally transformed leaders will always result in minimally transformed teams doing minimally transforming ministry. This is true even if the numbers are up and the programming is excellent. How could we expect it to be any other way? How can we expect to change the world for Christ if we ourselves are not being changed by him? In order to have any hope of dealing with immature or problematic team members, we have to focus first on our own spiritual transformation.

Personal Spiritual Development

At New Life, I always recommend that the first category listed for every leadership job description read, "Personal Spiritual Formation Development."

We start with ourselves. Why? Because the most important way we communicate the inseparable link between work performance and personal spiritual formation is to model it. When we make our transformation in Christ the first priority of our leadership, we instill that value in our culture and in our teams.

Geri and I are very intentional about modeling this. We meet with mentors and coaches. We attend training seminars, workshops, and conferences. We read voraciously. We look outside our context, North American culture, and our evangelical subculture for fresh perspectives and practices that will help us grow personally and professionally. In the twenty-nine years of our ministry, we've taken three sabbaticals to focus on learning, growing, and allowing God to transform broken areas in our lives and ministries. We share openly about what God is teaching us—in sermons, staff meetings, private conversations, and with members of our small group. In all of this, we communicate the fundamental value that we lead out of who we are. Thus, disciplining ourselves to invest time, energy, and money in personal development is not a selfish indulgence, but one of the most loving things we offer to those we serve.

Team Member Spiritual Development

Once we invest in and model the integration of work performance and personal spiritual formation, then we can intentionally and prayerfully dedicate ourselves to addressing the evident gaps in our team members. This is not an "extra" when it comes to being a Christian leader or something we sandwich in the cracks in order to get our "real" work done. It is core to what it means to be a servant leader for Christ. Let me illustrate this with a story about Phil, one of our New Life staff members.

Within six months of joining our staff, it was evident that Phil was conflict avoidant. As part of coaching Phil on this issue, Geri and I offered him the opportunity to serve as a case study for an upcoming Emotionally Healthy Leadership Conference. He gladly agreed.

Phil identified an event that had taken place during our recent Easter Sunday baptism service in which he had avoided a conflict with Myrna, his executive assistant. On the Saturday before Easter, Phil received a text message from his supervisor that a teenager named Emily was excited about being baptized. She had invited her family, who were not part of the church, to share in her big day. The problem was that her name had somehow not been included on the list of candidates. This meant it wasn't on the schedule for the service. When Phil's supervisor asked him to work it out so she could still be included, Phil responded, "Sure, no problem."

But it was a problem. In addition to being in the midst of his Sabbath, Phil and his wife were celebrating their one-year wedding anniversary. Nevertheless, he spent the next five hours sorting out the problem, ruining both his Sabbath and his anniversary. Phil arranged all the details himself, never calling Myrna, his executive assistant, who was responsible for scheduling the candidates and had evidently failed to include Emily on the list in the first place.

On Easter Sunday, Myrna approached Phil and apologized for her mistake with the scheduling. Phil smiled and answered, "That's okay. It wasn't a big deal."

When Geri and I became aware of what had happened, we worked with Phil on how he might have approached the issue differently. We invited him to use a tool we developed called "The Ladder of Integrity."[5]

CLIMB THE LADDER OF INTEGRITY

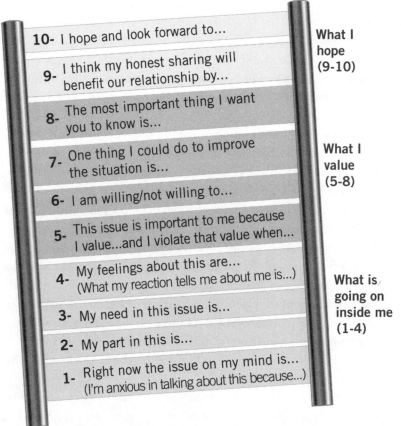

10- I hope and look forward to...

9- I think my honest sharing will benefit our relationship by...

What I hope (9-10)

8- The most important thing I want you to know is...

7- One thing I could do to improve the situation is...

What I value (5-8)

6- I am willing/not willing to...

5- This issue is important to me because I value...and I violate that value when...

4- My feelings about this are... (What my reaction tells me about me is...)

3- My need in this issue is...

What is going on inside me (1-4)

2- My part in this is...

1- Right now the issue on my mind is... (I'm anxious in talking about this because...)

Be sure to stick to one issue.

The purpose of the Ladder of Integrity is to help people discover what is going on inside them — to discern their values and assert themselves — in a respectful, non-blaming way. We call it The Ladder of Integrity because it provides a systematic approach that helps people to be honest and transparent as they prepare themselves to address problems and conflicts with another person.

Over the next six weeks, Phil spent a great deal of time reflecting on and then writing out his answers to the sentence starters on each rung of the ladder. He then practiced his responses in several meetings with

Geri and me. Slowly, he developed confidence in his ability to clearly and honestly assert himself with Myrna. At our conference, in front of three hundred pastors and leaders, we invited Myrna to join us on the platform. Phil then summarized his ladder statements with her in about five minutes. Here is what he said:

> Myrna, thank you for being willing to let me share something significant for me. It has to do with that scheduling conflict around Emily's Easter baptism. I appreciated that you apologized for your mistake. I then told you that it was "okay and no big deal." I lied. It was a very big deal because what I thought was only going to take five minutes ended up taking five hours and I basically ruined my and Debbie's Sabbath and the weekend of our one-year anniversary.
>
> My purpose in telling you all this now is because what really disturbed me was that I wasn't honest with you. I brushed it off like it was nothing, but that was far from the truth. In the end what grieved me — and scared me — was that I could so easily lie to you. As I reflected on all of this, I realized that in my culture [Phil's family is from India], it is an unspoken rule that a younger person never raise an issue with an older person or a more experienced staff person — even if that person is misinformed or made a mistake. We are to keep it to ourselves. We end up lying, and it damages relationships in churches and families.
>
> I am also a people pleaser and I want you to like me. I was afraid that you could be offended if I told you how it impacted me, and then distance yourself from me. I value truthfulness and having integrity within myself. When I am not honest with myself or others, I violate my own integrity. I want to be a leader who is authentic, and so thank you for allowing me to practice speaking truthfully.
>
> The most important thing I want you to know is that I respect you and value your work as an awesome executive assistant. And I need you to know how difficult it is for me to speak candidly because of my background — generations of people from my family and culture do not do this. I believe telling you this will benefit our relationship because you will

know that I can be honest with you. I look forward to more
opportunities in our future working relationship to be a sign
of the kingdom to our community. I hope that you feel free to
come to me as well.

Myrna smiled, hugged him, and said, "Thank you."

That was it.

You may be wondering if this was worth all the time and effort we put
into it. But let me ask you to consider a few other questions as well. Where
will Phil be as a leader—one, three, ten years from now—if he continues
avoiding conflict and stuffing his disappointments and hurts? What kind
of small groups and ministries will he build at New Life if he can't confront
his own immaturity? What will happen to his relationship with Myrna, his
coworkers, and his supervisors if he continues to hide behind the façade
of being a happy, good guy because he can't deal with conflict? And how
might all of this impact the health of the church overall?

Every member of your team will have different rough edges and areas
they need to develop—just as you do. It may be in the area of facing their
shadow and cultivating greater self-awareness. You may encourage them
to write about their feelings in a journal, see a mentor or therapist, read
a particular book. Another staff member may be so hard-working and
conscientious that they need to be challenged to work fewer hours and
devote time to be with God more intentionally. One of your single leaders
may have challenges related to creating delight in their life and setting
better boundaries around the ministry. You may want to brainstorm with
them about this. Last week, I spent almost two hours in conversation with
Ruth, our executive director of EHS, about this very thing.

The key factor here is that you are thoughtful and prayerful about
each member of your team. Like us, they lead out of their unique per-
sonhood, out of who they *are*. Just as we cannot give what we do not
possess—regardless of gifts and experience—neither can they.

The Elephants in the Room Are Acknowledged and Confronted

An "elephant in the room" refers to an obviously inappropriate or
immature behavior that remains unacknowledged and/or unaddressed.

Such elephants commonly roam wild and free among many teams. For example:

> ### EMOTIONALLY HEALTHY CULTURE AND TEAM BUILDING
> 1. Work and personal formation are inseparable.
> 2. **Elephants in the room are acknowledged and confronted.**
> 3. Time and energy are invested.
> 4. The quality of people's marriages and singleness is foundational.

- Jacqueline is an outstanding worship leader. Her gifts are a blessing to your church. But at weekly service planning meetings she is aloof, moody, and sullen, which seems to indicate she'd rather not be there. The other five members of the team can't help but notice this, but nobody asks her about it.

- Michael, a member of the church board, sends an e-mail to six members of the staff team, criticizing their decision to cancel the prayer meetings before and after Christmas. His tone is annoyed, bordering on angry. The lead pastor has a five-minute, perfunctory conversation with Michael in an attempt to quickly resolve his concerns. The short-term problem is smoothed over, but the tension remains.

- Rob is a gifted communicator. People love him. The problem is that he has a habit of misrepresenting the truth. For example, he routinely agrees to do things and then never follows through. He also exaggerates and embellishes facts. Those close to him have learned to tolerate it as part of the "visionary communicator" package.

- Nora's ministry is flourishing. But she shows up late to staff meetings and one-on-one meetings—a lot. She apologizes and offers reasonably good excuses, but the late arrivals persist. Others complain about her lateness, but no one holds her accountable for it.

- Patrick, the administrative assistant, has been on staff ten years, but he is not doing his job for the ministries he serves. He is highly critical of others, especially the new staff who don't have the history he does with the church. The church is changing and growing, but Patrick is not. His supervisor doesn't know how to talk to Patrick about it or what to do about all the complaints from those Patrick is supposed to be supporting. The elephant sits in the room year after year.

Overlooking unacceptable behavior in situations like these is so common in teams that when I suggest part of leadership is to expose and explore these elephants, leaders often look at me in disbelief: "Pete, you've got to be kidding. Do you know what would happen if I started confronting every elephant in the room? I might lose half my team. And I wouldn't have time for anything else!"

Depending on your situation, you may need to prayerfully prioritize how to go forward. I sure did as I transitioned our culture at New Life. Remember, elephants in the room rarely disappear by themselves. In fact, they often feed off the silence and grow into bigger, crisis-laden elephants over time. I know because I've ignored so many myself—and paid a steep price as a result.

For many years, I didn't see myself as the guardian of the values of culture at New Life. I didn't even know we had a culture. I didn't feel equipped. I hoped someone else would do it. I mistakenly expected my team as well as our staff, church board, and key volunteers to automatically "do everything right." I was surprised and often upset when they repeatedly brought their unhealthy ways of relating with them into New Life culture. *But what was I thinking?* Of course, they were bringing their immature behaviors and rough edges with them! What else could they do? That is all they knew.

The higher up we go in leadership, the greater the level of maturity is required. As people step into progressively wider spheres of influence and greater responsibility, unresolved issues in their inner lives will inevitably be exposed. Immaturity rooted in unresolved issues from their family of origin, trauma, issues with authority, and faulty thinking, for example, will reveal itself sooner or later. As much as we all wish leaders would arrive on our doorsteps as maturely formed, peak performers, that is rarely what actually happens.

Out of our commitment to rid New Life of unwanted elephants and create a new culture, Geri and I developed practical skills for our leadership and church over a sixteen-year period. The formula was simple: New skills + new language + intentional follow-up = transformed community.

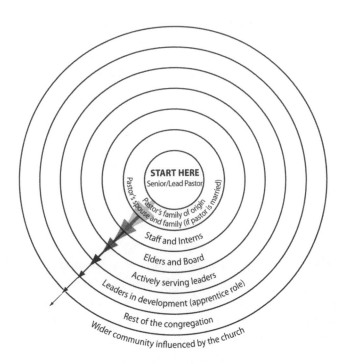

Our aim was to give people tools to love well in the new family of Jesus—beginning with our leadership team. We call these eight tools "emotionally healthy skills."[6] While they may look deceptively simple, each is built on a rich theological foundation and contains multiple levels of depth to understand and live out. They are:

1. The Community Temperature Reading
2. Stop Mind Reading
3. Clarify Expectations
4. Genogram Your Family
5. Explore the Iceberg
6. Incarnational Listening
7. Climb the Ladder of Integrity
8. Clean Fighting

Putting these skills into practice has given all of us a common framework for confronting the elephants in the room and wrestling with the difficult issues they represent. Using these skills also helped us to develop a new vocabulary. For example, when we are tempted to make a premature judgment, we might catch ourselves and instead model a more mature and loving conversation. Two simple but key concepts we have integrated into our New Life culture are *puzzles* and what we call *complaints with recommendations*. The latter involves using the phrase *I notice … and I prefer* when making a complaint. Allow me to illustrate how they work.

Being puzzled enables us to avoid assumptions and negative interpretations. For example, instead of saying, "Why did you leave such a mess in the office kitchen?" we can say, "I'm puzzled about why you didn't clean up after yourself." Instead of saying, "You should have returned my e-mail sooner," we say, "I'm puzzled about why you didn't respond to my e-mail sooner." Making "I'm puzzled" statements forces us to acknowledge that we don't know why. It helps us to pause and catch our heart before it jumps to judgment.

We also teach our team and members of the church how to make a healthy complaint in our culture as the new family of Jesus. To unlearn negative generational patterns from their family of origin, we encourage people to use the phrase *I notice … and I prefer* as the formula for making a complaint. For example, when a supervisor sends a Power-Point presentation to the tech volunteer at the last minute, instead of stuffing frustration and annoyance, he might say, "*I notice* that you sent me your PowerPoint two hours before your presentation, and *I would prefer* if you could send it one day ahead of time so I have time to upload it into our computer system." Instead of saying, "You were late for our meeting. If you don't show up on time, I can't work with you in the future," we might say, "*I notice* you arrived twenty minutes late for our leadership team meeting, and *I prefer* that you call when you are running late so I can adjust my schedule."

It's a simple phrase, but saying *I notice … and I prefer* effectively gives people training wheels to relate differently. It helps them to be aware of and take responsibility for the small irritations and annoyances that arise every day.[7]

What then does it look like to intentionally acknowledge and confront the elephants in the room in a way that serves people's maturing in Christ? Here are two simple but concrete examples.

Steve. Geri and I were meeting with Steve, one of our small group leaders, in our home. He recounted how, after he made a great presentation at work, his boss sent out an e-mail thanking everyone but him. "I knew he had it out for me," remarked Steve in anger. "He never liked me." Geri and I glanced at each other, knowing this was a teachable moment in which we could mentor Steve.

"Do you know that for sure?" Geri asked. "Has he told you that? Or might there be other ways to interpret what happened?" Based on the skill we call "Stop Mind Reading," I role-played how Steve might have wrongly interpreted what happened. I acted as if I was Steve walking into his boss's office, and Steve role-played his boss. "Mr. Simmons," I began, "I'm really confused about why you sent a thank-you e-mail to everyone on our team but me, especially when you seemed so pleased with my presentation in the meeting. Did I miss something?"

Andy. A pastor friend recently told me about his interaction with Andy, a musician on the church's worship team. Andy had complained to my pastor friend that worship team practice went thirty minutes overtime because of all the joking around the music director had permitted. A few days later, the music director, sensing Andy's annoyance, had asked, "Hey Andy, were you upset during rehearsal the other night? You left so quickly." Andy replied, "No, I just hurt my back the other day and wanted to get home right away." The problem was that Andy didn't have a bad back. He had played basketball with the church team the previous night!

My friend chose to approach Andy a few days later, being careful to not shame or judge him. "Hey, Andy, I'm curious," he said. "I overheard you tell the music director you had a bad back and that was the reason you went home early from rehearsal. What made you say that?" The conversation that followed was very powerful as Andy talked about his tendency to lie to avoid conflict. They talked about how Andy's family, when he was growing up, avoided conflict. They identified some of his faulty assumptions about "niceness" in church culture. They even considered how he might go back and redo that conversation with the music director.

These were important moments for both Steve and Andy to grow and mature. They served as opportunities to unlearn unhealthy patterns from their families of origin and to learn how we do life in the family of Jesus. Those who confronted their behavior were also building a healthier culture. As Steve and Andy change the way they relate and love, the larger communities of which they're a part will also be transformed. Time and time again, we have discovered that small, one-on-one mentoring moments like these have a sustained ripple effect through the culture that far exceeds their apparent importance.

Great wisdom is found in the ancient axiom "All roads lead to Rome." Just as spokes on a wheel lead to the hub, the Roman Empire's excellent road system led travelers directly back to Rome. In the same way, all surface issues in our lives will eventually lead back to the same unhealthy issues ingrained in the way we relate to ourselves and others. When we work with someone to fully unpack one—like the small incident between Andy and the music director—we can expect it to lead to the deep roots that inform other similar behaviors. Address this one thoroughly and light will be shed on the rest as well.

If we lead within the church or nonprofit sector, we may not be able to pay marketplace salaries. In fact, most of the teams we lead might well be comprised of volunteers. But we can offer something much more valuable—personal spiritual development to help those we lead become more like Jesus. That is quite a gift.

Time and Energy Are Invested in the Team's Personal Spiritual Development

Emotionally healthy leaders dedicate themselves to their team's personal development, and not just their professional or ministry skills. They know this will bear rich fruit and ripple though the ministry in powerful ways.

Jesus taught and led the masses, but he invested himself in a core team of twelve who, in turn, shaped the culture of the emerging church. As the time of his crucifixion approached, Jesus devoted increasing amounts of his energy to train them. In the same way, as Christian leaders we must shift

> EMOTIONALLY HEALTHY CULTURE AND TEAM BUILDING
>
> 1. Work and personal formation are inseparable.
> 2. Elephants in the room are acknowledged and confronted.
> 3. **Time and energy are invested.**
> 4. The quality of people's marriages and singleness is foundational.

a portion of our energy away from programs or the larger ministry to the intentional development of our core team. Like Jesus, we need a two-level focus—the overall leadership of the masses and the maturing of our team. If we are the senior leader of a church, ministry, or other large organization, we must identify our "core thirty" team. If we lead a smaller team within an organization or ministry, we must identify the key persons on our team and devote ourselves to investing in them.

Natural Church Development (NCD) is the leading organization researching healthy church growth around the world. Beginning in the late 1990s, NCD has conducted 93,000 surveys with over 70,000 churches in seventy-one countries. To assess the heart and health of a church, they survey *only thirty core people* in the congregation—regardless of church size.[8] Those in the core group must meet three criteria: (1) be members of a group within the church (choir or worship team, men's group, small group, etc.); (2) be actively involved in ministry (not just meeting socially); and (3) be committed to the life and growth of the congregation. When leaders of larger congregations ask if they can survey more than thirty people, here is NCD's response:

> It is possible, but is not advised because no more are required to produce a statistically accurate result. We recommend leaders take the time to reduce their list to the thirty people fitting the criteria whose opinion they value most or those they consider to have the greatest influence on church life. You are effectively taking a biopsy of the heart of the organism.[9]

When they want to assess whether or not the church culture has changed after a year or two, the church will again conduct an NCD survey with another sample of thirty people from the core of people who meet the criteria. Why? Because they know these are the ones permeating the entire culture with their values, ethos, behaviors, practices, and spirituality.

Although we have not formally done the Natural Church Development process at New Life, we do intentionally focus on our core thirty to forty staff, elders, ministry, and key small group leaders to integrate the principles you are reading in this book. In this way, the culture we seek to create spills out to the entire church.[10]

Here are a few recent examples of what it looks like to make this kind of investment in the team's personal spiritual development. At our last few weekly team meetings, we have devoted time to talking about practicing Sabbath, listening to God through the Examen, discerning our specific vocations as leaders, and recent discoveries from the neurosciences on how people change. We also pray a midday prayer from the Daily Office together each week. Then we move on to the business items on the agenda, such as upcoming events, changes in policy, problems, etc.

There are times, however, when this investment in our team costs more time and energy than we anticipated. The following situation took place two weeks before I made the official handoff to Rich as the new lead pastor at New Life. Rich had been formally leading the staff for the previous eighteen months, which meant my contact with Mike, the young staff member in this story, had been minimal up to that point.

It was Sunday, and Geri was delivering a message at our three services entitled "Hard Lessons Learned in Twenty-Six Years at New Life." Before the third service, I asked Mike, our paid staff person responsible for recording videos, to record her final message at New Life.

"No," he replied, "I only record the second service."

"I know," I said, "but this is a special Sunday. I want to get her best message on video, so please record this one."

Mike dug in his heels, "I'm planning to sit in the auditorium and participate in this service, so no."

I found myself growing angry and confused. *This fellow is twenty-five and on staff for one year. I have been senior pastor at New Life longer than he has been alive. Why isn't he doing what I'm asking him to do?*

I then went down a road of self-doubt (my own shadow). *Maybe I'm being perfectionistic. Why am I so uptight? Geri couldn't care less anyway.*

I named another staff person who had recorded services before and suggested Mike ask this person to record the message on his behalf.

"He doesn't know how to do it," Mike replied sharply as he walked away.

I was too stunned to respond.

Geri preached an incredible message in the third service. And I was furious it wasn't recorded.

A part of me wanted to fire Mike on the spot. But after saying good-byes to people following the last service, I realized I wasn't ready to talk to anyone about it, so I went home.

It took me Sunday night and all day Monday to calm down sufficiently, think clearly about what had happened, and identify the best way to go forward. I had other plans for Monday, but I knew this was an important cultural and spiritual formation moment for Mike, for the executive team, and for me.

I had to wrestle with a question: *Is this the way I will be treated when I step down in two weeks and transition to a new role?* That was precisely the reason a few senior leader friends told me not to do leadership succession in the first place. *Were they right?* The answer was clearly no. All my relationships with the church board, Rich, the staff, and members of the congregation were respectful and kind.

I also realized this could be a great moment for everyone — potentially, at least. So I typed up two pages of notes to get my jumbled thoughts together for a meeting on Tuesday morning with Rich and Mike's direct supervisor.

I opened the meeting by relating what had happened with Mike on Sunday. I talked about Mike's limited experience in the workplace, his family of origin, his level of personal maturity, as well as his giftedness. His gifts had placed him in a position of influence beyond his level of character development. And this quick rise to a position of authority within the church was having unintended consequences. Mike had come on staff part-time but soon moved into a full-time role with much greater responsibilities. He was performing his job well at one level, but no one was investing in him personally. In his twelve months on staff, he'd had two different bosses and little supervision. I was also aware that two other longtime staff had become concerned about his behavior in other settings as well. Mike's behavior and attitude were beyond anything I could write off to a typical twenty-five-year-old's mistake. Something was seriously out of order in his understanding of what it meant to be on staff at New Life and to represent us — regardless of his gifting.

Mike wasn't going to make it long term at New Life unless a supervisor focused on his personal development. The question was how to create safety for him in this crisis so that he could be mentored and developed. How could we help and not hurt him? To *not* address this would clearly be a serious failure on our part. We would be promising him a long-term future on our staff, a promise we could not keep if his behavior continued unchecked.

Before the meeting with Mike, I thought, *This young man is so talented. We are going to give him a painful gift that I pray he receives. But we need to offer it to him since few other workplaces will do this for him in the future.*

My recommendation was that we call Mike into the room to let him know that his behavior was unacceptable. We communicated the following: "Mike, if someone who is your superior asks you to do something on a day you are working, you do it. If you do something like this again to any person in authority at New Life, you will be fired. In another workplace, you would already have been fired."

The preparation for the meeting took me almost two days. And it took three of us on staff another hour to prepare for it. The conversation itself took less than ten minutes.

By God's grace, the story has a happy ending. Mike sincerely apologized.

Mike is still in process regarding his future at New Life. I know our commitment to him and to healthy teams and culture will likely require more conversations like this one down the line. But I trust that, as long as we at New Life dedicate the necessary time to his personal formation, he will be a great gift to many the rest of his life — regardless of where or how he serves Christ in the years to come.

As leaders, we make choices every day about how we will steward energy and resources — our own and that of the organization or team we lead. They are among the most important decisions we make.[11] There is no quick program or formula for transforming our culture or building our teams. Teachable moments often come to us when we least expect them. In addition, they often painfully intersect with our own lives and internal issues. But these transformational times are so powerful — for both our teams and our culture — that they are worth the time and energy it takes to steward them well.

One more crucial but often overlooked subject, however, must be carefully considered in our culture and team building — the quality of the marriages and singleness on our core team.

The Quality of People's Marriages and Singleness Is Foundational

If you work in a field such as education, local government, business, or health care, the state of your marriage or singleness is no one's concern. In some places, it is in fact against the law to even inquire about such matters. But the standards are higher for those of us who work within the church and for Christian organi-

EMOTIONALLY HEALTHY CULTURE
AND TEAM BUILDING
1. Work and personal formation are inseparable.
2. Elephants in the room are acknowledged and confronted.
3. Time and energy are invested.
4. **The quality of people's marriages and singleness is foundational.**

zations. We expect a certain level of moral conduct and stability. Behaviors such as extramarital affairs, using pornography, and sleeping around are unacceptable.

We would all say we believe in healthy marriages and singleness. And some of us might even ask our team members, "Is everything okay at home? In your personal life?" But I'd also guess that most of us always secretly hope that all we get in response is a quick "yes" because we have other important ministry work to do.

However, if we really believe that Christian marriage and singleness are meant to be living signs and wonders of God's love for the world, and that this aspect of our lives is the loudest gospel message we preach, we need to engage those we lead about this area of their marriage or singleness.[12] At New Life, one of the first questions we encourage leaders to ask their team members in one-on-one supervisory meetings is about their marriage or singleness. It offers an X-ray into the health and quality of their lives and leadership. We have found this to be true in every conceivable ministry context for the last twenty years.

For years, our personnel committee at New Life had been looking for a director to lead our Community Development Corporation, our ministry to the poor and marginalized in our community. We needed a leader with a strong business background who was committed to living in our community. At the same time, we needed this person to embody our values at New Life. We felt Redd, a member of New Life, was an ideal candidate. So we began discussions with him, asking if he would consider leaving his job as a construction project manager, take a one-third cut in pay, and join our staff.

During that process, the time came for me to talk with Redd and his wife, Aya. I drove to their apartment one Tuesday evening and took the stairs up to their fourth-floor apartment. One of the things I was eager to hear about was Aya's thoughts and feelings about the reduction in salary and what it would mean for her if Redd switched from construction to church work. Toward the end of the evening, it became increasingly clear that Redd would accept the job.

At that point, I asked him if he knew about "the-spouse-must-feel-loved" requirement for married leaders.

"No, I don't," he replied.

"Redd, it is not easy to get fired from New Life," I said, "but there is one reason you can count on for us letting you go. If you are working too much and Aya does not feel loved by you, we will fire you."

Aya smiled.

Redd looked at me in disbelief.

"I am not kidding," I continued. "We will fire you. The demands that will come your way will be overwhelming. We want our staff to lead out of marriages that overflow with the love of Christ. We will be routinely asking you, and Aya, if serving in ministry leadership is supporting or hurting your marriage."

Redd laughed. Then he answered with a smile on his face, "Well, this sure is different from the business world." Redd later told me that he received our conversation as God's reminder to him: *Redd, you are to love your wife and then your work—in that order.*

Redd and Aya loved the concern we demonstrated for their relationship, and Redd accepted the position.

That conversation flowed out of a conviction: Emotionally healthy organizations are inseparable from the level of health experienced by leaders in their marriage or singleness. The apostle Paul knew it was impossible for leaders to create a healthy church if their own home life was not in order (1 Timothy 3:8). For that reason, he made it one of the prerequisites for serving as an elder. I ask our single leaders whether they are protecting time to be in close community with a few people with whom they do life with the same intentionality and seriousness that I ask a married person, "Are you protecting time with your spouse?" I take an interest in their hobbies, delights, and interests outside work in the same way that I take an interest in the activities of a married person. I protect their Sabbath and work rhythms with the same intensity that I protect the Sabbath and work rhythms of those with families.

When Geri and I allowed God to do an extreme makeover of our marriage in 1996, we didn't set out to change New Life Fellowship Church. We simply did our best to learn new ways to negotiate differences, assert our preferences, manage our reactivity, differentiate with empathy, bond, and speak truthfully and respectfully — to name a few. God led us to break a number of negative legacies from our families of origin. We became different people with ourselves, with each other, and with God. Within a few years, this powerful change in our marriage began to overflow to our entire church. How could it not? God changed not only our relationship and behaviors with one another but our interior lives as well. It was inevitable that this transformation would then spill over into the rest of our relationships and the wider church culture.

When I teach this material to leaders, I often get comments like this one: "Pete, I know I need to ask questions about people's ministry tasks and how they are progressing with their work. But how am I supposed to ask about their personal and spiritual development?" My response is, "How can you *not* ask? There is no better way for you to serve God's purpose of transformation of your people. How can your team bring to others a life with Jesus they do not possess? Jesus himself knew he could not skip over this slow work of discipleship with the Twelve."

Ask the Four Questions

Use the following questions (based on the four inner life foundations from part 1) to reflect on your experiences and the state of your leadership when it comes to emotionally healthy culture and team building. You may also adapt or develop these questions as a starting place to begin discussing culture and team building with your team.

- **Face Your Shadow.** How am I growing in my awareness of my shadow so that it does not adversely affect the culture I am seeking to build with my team? When a recent situation with my team triggered an old automatic response, what might have calmed me down to respond in a more mature, thoughtful way? Who are the people with whom I am in relationship who can serve as mirrors for these blind spots and vulnerabilities?

- **Lead Out of Your Marriage or Singleness.** How well am I taking into account and nurturing my marriage or singleness as a model for building a healthy team and culture? What, specifically, am I doing to set a boundary between the demands of developing a healthy culture and my marriage/singleness? If married: What would my spouse say is the greatest challenge to our marriage? If single: What would my closest friends say is the greatest challenge to my singleness? What would I say?

- **Slow Down for Loving Union.** To what degree does my "being with Jesus" sustain my "doing for Jesus" in this challenging work of culture and team building? A little, a lot, not at all? What are the spiritual practices most helpful to me right now to help me slow down? What resources am I drawing from to grow in my personal relationship with Jesus that I can also bring to my team? What adjustments might God be inviting me to make so I can slow down, and help my team slow down, for loving union with him?

- **Practice Sabbath Delight.** How am I practicing my work-Sabbath rhythm in ways that model what we are seeking to build with other people? What do I find most replenishing and delightful during Sabbath, and how can that add value to our team? What is the greatest challenge I have to overcome to enter true Sabbath delight, and how is that similar to struggles others on my team experience? How can I build more play into my life to balance my work, and how can I help each member of my team to do the same?

I trust this chapter has given you a glimpse into the power of intentionally creating an emotionally healthy culture and team. Make no mistake about it. When we enter into this kind of leadership, we are a lot like Abraham, leaving "our country, our people, and our father's household and going to a land" that is unfamiliar (see Genesis 12:1). In other words, it is new territory that will feel uncomfortable, at least initially. But one thing is sure: you will meet God in unexpected ways and unleash a new beginning that will bless you, your team, your ministry, and the world you seek to serve for Christ.

Understanding Your Culture and Team-Building Assessment

If you took the culture and team-building assessment on pages 214–15, here are some observations to help you reflect on your responses.

If you scored mostly ones and twos, you probably have not given much thought to, or perhaps received much training in, building healthy cultures and teams. Becoming aware of how what you do — and don't do — affects the people around you is an important competency for leadership. You might take a first step by listing the desires and values you have for your team. Consider inviting a trusted mentor or team member into your process. Read carefully the four characteristics of healthy culture and team building, picking one to focus on and apply in your own setting.

If you scored mostly twos and threes, you are somewhat engaged in healthy culture and team building. I encourage you to take a few hours to prayerfully reflect — alone or with others — on your team and culture. Make a list of the characteristics that presently describe your culture and team. Then make a second list, noting the values, desires, and dreams God has given you for your team. Identify three to five specific steps you can take over the next three to nine months to bridge the gap between your current culture and team, and the culture and team you envision.

If you scored mostly fours and fives, congratulations! You are building a healthy culture and team. Reflect on specific examples and ideas from this chapter that would increase your effectiveness — or perhaps stir new ideas of your own. Consider clearly writing your values and vision to share with your team. And lead a discussion with them on how you can better implement your vision and values for the next season of your work together. You are also well positioned to multiply yourself by mentoring others on how to lead and develop their own teams.

Chapter 8

Power and Wise Boundaries

The most painful lessons I've learned in thirty-five years of Christian leadership have involved the exercise of power and having wise boundaries. Navigating the issue of power is a true test of both character and leadership. We're more than willing to talk about the abuse of power when news breaks about a scandal in someone else's life, but the minefields surrounding the use of power are rarely acknowledged, much less openly discussed, in Christian circles. This silence leads to consequences and significant harm, with the potential not only to wipe out a lifetime of good work but to undermine our ministries for years to come. The good news is that no matter where we are in our leadership journey, we can *learn* to steward power well and to set wise boundaries.

Who Made You the Boss of Me?

When we started New Life, we were mostly young families in our twenties and thirties who had a vision to live in community based on the Acts 2 model of the early church. Many of us intentionally moved to live in the same neighborhood. Our children played together. We shared our lives, our homes, and, at times, our finances. I was the senior pastor of the church, but I didn't necessarily see myself that way. I felt that all of us were simply friends and coworkers in Christ's kingdom, caught up together with God in an exciting adventure.

None of this was a problem for the first few years, but then a few fractures began to emerge. Among them was a disagreement I had with

Felipe, a key leader on our team. He and I began to clash over the future direction and ministry strategy of the church. Felipe had a developing vision for small house churches whose members would bear prophetic witness to Christ through their life together. I was mesmerized every time he spoke about it. However, I was also developing my own vision for the church. I wanted to build on small groups, but my focus was on making our Sunday celebrations central to our strategy by providing a safe place for both seekers and believers. Felipe and I shared the same goal—extending the kingdom—but we had two very different visions and strategies for how best to achieve it.

"Who gave you the right to decide on the direction of New Life?" Felipe asked during a staff meeting one week. "We have all given our lives for this." I was taken aback and didn't know what to say.

"We are all different parts of the body, equal in worth and contribution," he continued. "We're a family in this. Who gave you the right to unilaterally make this decision for us?"

"I'm the senior pastor," I uttered halfheartedly. It felt strange to say it.

"I can't believe it!" he said in disbelief. "In all our years, you have never pulled the authority card. And you pull it out *now*? Wow." He stared at the floor, unable to look at me. "And that is really sad."

I had nothing to say. He was right. My leadership was unclear and confusing.

In the end, we parted ways and Felipe went on to establish a vibrant house church. New Life bought a building and blossomed. The damage this did to our relationship, however, took years to heal. I considered it a very unfortunate personal disagreement but didn't think much about the theological or leadership issues raised by these tensions and the breakdown in our relationship.

Ten years later, the issue of power resurfaced, and I found myself at another crossroads. Geri and I were particularly close to several families in the church. We watched movies and went on vacations together, and all of the families had someone who served in leadership. Most were volunteers, but two were paid staff. Like Felipe, they were godly people who embodied our New Life values and culture. I deeply respected and loved them.

The church had grown slowly and steadily over the years. An elder board, an executive team, a staff team, and a personnel committee now added new layers of formal structure that went beyond this original group of families. There were others who now functioned in significant positions of influence. Because of this, my conversations with these friends changed, and I began to withhold sensitive information that seemed inappropriate to share in our informal gatherings, talking over a Sunday afternoon barbecue, or spending time on vacation together.

My friends began to notice that I was holding back, and I sensed the slowly rising strain in our relationships as I appeared more distant and withholding. When I engaged in some serious discussions with our personnel committee about the long-term staffing needs of New Life, I knew I was in trouble. My relationships with friends *who were also paid staff* were complicated and interlocked on so many levels that I found it impossible to be objective about their gifts and skills and whether or not they were still a good fit for their roles on staff. Others on the committee knew this was a highly sensitive topic and said little. I felt more conflicted and entangled than I could articulate.

I considered resigning, realizing I was in the terrible dilemma of being both boss and friend. I thought we had an unspoken understanding that, if you were a friend and you were on paid staff, your position was yours for life—unless, of course, a moral or ethical issue emerged. At the same time, as the senior leader of New Life, I was accountable to the church board to steward our resources well, which included hiring staff who could effectively advance our mission in their given roles.

In the end, after many a sleepless night, I chose to violate that unspoken rule and made some difficult decisions, removing friends from their existing staff roles. While I believe good eventually came from it, I didn't handle the process well. I was muddled and anxious. Looking back, I am embarrassed by how we did this. My understanding of how power affects relationships and the need for wise boundaries was woefully inadequate. I was trying to be both a good friend and a good "boss," but I was neither.

As a church, we lost trust—not just with the staffers who lost their jobs but within our close circle of friends. I lost several relationships I treasured and had spent years building. To this day, I consider this one of my greatest failures in twenty-six years as senior pastor of New Life. Even so, God used it to teach me more than I wanted to learn—about the nature of church and community, the proper exercise of power, and the importance of setting wise boundaries.

I know I'm not alone when it comes to making these kinds of mistakes. Almost every church, nonprofit organization, team, and Christian community I know bears deep scars and hurt due to a failure to steward power and set wise boundaries. Churches are fragile, complex, confusing systems. We are a community, a family, a nonprofit mission. Yet there is also a "business" side in that we steward resources (we hire and fire, comply with legal requirements, manage budgets, define success, etc.). What follows is far from a comprehensive treatment of the issue of power in leadership. I won't address every scenario you might encounter. But I hope to offer a few insights, some gold nuggets from experience, that I wish I had understood years ago. My sincere hope is that you will ponder them carefully as you seek to navigate this minefield with greater care and integrity than I did—not only for your sake, but for the sake of your family, friends, ministry, and the glory of Christ in the world.

Let's begin by defining "Christian" power.

What Is "Christian" Power?

The most elegantly simple description of power I know is this: *power is the capacity to influence.* As author Richard Gula writes:

> [Power] is what enables us to make things happen or not. In this sense, everyone has power, but we do not all have it to the same degree. Power as influence is always relative to our resources. One of the most important self-examinations we can do is to name our sources of power, for we are most at risk of ethical misconduct when we minimize or ignore our power.[1]

Part of what I find compelling about Gula's statement is its implication that virtually everyone is a leader. To a greater or lesser degree, everyone has influence, which means that everyone is power-full. And we all use that power—well or poorly, for good or for ill.

The problem is that so few leaders have an awareness of, let alone reflect on, the nature of their God-given power. As a result, some carelessly wield their power with aggression, exploiting it to their own advantage. They function as the proverbial bull in the china shop, careless and self-serving with their power. They are unaware of, or perhaps worse, unconcerned about, the impact they have on others or how others perceive them. Scripture offers us plentiful examples of such leaders, including King Saul and King Solomon.

On the opposite extreme are the leaders who shrink back from exercising their power. Their reluctance to assert themselves leaves the door open to the wrong people stepping into the power vacuum — which causes all sorts of chaos. It is not uncommon for these ministries or churches with weak leaders to fit the following description of God's people from the book of Judges: "In those days Israel had no king; everyone did as they saw fit (Judges 21:25).[2]

In my years of teaching and mentoring leaders, I've seen just as much damage result from this second group, the leaders who are ambivalent and uncomfortable with their power. Perhaps it's because I identify with them. For these leaders, it somehow feels wrong and unbiblical to grab the reins and take charge because power implies privilege, a higher social status, being above others. The thought of having *power* as a leader sounds detached and cold. So they prefer to deny or minimize the very real power they have. Some may even feel unworthy or afraid to exercise power, especially in God's name. As a result, they live in a fog, feeling powerless internally, yet responsible to exercise power to lead others.

So let me say it again. We *all* have power. Pastors, staff leaders, ministry directors, board members, small group leaders, long-term members, donors, parents, musicians in the worship band — we all have power. The problem is that we do not understand where that power comes from, nor do we understand how to exercise it responsibly. Our understanding of power is incomplete and narrow. This is true for leaders who are power hungry and for those who avoid exercising power. To get a feel for this in day-to-day leadership, consider the following scenarios:

- "I just preach every other weekend," says Henry, a teaching pastor at a large church. "I'm not running the church or even on the leadership team. There are others who do that." Henry remains unaware that his public role in the church and his communication gifts give him great power.

- "I am not voting for this new initiative," states Juanita, a church board member, at a congregational meeting. "But I am just one voice. Everyone needs to decide what they think is best." The discussion ends and the congregational vote is a no. Juanita's statement reveals a lack of awareness about the power church members project onto her because of her teaching abilities and her long history in the church.

- Dan has been the youth pastor at First Church for the last fifteen years. He grew up in the church, and seven members of his extended family are involved in various aspects of the ministry. The youth group is small but very tight-knit under Dan's leadership. Because it's hard for Dan to trust other people, he doesn't have other adults working with him. He is skillful in orchestrating activities and retreats, but weak in developing his students' spiritually. The ministry is stuck. His supervisor, the executive pastor, has tried to talk with Dan about it, but Dan is easily irritated and defensive. More than once he has abruptly withdrawn from the conversation and walked out of the room. He has twice threatened to quit when the lead pastor asked questions about the ministry. The church board feels powerless; if Dan resigns, they fear his extended family as well as several families of the students in his group might leave the church. While Dan does not consider himself unteachable or overly sensitive, he believes the youth ministry rightly revolves around him because he has invested fifteen years of his adult life to build it.

- "I'm married to the pastor, but I just speak my mind like everyone else," the pastor's spouse said. "I'm no different than any other member of the congregation." But the spouse of a senior leader is in fact *very* different than every other member of the congregation — especially when that leader is the lead pastor. The spouse is "one flesh" with the pastor. He or she sleeps with the boss! Together, they are a team of two through life—even if the spouse appears to be one volunteer among many. This gives the spouse enormous power by virtue of marriage. In some churches, the power of spouses behind the scenes is among the largest elephants in the room.

- Pastor James is an outstanding preacher, an excellent vision caster, and an effective fund-raiser. His church continues to grow steadily. James has set strong expectations for members—arrive at services early, attend midweek prayer and Bible study, tithe faithfully, and serve in at least one ministry of the church. James and his senior staff function as the church board, making all decisions about finances, property purchases, and personnel. James preaches regularly on giving, spiritual authority, and excellence as part of his teaching rhythm. The congregation admires James as a man of God, and one of their top priorities is to serve him and his family well. Pastor James is a good man with many fine qualities. There's no scandal here, and he loves his church. The problem is that he is unaware of how much power he actually wields and how it influences the congregation. People don't ask questions. An awkward silence prevails around finances in the church. James receives limited counsel, while the gifts of many lie dormant. James is unaware of how much his culture and his family of origin inform the way he leads.

In each of these scenarios, the leaders do not understand the multilayered nature of their power as it relates to their leadership. As a result, their ministries are curtailed and the communities they serve are hurt.

In order to really understand how we exercise power and influence others, we need to be clear about where that power comes from. Every leader needs to be aware of the six primary sources of power.[3]

Positional power. This is the easiest type of power to recognize because it's the power that comes with a position or a title. We are chosen for a specific role, such as pastor, director, board member, small group leader, chief financial officer, or worship pastor. This position provides a platform for influencing others.

Personal power. Personal power is anchored in what we do with the unique person God made us to be. It comes from such things as our gifts, personality, knowledge, education, and competencies. We acquire some of these assets at birth and others as a result of either privilege (such as advanced education) or through unique opportunities (having mentors, new experiences, open doors to learn, etc.).

"God factor" power. This refers to the sacred weight we carry when our role formally places us in a position to represent God. When we represent God and the church, people look differently at what we say and do. We symbolize something that goes far beyond us as individuals. In this sense, Christian leaders have greater power than politicians or Fortune-500 CEOs, more power than social workers and teachers, more power than any number of other helping professions. We represent God's presence, even if we feel inadequate to the task. We serve people in the name of Jesus.[4] People trust us.

Projected power. Projected power is the power other people unconsciously project onto us. The psychological term for this dynamic is "transference." It's what happens when others project unto us their own unmet needs and unresolved issues in hopes that we will meet those needs and help them resolve those issues. If we speak about and for God, we can expect that some people will project onto us their unresolved feelings of dependency, hostility, romantic desires, or anger from past authority figures or other significant relationships.[5] As a general principle, the more distressed a person is, the more invisible power he or she is likely to project onto a leader.

Relational power. Our power grows as people entrust to us their fears and secrets. Knowing things about people that few others know is an expression of intimacy. When we counsel someone, we prayerfully listen to painful experiences or unimaginable evils and hold them in confidence. We stand with people in their most vulnerable moments — as they face deaths (suicide, loss of family members, death of a marriage through divorce), transitions (births, graduations, retirements), tragedies (abuse, accidents, betrayals), and crises of faith (dark nights of the soul, doubts, broken relationships). Each time we are entrusted with one of these moments, it adds to our power.

Cultural power. Cultural power might include everything from age and race to gender and ethnicity. For example, Asian and African cultures grant power to their elders based solely on their age. In some cases, the eldest person remains leader of a group until he or she dies or grants that power to a younger person. Men carry more power than women in most countries of the world. Sadly, the color of one's skin and/or ethnicity conveys a greater or lesser amount of power, depending on the geographic, social, or historical context. Each of these factors impacts a leader's ability to influence others.

Whatever the source and to whatever degree we have power, or influence, we have it as a divine gift. And the more power we have, the greater impact we exert—intentional or not—on those around us. Our critical need is to become aware of *how* we exercise that power. We must learn what it means to use our power and then how to establish wise and healthy boundaries in our relationships with others.

How Healthy Is Your Use of Power and Wise Boundaries?

Use the list of statements that follow to briefly assess your use of power and wise boundaries. Next to each statement, write down the number that best describes your response. Use the following scale:

5 = Always true of me
4 = Frequently true of me
3 = Occasionally true of me
2 = Rarely true of me
1 = Never true of me

_____ 1. I am very aware of my God-given power and the influence I have on those around me.

_____ 2. I consistently monitor how my shadow impacts my use, or lack of use, of power.

_____ 3. I build safeguards into my dual relationships, seeking to be a friend with friends, pastor to parishioners, mentor to mentorees, and a supervisor to volunteers/employees.

_____ 4. I am sensitive to the impact that culture, ethnicity, gender, and age have on how I use power and how others perceive me.

_____ 5. I have reflected on how power was used in my family of origin and understand how that impacts both my use of, and response to, power in the present.

_____ 6. I take responsibility to carefully clarify roles and boundaries on our team, keeping them as clear as possible.

> _____ 7. I am attentive to how members of my team use, or neglect to use, their power and influence.
>
> _____ 8. I feel confident in helping others understand their use of power, offering them wise counsel and cautions on how to exercise their power wisely.
>
> _____ 9. I resist the temptation to take advantage of entitlements (perks and benefits) that are offered to me because of my leadership role.
>
> _____ 10. I seek wise counsel and engage in honest conversations with others before allowing members of the same family, or close friends, to serve together in leadership.
>
> Take a moment to briefly review your responses. What stands out most to you? At the end of the chapter (page 268) are some general observations to help you better understand the current level of health in your use of power and wise boundaries.

Characteristics of Emotionally Healthy Power and Wise Boundaries

A good test of a person's character is how they deal with adversity. But the best test of a _leader's_ character is how they deal with power. If we want to use our power well as Christ-followers, there are three things we must do:

- Identify and inventory our power
- Carefully steward our power so it comes _under_ others
- Acknowledge and monitor dual relationships

Let's take a careful look at each of these three characteristics.

We Identify and Inventory Our Power

Emotionally healthy leaders are keenly aware of the sources of their power as well as the nuances in their use of power. One of the best things we can do to develop this awareness is to identify and inventory the power God has granted us. And by "inventory," I mean we not only think about our power, we ponder it and own it. Before reading through the following list, I encourage you to grab a pad of paper or a journal. Then write down your responses as you consider the questions for each of the six categories of power. (If you find it helpful to have an example, see "Power Inventory Examples" on the following page.)

Positional power. What formal positions of influence has God entrusted to you? For example, small group leader, pastor, spouse of a leader, executive director, community organizer, CEO or CFO, greeter, teacher, board member, team leader, parent, etc. What privileges and opportunities does this position open up for you?

Personal power. What unique gifts, skills, and assets has God given you? Consider your experiences, education, competencies, natural talents, or other abilities. How has God uniquely crafted your personality in a way that contributes to your ability to influence people? Think of your introversion or extroversion, your ability to attend to details, to cast an expansive vision, etc.

"God factor" power. In what way(s) do you carry "sacred weight" with those in your church, workplace, family, and among friends? To what degree do people look to you for spiritual wisdom and counsel? Who are the people, inside and outside the church, who might perceive you as a spiritual authority who speaks for God?[6]

Projected power. What individuals and/or groups might attribute power and authority to you because of what you represent as a leader? How much of that attribution of power to you comes out of their unmet or unresolved needs? Who might idealize you from afar, attributing to you a greater wisdom, holiness, or skill than you actually possess?

Relational power. With whom, and for how long, have you built a relational history (people you have pastored, served, mentored, or walked with through life's challenges and transitions)? Consider individuals, families, and groups. How does their vulnerability and trust in you influence their perceptions and expectations of you?

Cultural power. How might your age, race, gender, ethnicity, or other cultural factors serve as a source of power or influence for you? How might this change from one group to the next in your setting (e.g., different cultures and ethnicities may treat you differently, young people may not attribute power to you, older people because of your position may respect and heed your words without question)?

Before continuing, take a few moments to read back over your responses. What stands out to you about the nature of your power and the people with whom you have influence? For a few minutes, invite God to speak to you about your inventory. Thank him for giving you the opportunity to influence others in his name. Ask for grace to stew-ard your power well so that your life and leadership might be a gift to those you serve, enabling them "to come more fully alive and flourish."[7]

Power Inventory Examples

Lead Pastor

Positional power

- As chief spiritual leader, I set direction and vision for the ministry.
- I speak for God. People sit and listen to me teach in his name for twenty-five to forty-five minutes each week.
- I have the strongest voice in determining distribution of the church's resources (finances, hiring and firing, staff and volunteers, use of facilities, determining priorities of people's time, etc.).

Personal power

- I am a gifted communicator and have the ability to move and influence people by what I say and how I say it.
- I am more familiar with the Word of God than most, with insights based on years of study as well as ministry experience.
- My gifts and abilities enable me to lead and manage the many different parts of a church, delegating responsibilities in order to sustain and build community.

"God factor" power

- When I speak and teach, people are listening for God to speak to them through me.
- People trust me as a pastor and representative of Jesus Christ, and they often tell me things about their lives few others know.
- People, some of whom are strangers, invite me into significant transition moments in their lives — deaths, life-threatening illnesses, births, weddings, graduations, and retirements.

Projected power

- Most weeks, people see my best gifts and qualities, but not my faults. Some idealize who I am beyond what is true. Others may be jealous of me or even despise me.
- People who did not experience a positive relationship with their earthly parent(s) look to me for the affirmation and love they never received growing up.
- Because of my personality, gifts, position, and apparent success as a leader, some people receive everything I say and do uncritically—they would never question me.

Relational power

- As a result of my years at the church, long-term members are deeply loyal and overlook my foolish mistakes and imperfections.
- Every time I offer pastoral care at key transitional moments in people's lives, their love for me and loyalty to me increase.
- Every time I serve as a pastor or teach and enable people to meet God, I gain a little more power and trust from those I serve.

Cultural power

- People from cultures heavily influenced by Confucianism honor my positional authority (and age, if they are younger), respectfully deferring to me.
- Immigrants in our church attribute to me additional power as an American and as a pastor who has influence in the community.
- African Americans, out of their history, treat me with a unique respect. Many Latinos, out of their deep roots in Roman Catholicism, and others from the Eastern Orthodox tradition view me with profound respect— almost like a priest—with access to the mysteries of God.

Small Group Leader

Positional power

- I set the agenda and parameters for small group meetings.
- I lead the discussion, directing it as I determine.
- I choose to delegate, or not to delegate, responsibilities to others.

Personal power
- Because I prepare and study in advance, I often know more about the topic we are studying than the rest of the group.
- People know I've been trained to be a leader by the church and can answer basic concerns they have.
- People trust my ability to integrate the different elements of a meeting into a meaningful spiritual experience.

Spiritual power
- Some people who are new Christians see me as a leader who speaks for God.
- People view me as a representative of the larger church.
- People trust I can shepherd and love them in Jesus' name, helping them with their basic spiritual needs and problems.

Projected power
- People look at my best gifts and qualities as a leader, not my faults. As a result, some idealize me.
- A few people view me as an authority figure and attribute to me wisdom and abilities I may or may not possess.
- People sometimes have unrealistic expectations of what I can offer because of my position as their small group leader.

Relational power
- Since people know I am good friends with the pastor and his/her spouse, people come to me for information about the ministry that exceeds my responsibilities and position as a small group leader.
- Because I attended a Christian college and took Bible courses, some people in my group look to me to answer difficult questions when they arise.
- People in our small group know that several years ago I attended a large and prominent church. Some assume I have more wisdom about leadership and running an effective small group than I actually do.

Cultural power
- Because of my education and my profession as a medical doctor, some group members assume I also have biblical and leadership expertise.

- Being a man offers me advantages and opportunities to lead that are not given to women, since some in our congregation are unsure about or uncomfortable with women in leadership positions in the church.
- The fact that I grew up in and have lived in our community for the last thirty-five years gives me credibility in our young, highly mobile, transient church.

We Carefully Steward Our Power so It Comes under Others

Ten years ago, I found myself being courted by a few Christian publishers. My literary agent at the time, a wise woman with over thirty years of experience in publishing, set up meetings in three different cities for me to meet with the various publishers and consider their contract offers. In each place, I was treated very kindly, almost like a potential star (it was nice while it lasted!). As the son of an Italian baker, it was also a strange experience for me, uncomfortable and intoxicating at the same time.

On the last day of our trip, I asked my agent a question: "You have been in this publishing business for a long time. You have represented some of the most popular Christian authors. What would you say is the greatest temptation I should be aware of?"

"That's easy," she said. "I can sum it up in one word: *entitlement*. Some authors have a lot of influence after they become well known. They change. They walk into a room, acting as if everyone owes them and the world revolves around them. It makes them miserable to work with."

I never forgot that conversation. I resolved from that point forward to treat every publishing door God opened for me as a sheer miracle of grace.

Entitled leaders act as if the world revolves around them. Their thinking goes something like this: *I've been blessed. I have gifts and influence. I have worked hard and deserve to be treated well.* This is what I refer to as "power over" others leadership.

The opposite of an entitled leader is a grateful leader. Grateful leaders continually marvel at all they have received from God. But as a leader's sense of gratitude shrinks, their sense of entitlement grows in equal measure.

While the world practices a "power over" strategy characterized by dominance and win-lose competitiveness, Jesus taught a "power under" strategy characterized by humility and sacrificial service. In the world, says Jesus, leaders throw their weight around, "[but it is] not so with you.... Whoever wants to become great among you must be your servant" (Mark 10:42–43). While Jesus is the invisible God who holds all things together — Almighty, eternal, immortal, and infinite — he became human, temporal, mortal, and finite. Jesus demonstrated his power not by force or control, but by choosing to come *under* us, humbly washing feet and dying for our sins. He carefully stewarded his power: "[Christ Jesus,] who, being in very nature God, did not consider equality with God something to be used to his own advantage; rather, he made himself nothing by taking the very nature of a servant" (Philippians 2:6–7).

The church is not a corporation. We are not corporate executives who make tough decisions to "get the job done." We are not CEOs implementing best practices in order to expand our impact or market penetration. The church is not our family business. Instead, we are the body of Christ, the temple of God, the new family of Jesus, the bride of Christ. As leaders, we are stewards of delegated power gifted to us for a short time by God. The choice of the word *steward* is important. The church belongs to God, not to us. We must never forget that the power we exercise belongs to him. Our power is *given* to us to come under people for their good, for them to flourish, not so we will look good.

The failure to come under people with our power can take many different forms. Consider the story of Patrick and Ken. Two years ago, Patrick and his wife moved from New York to West Virginia so Patrick could take a position as a youth pastor in a rural church. Before the move, he had served as a volunteer youth ministry leader at First Assembly, a church in their home state of New York. During a recent trip back to New York to visit family, Patrick contacted Ken, First Assembly's senior pastor, and asked if they could have lunch. Ken was initially reluctant because he and Patrick hadn't parted on the best of terms, but he was also curious and agreed to meet.

When they met, Patrick surprised Ken by asking forgiveness for his lack of submission to authority and for his rebellious spirit when he served as First Assembly's youth leader. He described how the senior pastor at their church in West Virginia had confronted him and helped him see his blind spots and arrogance.

Ken couldn't believe what he was hearing. He'd been relieved when Patrick moved to West Virginia because he was so difficult to manage. Patrick's inappropriate remarks and behaviors had caused Ken many a sleepless night, but he had never said anything. Why? Ken hates conflict and relational messes. But Patrick was now clearly a different person — broken, humble, and repentant. A few days later in a conversation with me, Ken wondered if he should now take Patrick out to lunch and ask his forgiveness for never confronting these issues when Patrick was under his leadership!

Note that Ken failed to exercise his God-given power to come under Patrick — to love him well. He failed to serve Patrick, allowing his aversion to conflict to cause him to abdicate his power and authority. I advised Ken that I thought it would be good for his soul to take Patrick out for lunch in order to ask his forgiveness.

One of the ways we know we are intentionally using our power to come under people is when we do something difficult and hard for us because it will benefit someone. This is what Ken should have done for Patrick even though it might have cost him Patrick's approval or even the relationship.

Another indicator I monitor in my own life to ensure I am using my power to come under others is to examine my heart. I watch to see if I am still grateful for the privilege to represent Jesus and have a level of influence in the lives of other people. Perhaps the best test I know for alerting me that I have strayed from a healthy use of power is when I resent people treating me like the servant I claim to be.

Ten Principles for Exercising Power and Wise Boundaries

1. **Do an honest inventory of the power God has granted you.**
   To be faithful, we need to be profoundly aware of the sources of power God has granted us. We are at risk of using power poorly if we ignore or minimize the extent of our power.

2. **Meet with a mature spiritual companion when you find yourself triggered.** You can expect unresolved family-of-origin dynamics to reassert themselves anytime you have responsibility and power. The workplace and church are key places where our triggers and hot buttons will emerge.

3. **Enlist wise counsel to monitor dual relationships.** Mentors, therapists, elders and church boards, and mature friends give us perspective and counsel. It is critical that we know our limits and defer to the discernment of others when dual relationships (e.g., employer and friend) are part of our leadership.

4. **Watch for early warning signs of danger.** People change. We change. The church changes. What works now may not work a few years from now. Have honest conversations with people when your relationship with them experiences tensions and awkwardness. Talk about the risks, drawbacks, and challenges before you.

5. **Be sensitive to cultural, ethnic, gender, and generational nuances.** The cultural and historical differences around power, authority, age, and gender are vast. Be a learner. Ask questions. Your history and experience with power is likely very different than that of other cultures, age groups, or even gender. Invite people from the different groups to share their unique perspectives with you.

6. **Release people (paid and volunteer) in a loving way.** This is one of the most difficult tasks for leaders, especially since we represent God and carry a number of different roles with people — employer, pastor, spiritual guide, mentor, etc. Be sure to get wise counsel to ensure you use your power fairly, honestly, and in a caring fashion.

7. **Remember that the burden to set boundaries and keep them clear falls on the person with greater power.** Even though a person in our ministry may manipulate a situation, the greater burden falls on us. Why? God has entrusted us with greater power.[8]

8. **Be friends with friends, a pastor to parishioners, a mentor to mentorees, and a supervisor to volunteers/employees.** Monitor and avoid dual relationships (such as, friend and employer) as much as possible. Ask yourself, "What role is primary for me in this relationship? Who am I to this person? Who is this person to me?"[9]

9. **Meditate on Jesus' life as you encounter the suffering and loneliness of leadership.** Exercising the self-discipline needed to steward your power well can be difficult and lonely work. Align

yourself with Christ by allowing extra time to read and meditate on the life and passion of Jesus.

10. **Ask God for grace to forgive your "enemies" — and yourself.** You will make mistakes and hurt people. Ask for forgiveness and reconcile whenever possible. At some point, deservedly or not, people will feel betrayed by you; you will feel betrayed by them. I have yet to meet a Christian leader who has not experienced betrayal. These wounds cut deep and often lead us to a dark night of the soul. But as we pray daily for the miracle to forgive our "enemies" (and ourselves), we may experience some of our greatest seasons of maturing and deepening as leaders.

We Acknowledge and Monitor Dual Relationships

Exercising power and setting wise boundaries in leadership can be complex, regardless of the setting. But the exercise of spiritual power, or the "God factor," in the church and in other Christian organizations introduces additional complexities. Perhaps nothing is as complex for leaders as the challenge of navigating dual relationships with family and close friendships. Consider the following story in which this was ignored, resulting in a twelve-year downward spiral in one church.

Paul, a lawyer, had been chairperson of the board in his church for over fifteen years. In that role, he effectively served as "the boss" for the lead pastor and the staff. At the same time, he was also best friends with Ben, the lead pastor. They enjoyed each other's company and routinely went to lunch and attended sporting events together.

The church was growing and all seemed to be going well until the day the board was informed that Ben had been caught kissing a woman in the church who was not his wife. Members of the board and the church felt betrayed. At that point, Paul felt compelled to assert his role as both supervisor and spiritual authority over Ben. This was what the church constitution mandated for the relationship between the board chairperson and the senior pastor, even if they hadn't previously operated that way in their friendship. Ben resented the sudden shift in their relationship as well as the intrusion and forced accountability. He resigned and he and Paul haven't spoken since.

"What happened?" I asked Paul. "You two spent so much time together. How did you miss what was happening with Ben?"

"Well," he admitted, "I really didn't miss it."

"What do you mean?" I asked.

"He flirted once in a while," Paul responded. "I saw him cross a few minor lines, but I thought, who am I to challenge him? He was sloppy in other areas too — his personal finances, even his preaching. But his gifts carried him. Even when he wasn't fully prepared when he preached, people couldn't tell the difference. But I could."

Paul looked down at his coffee, deep in thought. There was a long silence and then he said, "Actually, the person I'm most mad at is me! I didn't do my job as an elder and chairperson. We were such close friends. That's why the discipline and restoration process went so poorly. What a massive mess."

Paul found himself in a dual role — that of both friend and boss/spiritual authority. This led to blurred boundaries and confusion around their relationship that couldn't survive the sudden shift in roles the crisis required.

The Challenge of Dual Relationships

A dual relationship is when we have more than one role in someone's life. We observe this, for example, when a small group leader builds her real estate business by soliciting members of her group, when a doctor becomes a patient's golfing buddy, when a pastor hires his son to work for him. When you go to a doctor, a lawyer, a therapist, a teacher, an accountant, or a professional coach, the relationship is meant to have certain boundaries. The professional offers you a service and you pay them for it. You each have just one role in the life of the other person. You don't go on vacation together. You don't go out for dinner that evening. You don't offer them advice for their personal problems. You have a one-role relationship in which the boundary lines are relatively clear.

There is an implicit recognition of the unequal power in these relationships. They are the experts. You are the recipient of their services and expertise. The professional, for example, a doctor or lawyer, must adhere to a code of ethics and laws in order to be licensed. Therapists are not to date their clients. To do so would be a violation, an abuse of the therapist's power.[10]

I do not believe it is healthy or biblical to try to entirely eliminate dual relationships from Christian leadership. Drawing rigid professional boundaries in a church or para-church organization may well limit what God is doing. These boundaries simply need to be prudently and carefully monitored.

Paul was in a dual relationship with Ben. They were friends and, as board chair, Paul was also Ben's supervisor. They felt the tension at times but didn't have the language or relational maturity to talk about it. Paul's relationship with Ben was not equal. He was the chairperson of the board; Ben worked for the board. The board could fire Ben; Ben could not fire the board.

When we find ourselves in a dual relationship, it is important to define the boundaries around our roles. Boundaries are like fences; they help us to know where our yard ends and our neighbor's yard begins. With proper boundaries, we know what we are, and are not, responsible for. For example, in the situation with Paul and Ben, establishing wise boundaries at the beginning would have involved talking openly about their differing roles and responsibilities at the church. They could have invited other board members into the dilemma, discussing potential conflicts of interest. Perhaps Paul could have stepped down as board chair or from the board altogether. They could have discussed the implications of their dual relationship at the beginning to ensure they exercised their power wisely.

The responsibility to set a healthy boundary rests first with the leader, not with those he or she serves. Why? The leader has been given the greater power. Following through on this responsibility isn't easy. It requires self-awareness, thoughtfulness, the ability to have honest and clear conversations, and a healthy level of confidence and personal maturity. How do I know? Through my mistakes. Lots of mistakes. The following is one painful example.

For years, I allowed myself to become like a father to Joan, our former youth pastor. Geri and I invited her over for the holidays, had dinners together, and offered her lots of personal help to succeed in her job. Our girls admired and loved her. In the process, I became something of a surrogate father, pastor, and mentor all rolled into one. She was deeply loyal and grateful.

A time came, however, when things were not going so well in both her ministry and her personal life, and several members of the church board raised concerns. At that point, I needed to step in and assert myself as her supervisor. In order to remain on staff, she needed to make some significant changes in her life. At the time, I was unaware of how terribly confused our boundaries and roles had become. When I had the hard conversation with Joan about her performance, she felt hurt and betrayed.

"How could you treat me like this? How could you do this to me?" she cried.

My offer to find her another position within New Life fell on deaf ears. My betrayal of her felt too deep.

I understand why. As far as she was concerned, I was her biggest cheerleader and champion, the one older man in her life she could depend on if all else failed. I was the one who had invested years to help her grow from a position as an intern to an influential leader over a vital ministry. I was the pastor who loved her, like God, without conditions. I was not her "boss."

I was unaware of all this and sloppy with my power.

She resigned.

One of our daughters was a member of the youth group and found herself in the middle of that painful transition. She knew nothing of the board issues or the boundary violations I had allowed. She felt deeply hurt, and it took her years to recover. How many children of pastors and leaders have been needlessly hurt because of a parent's lack of wisdom in the use of power and setting wise boundaries?

It was unfair for me to have put Joan, our youth pastor, in that position. As her supervisor, I had much greater power in the relationship. I should have limited my mentoring and handed the mentoring of her to others. I also should have ensured that a serious job review and job evaluation was done for her as it was for other staff. Because I treated her like a member of my family, I allowed myself to have different expectations for her. In fact, this dilemma can be even more challenging when the dual relationship is with someone in our own family.

The Challenge of Family

Believe it or not, entire books have been written about the pros and cons of hiring family members in organizations. Some experts argue it is more productive and enriching for both the organization and families, particularly in dual-career couples. For others, favoring family members is seen as a bad thing and organizations should not tolerate this practice because of fairness and justice issues, even if it achieves their objectives.[11]

There are many wonderful examples in history and in the contemporary church of family members working well together. In Scripture we observe many family members serving together in leadership positions.

- Moses served as the senior leader, along with his siblings, Aaron and Miriam.
- Aaron and his sons served together in leadership as priests.
- David handed down leadership to his son Solomon, who handed it to his son.
- Peter led the twelve apostles while Andrew, his brother, served on his leadership team.
- Brothers John and James were both on the same apostolic team.
- Scripture implies that Peter, Andrew, James, and John were business associates in the fishing industry in Capernaum.
- Priscilla and Aquila were a married couple apparently on staff together in their church.
- James, the brother of Jesus, led the Jerusalem church, as described in the book of Acts.

In each case, these were family members tied to one another by blood. Yet they were also gifted and called by God to serve together in leadership. To be sure, we have a few hints of problems (for example, disagreements among Moses, Aaron, and Miriam, also with David and his sons), but we don't know very much beyond that.

On the other hand, we also have tragic examples of families and churches that were destroyed when one family had too much power.[12] Some churches and organizations have had such bad experiences with multiple family members on staff that they now forbid it. Yet even though significant dangers and challenges exist in having family members serving together in leadership, it's my belief that Scripture clearly leaves the door open for this. If we allow this, we must work to protect everyone involved by openly discussing issues of power and dual relationships and establishing boundaries and checks and balances. A mature, disciplined, differentiated leadership will need to monitor the impact family members have on the health of the larger body to ensure that no lines get crossed that could be interpreted as favoritism or nepotism.

Before Rich became lead pastor at New Life, we wanted to hire his wife, Rosie, as the director of our children's ministry. She was the most qualified person for the job, but the board openly talked about the potential risks. If things didn't work out with Rosie, we could lose both her and Rich. That was no small loss since Rich had begun the process to assume my role. We discussed that risk with the board and with Rich and Rosie. Eventually the elders, as ultimate custodians of our culture and values, decided Rosie would report to the director of pastoral ministry, who would meet with the head elder once a year to report on her performance. It was understood the head elder would back the pastoral ministry director if he concluded at any point that she was no longer the right fit for the children's ministry director position. We hired her, believing we had the margin, capacity, and maturity to navigate that particular complexity.

When family members are able to serve in leadership and it works well, it is amazing. When it doesn't work well, it is very bad and difficult to unravel. So, like any decision, it must be carefully discerned and discussed.

The Challenge of Close Friendships

Let me repeat this: I do not believe it is healthy or biblical to try to eliminate dual relationships from Christian leadership. This applies not only to family members but also to close friendships. These too need to be prudently handled and supervised. Navigating dual relationships in close friendships has been one of the painful blind spots in my leadership over the years. Sadly, I am not alone in this. Too many of us

routinely violate appropriate and necessary boundaries in close friendships and then find ourselves deeply entangled in a painful situation.

Friendships work best among equal peers with equal power. This balance is compromised when one person functions in a position of spiritual
leadership or supervision of the other. Ethics scholar Martha Ellen Stortz
has written an excellent description of the core qualities of friendship and
how these conflict with Christian ministry and leadership.[13] In what follows, I've summarized a few of the qualities of friendship she identifies:

Choice. Friends choose each other. This means they *don't choose*
other people; they exclude them. As leaders in a community, when we
exclude people, we risk taking sides and inadvertently defining who is
"in" while others are "out." In the early years of our church, my executive assistant often commented on what she described as my favoritism
toward my inner circle of friends. She said that I treated them differently. I dismissed her observations at the time, but she was right. Our
friends have more access to us than other people. And this gives them
greater influence than most other people with whom we serve.

Equality. Friends are equal in power and status. As senior leader, I
had doors opened to me that others in my friendship circle did not—
from vacation opportunities from donors to growth opportunities along
with the authority to hire and fire. As lead pastor, I could also open
opportunities for my inner circle of friends at New Life that they could
not open for me. Because of my particular mix of positional and personal power, all things were not equal in my friendships with those who
were on staff. This inequality is one of the reasons dual relationship
friendships may become confusing and problematic.

Reciprocity. Friends give and receive equally. I attempted to maintain reciprocity in my friendships, but it was sometimes impossible.
Because the friends in our inner circle had served with me through the
challenges and stresses of leadership, a few of them wanted to pastor
their pastor, inviting me to let down my guard and share anything I
wanted without holding back. The problem was that the difficult issues
the board and I were discussing at the time, for example, weren't appropriate to share in a coffee chat at the local diner. In fact, they weren't
appropriate to share with anyone who was not on the board. Friends

give and receive equally, but I was intentionally holding back from my end. This created a larger and larger gap over time.

Knowledge. Friends invite truthful self-disclosure. This especially applied to those for whom I was both pastor and friend. There were times when I wanted to do the same with them. But all things were not equal. Because of my positional power, my words carried extra weight. To share as openly and truthfully as some in our inner circle wanted me to do would have been imprudent and inappropriate. Had I critiqued them in the way they critiqued me, they would have been crushed. I remember, for example, receiving a lengthy, exhaustive critique of a spiritual formation retreat I had led in which a number of my "close friends" participated, an evaluation that did not include the "things that went well" category. We don't have the luxury of doing that to people who serve under us when we have more power than they do. Otherwise, we do more damage than good. When we as leaders give critique, our words need to be chosen carefully, sandwiched with positive affirmation, and given in a safe environment that protects people's dignity.

I offer you these four characteristics of friendship as a framework to help you determine whether your dual relationships with friends meet these particular standards of friendship.

Does all of this mean that I am opposed to senior leaders having close friends in their church? Absolutely not. But I will say that after more than two decades of ministry, I've seen many tragic endings. Only a few leaders are sufficiently self-aware and skilled enough to navigate the dangers wisely and well. I can testify that it *is* possible to do this, and I believe my relationship with Andrew, a faithful member of New Life, illustrates this well.

I served as Andrew's pastor for many years, and we enjoyed each other's company. He also participated in a small group I led, and Geri and I occasionally had dinner with him and his wife. On a hot summer day, for example, we would drive to their home and enjoy cooling relief in their pool. We talked about New York sports and his love for trains.

Six or seven years into our friendship, Andrew was elected chairperson of our board of elders. At that point, he became my direct boss. I was expected to send him monthly reports. He led the board in regular evaluations of my performance. He watched over my character and integrity. He had power and authority to demote me, fire me, or grant me a raise. I could not demote, fire, or grant him a raise.

I was the pastor of his family and he was now my boss. We talked about our roles. We joked about not going on vacation with one another. We remained friendly and continued to enjoy each other's company. But our relationship changed. It was no longer equal.

That's not to say that the relationship ended. Our respect for one another has grown over our twenty-seven years together as a result of our willingness to talk openly about the changes in our relationship. Understanding those changes and acknowledging them has kept the boundaries of our relationship healthy and clear. At the same time, our love and appreciation for one another has only grown over the years. His term as both the board chair and as a board member will soon expire. It will be interesting to see how our relationship evolves from that point forward.

New Life Fellowship: A Case Study on Clarifying Multiple Roles among Pastoral Staff

I began this journey of wrestling with emotionally healthy power and wise boundaries at New Life in 2007. I wanted to give our people language we could use to talk about our relationships as staff while cultivating a healthy respect for the legitimate power of those in authority at New Life. We needed help because we found ourselves continually wrestling with the dual roles between pastoral staff and the board, with each other, with supervisors, and with members of the congregation. We discovered that when we hired and paid people (transitioning them from serving as volunteers), this added another level of complexity. We needed a common frame of reference to help us navigate the overlapping complexity in all of these relationships and our employment process at New Life, and we needed to do this with wisdom and clarity.

The result was a Rule of Life for the pastoral staff (and later for the administrative staff and church board) that continues to guide us to this day.[14] This excerpt describes the three distinct yet overlapping roles of pastoral staff and how we are to navigate them well in our relationships with one another:

Using their God-given talents, our members work and serve as volunteers out of a sense of passion and mission. We too work and serve out of a sense of passion and mission; nevertheless, we function in a dual relationship with the New Life Fellowship (NLF) Board and congregation as "employees." In fact, we have at least three roles in the community of NLF: we are family members, leaders in this church family, and employees. These roles carry challenges in how we relate to one another and to NLF.

Each year, we are set apart by the board of elders to serve the body at New Life Fellowship in a unique way. Whether full or half time, we are given a salary in order to fulfill this special calling free from the constraints of secular employment. The body as a whole supports us financially so that we can devote ourselves to serving the body — praying, pastoring, and equipping the saints to do ministry (Ephesians 4:11ff). This is our privilege and our joy.

At the same time, the elder board is responsible for the stewardship of the church's resources in our dynamic, changing environment. Our call from God to pastoral leadership may last our entire lives regardless of our employment at NLF. Yet we recognize the fit of what NLF needs and desires may change over time. Thus, our status as employees is subject to the direction God is taking the church, her resources, and our leadership effectiveness. Furthermore, we are each subject to periodic reviews regarding our job description, status, and contract.

These clarifications have guided our thinking, given clarity to the staff, and provided a framework for us to manage our boundaries and relationships as leaders seeking to serve New Life with integrity.

Ask the Four Questions

There are great risks you take in leading God's church. You may lose relationships you cherish or harm the ministry you love. Like everything else we've discussed in being an emotionally healthy leader, managing the multidimensional challenge of power and wise boundaries goes beyond a particular set of techniques — it is about the core of who we are. These issues of power and boundaries touch on our insecurities and our need for validation. They reveal our level of personal maturity like few other challenges. They are influenced by our shadow.

As we close this chapter, I again invite you to ask yourself and your team questions based on the four key elements presented in part

1. This will enable you to mature in your exercise of power and wise boundaries — both personally and as a team.

- **Face your shadow.** How might my shadow be impacting my use, or lack of use, of power in my leadership? How might it be motivating or complicating my dual relationships? What patterns from my family of origin or culture contribute to my ambivalence about exercising power or the temptation to wield it too strongly? What past experiences with power figures contribute to the way I understand power and set, or fail to set, boundaries with others?

- **Lead out of your marriage/singleness.** As a married or single leader, how aware am I of the projections of others and the ways in which they might idealize me? What boundaries do I need to set to ensure that I serve people with integrity out of my marriage or singleness? What safeguards do I need to build into my leadership in order to protect my spouse, children, or close friendships?

- **Slow down for loving union.** In what ways might my time in loving union with Jesus help me to gently, wisely, and more effectively steward my influence and power? How might I listen more closely to other perspectives about my use of power and how I can more prudently navigate my relationships? How can I use my capacity to influence to help others develop a healthy relationship with their own power?

- **Practice Sabbath delight.** How can Sabbath serve as a weekly reminder for me and my team of the transitory, short-lived nature of my earthly power? In what ways can Sabbath serve as a safeguard not to take myself too seriously as a leader? How can I engage these weighty, challenging issues around power and wise boundaries with a sense of Sabbath playfulness and lightness?

Managing power and establishing wise boundaries are among the most challenging tasks of leadership. I wish there were easy steps I could give you to cover all of the issues you will face. If I had known the principles I share in this chapter at the beginning of my leadership, I believe many of my biggest mistakes could have been avoided. There is no substitute for being thoughtful and prayerful. Build in checks and balances with those you trust and seek wise mentors. You will be glad you did.

This ability to think clearly about power and boundaries equips us to hold lightly to the roles and responsibilities God grants to us. As we do this, we learn that the power and responsibility we enjoy now will one day come to an end. And as we will see in the next chapter, this helps us to understand and prepare for the future, that out of these endings God calls us to new beginnings.

Understanding Your Power and Wise Boundaries Assessment

If you took the power and wise boundaries assessment on page 247–48, here are some observations to help you reflect on your responses.

If you scored mostly ones and twos, this topic is probably new for you. You may even feel overwhelmed by the number of issues raised by the assessment. Don't worry. Growing in this area of your leadership is a process. Begin by taking an inventory of your power (see pages 250–54). Focus on one issue that applies to you now (for example, dual relationships, family, friendships). You can return to the rest at a later time. Relax. Go slowly. I learned the lessons in these pages over decades, not months. And I'm still learning.

If you scored mostly twos and threes, you are partially aware of your power and influence on those around you. It is important for you to clarify the nature and extent of your own power, even if you feel you don't have much. Use the power inventory (pages 250–54) to clearly identify the power you have. Reflect on any issues from your family of origin, along with any previous workplace or church experiences, to determine how these influences might be impacting your use of power and boundaries. You will want to understand the concept of dual roles, building in safeguards as appropriate. Let me encourage you to read this chapter carefully now and return to it one more time over the next year.

If you scored mostly fours and fives, you are in an excellent place to help others navigate their complex challenges with power, dual roles, friendships, family, and boundaries. Use the language and categories from the chapter as a framework for talking with team members about these issues *before* they find themselves in great difficulty. These themes are multilayered, with as many variations and complexities as there are ministries and churches. Expect to gain new insights as you continue to learn and apply these principles in your leadership.

CHAPTER 9

ENDINGS AND NEW BEGINNINGS

Pastor Tom led New City Community Church for thirty-one years. When he first arrived, the church was in a season of decline. Yet under his leadership, the church soon began to grow — from seventy-five to over four hundred in twenty years. The last eleven years, however, have been difficult. Gradually, more and more young people and families drifted away to a newer church on the other side of town. The congregation dwindled. They loved the contemporary worship and opportunities to meet other young families and singles. Tom saw that the culture around him had drastically changed, and he tried to help the church keep up. The church changed worship to include more contemporary songs, engaged social media for the first time, and hired a bright and energetic assistant pastor. Yet the church continued to age, with most members being fifty or older.

Tom loved being a pastor. After making a full recovery from a heart attack five years ago, he returned to work with a renewed commitment to continue his morning radio program each day and to lead New City. Three months ago, however, Tom had a minor heart attack and he agreed, at the insistence of his doctor, to retire. He was sixty-six years old.

The church, now numbering 120 people, was unprepared for Tom's sudden departure. The denomination secured an interim pastor for a one-year term, but he stayed just six months. "He just wasn't Pastor Tom," lamented Susan, a longtime member. After cycling through two more interim pastors over the next three years, the church declined to fifty-five people. They struggled to pay their bills for building upkeep and staff salaries. In a last-ditch effort to save the church, the board decided to let the longtime children's director go to free up sufficient funds to hire a young seminary graduate to resurrect the church. This didn't go well. Within three years, the church closed and the building was sold.

There was obviously no scandal here, so what happened? Why did this church fail? The failure wasn't a moral one, but it was failure nonetheless—a failure to discern the reality and necessity of the endings and new beginnings that were staring at them as a church. In addition to the heart attack warning signal of Pastor Tom's fragile health, there was the fact that he was rapidly approaching retirement age. No one acknowledged or discussed this, including Pastor Tom. The church had no biblical framework to provide wisdom and courage as they approached this necessary ending, and so the board did too little too late.

The Continuum of Endings in Leadership

Embracing endings in order to receive new beginnings is one of the fundamental tasks of the spiritual life—and this is especially true for Christian leaders. Not every problem can or should be solved or overcome; some things just need to be allowed to die. This isn't necessarily a failure. Often it is an indication that one chapter has ended and a new one is waiting to be written. This happens in our personal lives as well as in leadership.

We experience personal endings in many ways with those we love and care about. A loved one dies, suffers cancer or another serious illness, or we experience divorce, job downsizing, economic hardship, an affair, a broken dream—even the aging process itself. This is the inevitable suffering that comes during the seasons of life: "There is a time for everything, and a season for every activity under the heavens" (Ecclesiastes 3:1). We cannot control or stop the seasons. They simply come in God's time.

Like the ending of the seasons, we experience leadership endings with those we serve. In fact, I would say leaders experience even more endings and losses than the average person. Such losses may span a continuum from large to small, but a loss is a loss, and each one leaves its mark on us. To a greater or lesser degree, these endings drain our energy and diminish our ability to rise for the next challenge. They knock us off balance — at least for a time.

On one end of the continuum are the smaller endings that carry their own unique pain:

- Your church sends out fifty people to start a new church. You are both excited and sad as you realize your relationship with these folks will never be the same.
- The ministry you lead quickly grows from twenty-five to over a hundred. Members of the original group feel displaced and miss the closeness and sense of connection they felt when the group was small. You too are disoriented and struggle with this new normal.
- You begin to realize that the demographics of your church no longer reflect the surrounding community. You set up a meeting with the pastor and a member of the board to talk about the need to make changes and develop a long-term plan.
- Your assistant informs you that a gifted family of six who visited recently decided to attend a neighboring church because that church has a stronger ministry to children.
- The women's ministry, which has been without a paid staff leader for the last two years, struggles when a new director is finally hired. You've led the volunteer team that held the ministry together in the interim, and it's hard not to feel displaced and unimportant.
- Your most supportive board member has received a well-deserved promotion at her job and will soon be relocating to the company's corporate headquarters in another state. You are happy for her achievement but feel the loss of support and partnership. Leadership at the board level just got much harder.
- One of your best donors the last five years — your "go-to" person in difficult moments — informs you she is reducing her contributions so she can invest in other charitable projects.

On the other end of the continuum are the large endings, the kind that stop us in our tracks, keep us awake at night, and mark an indelible "before and after" on our lives:

- A trusted leader is discovered in a long-standing affair with the spouse of a prominent church member.
- You are diagnosed with cancer and have to make radical adjustments to your role.
- After fifteen years of providing excellent leadership, your associate pastor abruptly resigns to take a position at a larger, more affluent church in a different state.
- After ten years of working with a dynamic and growing nonprofit in your city, you realize that God is in your restlessness, and it's time for you to leave and launch a new career.
- A key ministry couple in the church divorce.
- One hundred people abruptly leave the church, disgruntled and discouraged about a recent ministry decision.
- Your organization or ministry reorganizes, and your position is eliminated.
- A person you trusted sends a letter to your supervisor detailing false allegations about your character or behavior.

Change is difficult for most people. We experience it as an unwelcome intruder derailing our hopes and plans. We prefer to remain in control and to operate in familiar patterns, even when they fail to serve us well. We might acknowledge intellectually that God can bring new beginnings and precious gifts out of our losses, but it somehow doesn't ease the sting of loss or prevent us from trying to avoid it. It isn't easy to trust the inner voice of the Spirit inviting us to cross over into this painful and unknown new territory.

If we accept the broader culture's view of endings—as failure and something to be avoided—we will neglect one of the most essential tasks of leadership, helping others navigate endings and transitions well. To navigate transitions well means leading with care, helping others to avoid the traps of bitterness, hardness of heart, or resistance to the new thing God might be unfolding in our midst. To be able to do this, our view of endings must be shaped by the truths of Scripture. And yet, too often we are shaped instead by our cultural values. Let's briefly consider how endings and new beginnings are commonly viewed today in churches and Christian organizations.

How Healthy Is Your Practice of Endings and New Beginnings?

Use the list of statements that follow to briefly assess your approach to endings and new beginnings. Next to each statement, write down the number that best describes your response. Use the following scale:

5 = Always true of me
4 = Frequently true of me
3 = Occasionally true of me
2 = Rarely true of me
1 = Never true of me

_____ 1. I am intentional about embracing endings and losses rather than trying to avoid them as a sign of failure.

_____ 2. I am able to rest in God's love, goodness, and sovereignty even when I am disoriented and confused by loss.

_____ 3. I initiate change to do what is best for the ministry rather than waiting until the last possible moment when things are falling apart.

_____ 4. I experience waiting attentively on God in the midst of disorienting change as life-giving and foundational to my spiritual growth.

_____ 5. I allow myself to feel painful endings in the context of leadership. I view them as a means of growth and a way to know Jesus and know "participation in his sufferings" (Philippians 3:10).

_____ 6. I regularly ask God's leading to discern whether I have completed what I can (or should) do in my position.

_____ 7. When a program or initiative is falling apart, I resist the temptation to take excessive measures or work twice as hard to keep it from failing.

_____ 8. When I am in the midst of a disorienting leadership transition (my own or that of others), I consistently seek out objective, wise counsel.

_____ 9. I am routinely able to engage in necessary endings — such as discontinuing programs, releasing a key volunteer, having a hard conversation — in order to open the door for new beginnings from God.

_____ 10. I am continually developing people who can someday replace me — with joy, faith, and a lack of fear.

Take a moment to briefly review your responses. What stands out most to you? At the end of the chapter (pages 299–300) are some general observations to help you better understand the current level of health in your approach to endings and losses.

Characteristics of Endings and New Beginnings in Standard Practice

Why are endings and transitions so poorly handled in our ministries, organizations, and teams? Why do we often miss God's new beginnings, the new work he is doing? We miss seeing what is ahead in part because we fail to apply a central theological truth—that death is a necessary prelude to resurrection. To bear long-term fruit for Christ, we need to recognize that some things must die so something new can grow. If we do not embrace this reality, we will tend to dread endings as signs of failure rather than opportunities for something new.

We View Endings as Failures to Be Avoided

Endings feel like a failure, and failures are painful. So what do we do? We avoid them by whatever means possible. We mistakenly believe that our responsibility as a leader is to always keep things going—even if they aren't working—and to keep our people from experiencing the pain of loss. See if you recognize yourself in any of these examples:

- George, a men's ministry leader, is not doing well in his role and hasn't been for years. You hear complaints, but you avoid having the difficult conversation with him. You've experienced him as defensive and self-protective in previous interactions; you strongly suspect any questions from you will be interpreted as a personal attack, and he might resign. Then the ministry would wander and people would scatter. And your job is to add, not subtract, ministries that enable people to connect to one another. So you spend weeks trying to figure out how to keep the ministry going without losing George. From sending in an assistant with leadership gifts to reassigning George to a new ministry, you imagine all the possible solutions. None seem like they will work, so you decide to leave things as they are, concluding that having someone in that position is better than having no one.

- Your church has formatted the Christmas outreach service the same way for the last ten years. It was good the first two or three years, but the time for a change is long overdue. You're not certain that the faithful volunteer who invests countless hours every year to orchestrate the service is capable of going in a whole new direction. If you insert yourself or invite other creative people to give input, your faithful volunteer might take it badly, which in turn could create a messy ending. After weighing the pros and cons, you're not sure it's worth the risk. It's just one service, after all. So what do you do? You decide to leave things as they are, concluding something is better than nothing.

- Caroline finished her graduate degree in social work last year and is excited to lead her first small group at her new church. She met with the pastor, received training, and launched with eight people. However, Caroline quickly discovered that leading a group was much harder than she'd anticipated. A young married couple, clearly in pain, wouldn't open up about the source of their anguish. A twenty-year-old talked way too much and dominated discussions. His two sisters, also members of the group, later informed Caroline that he has a mental disability and can't help himself. The two remaining singles, both new to the church, were more observers than participants. They said little. By month four, the two singles had dropped out and the group was down to five. Caroline dreaded their painful weekly meetings. She wanted to end the group but worried where people would go. She also worried the pastor might not let her lead again. She decided to leave things as they are, concluding that something is better than nothing.

It's not hard to see that necessary endings[1] are required in these situations. Undoubtedly, they will involve painful conversations and require a great deal of wisdom. In each scenario, the underlying problem is the leaders associating endings with failure. They don't see that embracing the end is the only way to open up a new future. In fact, if they could model openness to and acceptance of endings, they would help those they lead to see an ending as normal and of value, not a failure. When the leader is open about the need to end a program, others will no longer have *carte blanche* to pretend everything is fine when it is not. But viewing endings as failures to be avoided is only our first problem.

We View Endings as Disconnected from Spiritual Formation in Jesus

For most of my leadership life, I have viewed endings as obstacles to be removed or fixed — quickly. My anxiety level, often accompanied by heaviness and tension in my body, increased exponentially when I realized some person or program wasn't working. I ramped up my efforts to fix things in a misguided effort to avoid any potential future pain. I viewed these situations as the inevitable "blows and arrows" that accompany leadership. I never once connected any of them to my personal maturing in Christ. If anything, I listened less, not more, to what God might be trying to communicate through the pain. Allow me to share an example.

Kevin, a gifted assistant pastor, informed me over lunch one day that his family had decided to leave Queens. "Life is too hard in the city," he said. "We don't want to raise our children here. If we move to the suburbs, we will be able to buy a beautiful house for half the price of a home here."

My first thought was, *How could you do this? Don't you realize that your leaving for the suburbs may encourage others to do the same? Don't you care how that will impact us? What about those of us who are left here?*

All I could see was how much time and work it would take to find a person to fill Kevin's position. Loneliness flooded my soul. I put the disappointment out of my mind and tried to keep moving forward to build New Life. It didn't occur to me to wonder what Jesus might be doing in and through me in this situation. It never entered my head to ask:

Lord, how are you using this to help me depend more deeply on you?

In what new ways might you want to speak to me through Scripture about what it was like for you in lonely times?

What new beginnings might be hidden as a gift within this loss? How might I and those I lead be on the threshold of resurrection and new life we couldn't experience any other way?

Do you see how much we are missing out on when we fail to connect the pain of endings with our maturing into spiritual adulthood, when we fail to allow it to lead us to a deeper connection to Jesus? Because so few of us have a biblical understanding of what it means to truly wait on God, we fail to grow and mature through the inevitable endings that accompany all leadership. Instead, we begin to develop a hard protective shell, the emotional armor we feel we need to survive the many blows and arrows that will surely come. Our superficial theology fails to grasp that Jesus' death and resurrection is not only the central message of Christianity but also the necessary pattern of our lives.

We Disconnect Endings from Our Family-of-Origin Issues

Issues rooted in childhood and our families of origin leave a deep, often unconscious imprint on us. Only as we grow older and gain perspective do we begin to realize the depth of that influence. However, this family imprint isn't something that remains quietly in the past. It functions as a living presence inside us that must be acknowledged and transformed through our participation in the new family of Jesus. Thus, as Christian leaders, it is imperative that we consider how the families we grew up in dealt with the pain that accompanies endings and losses—large and small. We must ask ourselves questions like these:

- Did my family deny or minimize loss and endings?
- Did my family blame others, demanding that someone or something was always to blame for a loss?
- Did my family members blame themselves for endings and losses, retreating into isolation or depression?
- Did my family members distance themselves from endings and losses by intellectualizing them or manufacturing half-truths to soften the painful reality of what really happened?
- Did my family tend to medicate the pain of loss through self-destructive, compulsive, or addictive behavior?
- Did my family retain a sense of hope and expectancy of what the future might bring—even when things were at their worst? Or did they resign themselves to despair and hopelessness when confronted with difficult transitions?

I can tell you exactly how my family felt about change, transition, and loss: *they hated it.* My grandmother, Pasqualina Scazzero, emigrated to New York City from Italy to build a better life for her six children.

278 The Emotionally **Healthy** Leader

When her husband died prematurely at age forty-eight, she wore black the rest of her life as a sign of mourning. And things didn't improve much in the next generation. On the threshold of every change in my mother's life, she cursed, blamed, and raged at those around her. She hated everything—from moving, to job changes, to adjusting to the developmental phases of her four children. (My mother suffered from mental illness.) My father, on the other hand, was upbeat and optimistic. But he still didn't do change well. He escaped the pain of endings and loss by working, often seven days a week for months on end.

Is it any wonder that I hated change and brought this aversion into my adult life? As an entrepreneurial and visionary pastor, I was great with new beginnings—as long as they didn't first involve awful endings. Failing to understand biblical endings and new beginnings blocked me, and the church I led, from growing spiritually and emotionally.

Our society doesn't teach endings. Our churches don't teach endings. Our families don't equip us to embrace endings as part of the rhythm of life. When we add our own insecurities and fears, it seems obvious that we consider endings as interruptions to be avoided no matter what it takes. The problem is that, in the process, we block the new beginnings God wants to birth in and through us.

If these characteristics represent the standard way Christian leaders today treat endings, then what might it look like to engage in emotionally healthy endings and new beginnings? The answer, we shall see, is grounded in a biblical countercultural truth that takes us to the heart of the Christian life.

You Know You're Not Doing Endings and New Beginnings Well When . . .

- You can't stop ruminating about something from the past.
- You use busyness as an excuse to avoid taking time to grieve endings and losses or to allow for the possibility that you might meet God in the process.
- You avoid acknowledging the pain of your losses rather than grieve, explore the reasons behind your sadness, and allow God to work in you through them.

- You often find yourself angry and frustrated by the grief and pain in life.
- You escape or medicate the pain of loss through self-destructive behaviors such as overeating, use of pornography, inappropriate relationships, substance abuse, overengagement with social media, or working too much.
- You struggle with the envy you feel toward those who don't seem to be hit by the same hardships in life that you experience.
- You often dream of quitting in order to avoid the pain, disappointments, setbacks, and endings that routinely characterize leadership.
- You are not honest with yourself about the feelings, doubts, and hurts deep beneath the surface of your life.
- You rarely acknowledge directly that a program or person has outright failed. You avoid that pain by spinning the truth and glossing over the losses, disappointments, and struggles.
- You rarely think about change in your role or position because you dislike change.

Characteristics of Emotionally Healthy Endings and New Beginnings

Although I have been reflecting for many years on how God enlarges the soul through grief and loss in our personal lives, it's only been in the last several years that I've been able to apply this truth broadly and deeply to leadership. Although the process of navigating endings and new beginnings is almost always complex, we can say we are making a healthy transition when our process takes us through four phases:

- We accept that endings are a death.
- We recognize that endings and waiting in the confusing "in-between" will often take much longer than we think.
- We view endings and waiting as inextricably linked to our personal maturing in Christ.
- We affirm that endings and waiting are the gateway to new beginnings.[2]

These phases each have distinct characteristics, but they don't necessarily happen in a step-by-step fashion. In fact, they often overlap. As we shall see, it is possible to experience all four at the same time!

We Accept That Endings Are a Death

Before a new beginning can emerge, an ending must take place—and that ending must be *final*.[3] For most of my leadership, I routinely tried to hang on to the old while at the same time attempting to seize the new—just in case. It never worked. Endings are a death—and death is final.

Nothing new takes place without an ending. Or, in the words of the Roman philosopher Seneca, "Every new beginning comes from some other beginning's end." The failure to identify and prepare for endings and the accompanying loss is perhaps the biggest obstacle that prevents so many of us from moving on to something new.

Job had to accept that endings are a death when he lost his wealth, his ten children, his health, and his previous understanding of God. The prophet Jeremiah experienced loss as a death when Jerusalem and the temple were razed to the ground. The twelve disciples experienced a real death when Jesus did in fact die, taking all their hopes and dreams with him to the grave.

However necessary endings may be, they are almost always disorienting. A real ending—a final death—often feels like disintegration, falling apart, a coming undone. It feels that way because that is what death is. It is an ending that requires walking through a completely dark tunnel not knowing when or if any light will come again.

Most of us tend to live under the illusion that God wouldn't intentionally lead us into such pain—especially multiple times. We can't make any sense of why the people and things we love must literally and figuratively experience the finality of death. So we are shocked, anxious, confused, and often angry when endings come.[4]

While some endings happen quietly, others might more readily be characterized as a brutal crucifixion. Leadership, in particular, introduces us to the unique experience of following Jesus' way of leading. It is, believe it or not, one of the greatest gifts we receive from him. None of us would choose this kind of death, but it nonetheless becomes a means of grace as we come to know Jesus in the "participation in his sufferings" (Philippians 3:10). Paul refers to our leadership sufferings as one way we participate in the redemptive mystery of "fill[ing] up in [our] flesh what is still lacking in regard to Christ's afflictions"

(Colossians 1:24). In an effort to understand that text, I once asked a number of wise mentors for their perspective on this passage. Each talked about how our losses and griefs for Christ's church advance the kingdom of God in some mysterious way that transcends understanding. If we embrace these losses for the severe mercies they are, God does a profound work in us and through us in ways that are similar to what the apostle Paul describes as "death is at work in us, but life is at work in you" (2 Corinthians 4:12).

Having personally walked through a number of difficult endings, I understand why so few leaders and organizations are willing to surrender themselves to this kind of pain. As a young adult in my twenties, I served as an elder in a small inner-city, bilingual church of sixty adults. We met in a decaying church building with fixed pews that sat six hundred people. The board and senior pastor recognized that the ministry needed to drastically change in order to be welcoming and relevant to our poor, Spanish-speaking community. However, when serious discussions took place, it became clear that significant change would require several painful endings and losses, all of which seemed too difficult to bear. Multiple staff members would have to be let go to make room for new leadership. The music and programming would need to change completely. We would lose the tight sense of community we had as a small congregation. As a result, we never summoned the resolve for such drastic measures, and the church continued its slow decline.

I later attended a church with a tradition-rich history and a dynamic pastor. Rapid numerical growth forced the leadership team to consider possible building expansion, incorporating more contemporary music, hiring younger and more innovative staff, as well as other new initiatives. As a young seminary intern watching from the outside, it seemed obvious that God's future for this church was glorious. What I didn't understand was how the pain of the ending was necessary in order to make way for the new. This transition process was so painful and difficult, the pastor grew weary of trying to manage a seemingly endless stream of internal conflicts. He eventually gave up and moved on to another ministry.

As a person who tends to resist accepting the necessity of endings, I consistently do four things to keep me on track:

- I face the brutal facts of situations where things are going badly and ask hard questions, even when everything inside me prefers to distract myself or flee.
- I remind myself *not* to follow my feelings during these times of embracing endings as a death. My feelings inevitably lead me to avoid what I need to face.
- I talk with seasoned mentors who are older and more experienced, asking for their perspective and wisdom.
- I ask myself two questions: *What is it time to let go of in my personal life and in my leadership?* And, *If I embrace this death, what new thing might be standing backstage, waiting to make its entrance in my personal life and in my leadership?*[5] This second question especially encourages me to move beyond my fears, reminding me that God has something good for me in the future—even though I may not yet see any hints of what that might be.

While you may find one or two things from this list helpful for your endings, I encourage you to develop your own list of things to help keep you on track whenever you find yourself in a "death" season of endings. It's important to have anchors because endings thrust us into a confusing in-between where something is over, but nothing new has yet emerged. We find ourselves in a season of waiting.

We Recognize that Endings and Waiting in the Confusing "In-Between" Often Take Much Longer than We Think

No one enjoys waiting. But waiting for God is one of the central experiences of the Christian life. It is also one of the most difficult lessons we need to learn as leaders.

- Abraham waited almost twenty-five years for God to follow through on his promise of the birth of Isaac.
- Joseph waited somewhere between thirteen and twenty-two years to see his family again after being betrayed by his brothers.
- Moses waited forty years in the desert for God to resurrect a purpose for his life.
- Hannah waited years for an answer to her prayers for a child.
- Job waited years, not months, for God to reveal himself, redeem his losses, and take him into a new beginning.

- John the Baptist and Jesus waited almost thirty years before the Father's time for their ministries came to fulfillment.

"Yes, Pete," you might be thinking, "but *how long* do I have to wait for a new beginning to come out of my ending?"

My answer: "This waiting is much harder and will likely take much longer than you think."

When I planted New Life in 1987, my dream was to establish a dynamic, multiracial church in Queens that served the poor and marginalized in our community and was strong enough to reproduce itself—all, eventually, without me. This has required a lot of waiting and confusing "in-between" times.

I waited years for a core group to develop and then for a fledgling leadership to form. It took me eleven years to begin to understand what it meant to be a pastor and to free myself and my leadership from the unhealthy entanglements of my family history (and I'm still learning!). We waited sixteen years to finally buy a building and eleven more to renovate it (an ongoing process to this day). I waited more than twenty years for my successor and the long-term director of our community development corporation to emerge. I waited almost twenty-five years for the doors to open wide for us to impact the global church out of God's work in New Life. (This happened explosively and suddenly through the ministry of Emotionally Healthy Spirituality only a few years ago.) The list goes on, but I think you get the point. Waiting in the confusing "in-between" not only takes longer than we think, it is the normal condition of a Christian leader.

Why is waiting so important? God's purpose in endings and losses is not simply about changing your external environment or circumstances. He is doing something even greater—initiating a deeper level of transformation in and through you far beyond what you may want.

We View Endings and Waiting as Inextricably Linked to Our Personal Maturing in Christ

Jesus Christ is deeply formed in us when we trust God enough to embrace endings and losses. Endings and waiting bring us face-to-face with the cross, with death, with the refining fire of what John of the Cross described as "the dark night of the soul." A dark night is an experience of spiritual desolation and the ordinary way we grow in Christ as leaders. Here is how John of the Cross describes the purpose of the dark night:

> God perceives the imperfections within us, and because of his love for us, urges us to grow up. His love is not content to leave us in our weakness, and for this reason he takes us into a dark night. He weans us from all of the pleasures by giving us dry times and inward darkness.... No soul will grow deep in the spiritual life unless God works passively in that soul by means of the dark night.[6]

In this dry season, we may feel helpless, weary, empty, and consumed by a sense of failure or defeat. We have no consolation from God or any sense of God's presence. There is no way back to the way things were before, and we can't see the future. God sends us into what John of the Cross describes as "the dark night of loving fire" in order to purify and free us. It is his way of rewiring and "purging our affections and passions" so that we might delight in his love and enter into a richer, fuller communion with him.[7]

Much of my growth as a leader has come out of these kinds of painful, mysterious, and confusing experiences — the in-between times — over which I have so little control. When I have resisted God in such times — by simply getting busier and adding new programs, for example — I have missed the new beginnings God had for me and those I led. When I have remained with him, I discovered this in-between land of confusion was rich in insights and mercies. What looked like an empty, blurry, inactive time turned out to be the place of my most profound transformation.

Even this book you are reading was written out of a dark night of the soul, a dark night so painful that I wondered if I would survive it, let alone write a book out of the experience. In fact, I can identify four or five significant dark nights during my almost forty-year journey with Christ. The last one, however, the one I described at the beginning of the book as my fourth conversion (pages 12–21) was particularly long and intense.

At the time, I was dealing with a number of family-of-origin issues that had recently surfaced in my leadership, particularly around my difficulty in having honest conversations with key leaders. Digging into why I lied and lived in half-truths took me to places in my history I preferred to avoid. This led to a season of therapy and spiritual direction that was both painful and liberating. At the same time, I began to lead more clearly and strongly in New Life, making needed changes for the long-term future. In the middle of all this, I experienced a painful misunderstanding with a few friends that hurt deeply. Their critiques of me were valid (which made it even more difficult), and my self-doubts soared to new heights. While those two to three years felt terrible, I knew God was purging me and teaching me things I couldn't learn any other way. Many of the insights in this book emerged from my journals during that period.

Through it all, what kept me going was one truth — death always leads to resurrection.

We Affirm that Endings and Waiting Are the Gateway to New Beginnings

The central truth that Jesus is risen from the dead is what enables us to affirm that endings are always a gateway to new beginnings — even when we can't discern that anything redemptive could emerge from our loss. The key is to be willing to wait. And while we wait, we spend extended amounts of time alone with God. We process our thoughts and emotions with others or in a journal. We position ourselves as expectant pilgrims on a journey — we listen and learn, looking for and expecting to see signs of new life.

And then it happens. In the midst of our dark tunnel, a sliver of light crosses our path. It comes from the other side of an open door, one we never knew existed. Author and educator Parker Palmer says it well:

> On the spiritual journey ... each time a door closes, the rest of the world opens up. All we need to do is to stop pounding on the door that just closed, turn around — which puts the door behind us — and welcome the largeness of life that now lies open to our souls.[8]

I wish I could say that my leadership has been characterized by consistently putting closed doors behind me and welcoming the "largeness of life" God was calling me to, but that hasn't been the case. I've been a door-pounding leader, trying hard to get those closed doors back open. However, as the following story illustrates, those closed doors can be the gateway to the new beginnings God has for us.

Peter has been on New Life staff for twenty-two years. For the first twenty, he served as a worship pastor. He did an amazing job of raising up worship teams in our multiracial, cross-cultural context. My impending transition to a new role at New Life has brought with it a sense that Peter's role might also need to change. At that point, the ending was clear — Peter would no longer lead the worship teams — but the new beginning was not as clear. Over the next two years, the church leadership and Peter wisely discerned that his time at New Life might not yet be over. Because of Peter's wisdom and maturity, he was offered a new position on the executive leadership team. It was actually a role he had been offered years earlier but had rejected. He now accepted it and found he really enjoyed his new role. The following summer, when the two members of the executive team went on vacation, Peter stepped in as the person in charge of the church for a month.

As I observed Peter during that month, I was stunned — he was a wonder to behold! So much leadership, passion, wisdom, and authority came out of him that I called Geri after a staff meeting and said, "Geri, you're not going to believe this, but Peter is a different person. I barely recognize him. Remember the old Peter who never wanted to venture beyond his worship leader responsibilities? Well, he's gone. Somebody new is here in Peter's body — and he is doing an incredible job!" Peter followed that summer with a three-month sabbatical to help him retool for the next phase of this new role that was unfolding before him.

Was Peter disoriented for the two years that we were in transition? Absolutely. Did he struggle with the excruciating death of letting go of the worship team role he had so carefully built over most of his adult life? Yes. Did he experience the confusing in-between season of waiting? Yes. In fact, he is still figuring out his new role. Although the new beginning hasn't fully emerged, Peter is now supervising our pastoral staff and doing an excellent job.

This new beginning for Peter might have been derailed if Peter, his supervisors, or the board had not been able to live with the tension of the truth that endings and waiting are gateways to new beginnings. And

Peter's ability to pay attention to the different shifts and emotions he experienced enabled him to remain patient during the waiting period until the new thing God had for him began to take shape.

My Transition at New Life Fellowship
After Twenty-Six Years: A Case Study In Succession

The last six-and-a-half years have provided an immersion course for me in endings and new beginnings as I have transitioned from serving as senior pastor to a new role as a teaching pastor/pastor-at-large. It has not been an easy process, but it has helped me to discover unanticipated riches within the complexity, depth, and nuances of this powerful biblical theme of endings and new beginnings. And so I want to share with you my experience of succession, of intentionally stepping out of my role as senior pastor of New Life. My goal is not to repeat the many insights and principles outlined in other excellent books on succession,[9] but to offer you an inside look at how the inner life of a leader is what makes the outer life of endings and new beginnings possible.

Initiating Succession

Believe it or not, I first began thinking of my succession plan during the earliest days of New Life. I had been taught that I was to give away what God had given me, that I was to follow the path of the apostle Paul: "And the things you have heard me say in the presence of many witnesses entrust to reliable people who will also be qualified to teach others" (2 Timothy 2:2). But it wasn't until the purchase of our building in 2003 that I begin to consider it in earnest. I felt a heightened sense of responsibility as our church made such a large financial investment, and I became deeply concerned about the long-term impact of New Life in our community beyond my tenure.

Over the next few years, I talked to the elders multiple times about the need for a succession plan, but the church was growing and doing well, so there wasn't much urgency. They knew I was happy. The church was happy. Two board members had witnessed disastrous successions in previous churches and were not excited about possibly following a similar path at New Life.

Even so, I took intentional steps to prepare the church for a change in senior leadership. We slowly transitioned to a preaching/teaching team so people could get used to having other shepherds in the pulpit. I intentionally mentored young staff who might serve as potential successors. I chose not to expand the church in ways that might increase its dependence on me. I prayed and began looking around for successful succession models.

I didn't want to move to another church or take another position, such as teaching in a seminary. I wanted to stay at New Life under a new leader and model a supportive, servant role. I had seen it done successfully in religious orders such as Trappist and Orthodox monasteries as they implemented the Rule of St. Benedict with its emphasis on the breaking of self-will through submission to authority.[10] I knew one monk, in particular, who had formerly been an abbot (the leader of the community), who stepped out of his role to once again return to being a member of the community. He didn't miss his former role at all. In fact, he was thankful to have more time for prayer and contemplation! His identity was so grounded in the love of Christ that the transition for him was one of pure joy. And I believed that the journey of emotionally healthy spirituality had done a work of transformation in me, and in the congregation at New Life — making succession possible. I wanted to use my power and position as church founder to ensure a vibrant New Life for the next generation.

In February 2009, I wrote a formal letter to the elders stating my resignation as effective in the fall of 2013. This gave us over four and a half years to transition well. The letter changed everything. At that point, everyone knew an era was ending. Uncertainty filled the room that night at the board meeting.

"Pete, why do such a thing now?" one elder asked. "You're young [I was fifty-three]. The church is growing and doing great."

"Do you really think this is God?" another elder asked.

"I do," I answered without hesitation. Then I explained this was perhaps the most important leadership contribution I could make at New Life for the next twenty-five years. I talked about the succession of Moses and Joshua, Elijah and Elisha.

Then came the question I knew someone would ask.

"Suppose we don't find anyone in time. Would you stay longer until we do?"

"No," I answered calmly.

The room grew very quiet. Having a firm date changed everything.

At that point, I had been at New Life almost twenty-two years. To many people, I wasn't merely the founder, I was New Life itself.

I informed the elders that I had set up a video conference call for the board with an experienced consultant who specialized in succession. His work with a wide variety of denominations and ethnic churches was an ideal fit for our unique context. Because he came from outside our church, he brought a clear, unemotional, experienced perspective to the process. While he reminded us that only 33 percent of successions from founding senior pastors actually succeed, we appreciated his frankness.

I went home that night badly shaken up. Something powerful and unexpected had been unleashed by putting a date in writing. *Where was this going? Suppose this turned out badly? Would New Life split along racial lines?* (We had people from seventy-three nations.) *What would my role be at NLF? What do I do if the new lead pastor doesn't want me around?* In the back of my mind was one other question: *Why didn't the board argue more strongly against me stepping down? Were they secretly relieved?*

Waiting

Our process lasted the full four and a half years.

The elders and I researched how other churches had transitioned from a founding pastor to a new leader. There were very few success stories. A healthy transition would lead to another generation of fruitful service and impact for God's kingdom. A poor process would lead to years of faltering before New Life righted herself, if ever, and stabilized. Most churches, we learned, never recapture the "glory days" enjoyed under the founder's leadership. Yet I remained convinced that New Life's best days were still ahead of us.

During this waiting period, a number of pastors and leaders counseled me against proceeding with succession.

"Don't do it!" one pastor friend said. "That's your church that you built with your blood, sweat, and tears. Once you open up that power vacuum of you leaving, all hell will break loose, and they will want you out of the church as soon as possible."

Another pastor whom I greatly respect, a person with forty years of experience, wrote me a long e-mail, warning that it was likely the church would hurt me, and my family, in the process. They wouldn't empathize with our situation. He recommended I give the church a six-month notice when I was ready to leave, get out of town, and never look back.

Yet another pastor/leader of a very large church informed me he had legally, albeit secretly, put the church building and assets in his family's name in case someone attempted to take the church from him.

"Pete, you'll miss the power and the perks of calling the shots when you don't have it anymore," another warned. "You may think you want to empower young leadership, but it will be very different when they are in charge. End this foolishness as soon as possible!"

Finally, a former pastor, now a consultant, told me, "Pete, you think you can sit there in a staff meeting following the lead of a young pastor with less than half your experience? You have got to be kidding!"

The chairperson of our NLF board also voiced to me in private that he didn't think I would really follow through on the seven-stage transition plan we worked hard to develop. He was pessimistic about the outcome and secretly wondered how many years it would take New Life Fellowship to recover.

The Seven Stages in Our Transition Process

The following are the seven stages of the transition process developed by the board and me. I shared these stages with the congregation in 2011.

1　***Define the founding pastor's new role.*** Since I would be staying at New Life, the first thing we had to determine was what my role and contribution would be once a new senior leader was in place. This would have a significant impact on the contours of the next senior leader's job description. I was convinced it was God's will that I surrender my power and come under a new lead pastor for the future of New Life.

2　***Define the new senior pastor's role.*** We determined the job description for the new senior leader and his or her relationship to the elder board.

3 **Establish a task force.** The elders commissioned a transitional task force to begin the search for a new senior leader.

4 **Identify potential candidates.** The task force and the elders concluded that we had two potential internal candidates at New Life. We began conversations with each of them to discern God's choice for this role. During this process, one of the candidates determined that remaining at New Life was not God's will for him.

5 **Complete a year of "testing."** The elders then set up a one-year framework for "testing" Rich, the remaining candidate, and possibly choosing him as the next lead pastor.

6 **Affirm a new leader.** That year of "testing" concluded successfully in December 2011, and the elder board affirmed Rich as the new lead pastor who would follow me. At that point, Rich began functioning as my "number two," with all church staff reporting to him.

7 **Communicate the transition publicly.** We made a formal announcement at the New Life Annual Vision Meeting in June 2012, informing the congregation of the transition that would take place in September/October 2013. This gave us fifteen months to train and develop Rich for his new role. It also gave New Life members fifteen months to prepare emotionally for the change.

What Happened Inside Me During the Transition Process

On one level, I was elated about guiding our church through a difficult process and pouring my life into a new leadership for the long-term future. In the early years of starting New Life, I had longed for an older pastor/mentor to guide me. I promised myself I would do this for the generation that followed me.

I understood that I was a steward of the people of New Life—their money, their time, their energy, the DNA of the church, and the unique mission to which God had called us.[11] This was God's church, not mine. I firmly believed that a successful succession was probably the greatest gift I would give New Life in my twenty-six years of leadership.

Geri too felt this was the right season to do it. We were still relatively young. Who knew what God might have planned for our lives? She too loved New Life but longed to see me free from carrying the day-to-day pastoral weight of being the senior pastor.

So that was all on the upside.

At the same time, however, a profound sadness settled over me.

Leaning into Grief and Depression

I grieved for almost two years. I couldn't figure out fully why I was depressed since I was the one who had initiated the process in the first place. Succession was biblical. I was utterly convinced this was God's will. But another part of me wanted to return to the familiar role I had enjoyed for so long. People were already treating me differently.

Scripture is clear that getting wise counsel is key to doing God's will. "Plans are established by seeking advice; so if you wage war, obtain guidance" (Proverbs 20:18).[12] My emotions were so raw, I knew I needed good, wise counsel. So I found people who had successfully walked through such transitions themselves or helped others with the process. This proved invaluable. I met with three key people over that two-year period.

The first was a Christian counselor I highly respected. We explored issues related to my family of origin and how this impacted my emotional state. I met with a longtime mentor who had known me for over thirty years; I listened to his wise perspective. Then I spent time with an older pastor who had walked through succession after serving in his church for over thirty years. He shared openly about the mistakes he had made (they lost thousands of members in the process). And his internal struggles were remarkably similar to mine.

These three men kept me steady. I never doubted that succession was God's will during the four and a half years. But I did wonder if I would survive the very painful pruning God was doing inside of me. Letting go was a death much messier and bloodier than I had anticipated.

Leaning into God

The church bore fruit and grew throughout the entire transition process. Over time, I allowed myself to feel the loss of the role I had grown accustomed to for almost three decades. Our pastoral staff takes a day alone with God each month. I added a second day per month for me. I found myself irresistibly drawn to increased time alone with God.

For the first time in my life, I spent countless hours meditating on the passages of Scripture related to Jesus' journey to the cross. How did Jesus let go of everything (literally!) to the extent of dying naked on a cross, his whole life and message misunderstood? My life verse during this period became Jesus' words to Peter: "Very truly I tell you, when you were younger you dressed yourself and went where you wanted; but when you are old you will stretch out your hands, and someone else will dress you and lead you where you do not want to go" (John 21:18).[13]

It was a humbling experience to allow my power to decrease as Rich's power increased in the years leading to the actual succession. I watched him lead our staff with an inner confidence and naturalness that took me aback. His decisiveness and clarity surprised and impressed me. The church continued to function and grow as if nothing changed. And Rich made noticeable improvements in a number of areas in the church. He cast an exciting vision for a five-to-ten-year future. People who had once needed a hug from me each Sunday now went to Rich. The number of messages on my phone decreased 50 percent. In my head, I knew this was good. In my heart, I struggled with my dead mother's voice that whispered, *See, they don't need you. Leave now. You didn't really know what you were doing. Thank God you got out of the way before they pushed you out.*

I was being led where I did not want to go — into a place of vulnerability I could not control. I didn't want to embrace a path of downward mobility leading to the forgotten place of the cross. God was inviting me to die with him on a whole new level — and it wasn't pleasant.

Finding a New Identity at the Cross

I finally accepted the fact that my identity was at least partially wedded to my role as senior pastor. After twenty-six years, it was only natural that my identity had attached itself to a particular role — Pete Scazzero, senior pastor of New Life Fellowship Church.

Now there was a tearing, a separation. The best words to describe this kind of emotional cutting is *bloody*, *excruciating*, and *horrific*. I thought I was going to die — literally. John of the Cross, in the sixteenth century, described a second dark night of the soul that was so violent internally that you wondered if you would survive. The succession process opened up for scrutiny my strengths and weaknesses, my gifts and my limits, my successes and my failures. It was hard to see others slowly assume leadership and do things so much better. I remember watching Rich lead staff meetings. He brought a more natural gifting and creativity to our times together. I learned from him.

Shaming internal voices, along with one or two external ones, bombarded me:

What good are you? Why didn't you do that when you were leading?

Thank God you are leaving. People were probably praying you would give the senior role to someone else.

Pete, you should have done this earlier. Look how much better things are.

All endings require inner work. Succession demanded a profound inner work that touched deep vulnerabilities and unhealed wounds. Now I understood why so few churches around the world do succession well. The pain is profound and unrelenting—particularly for the one letting go.

I had a strong contemplative dimension to my relationship with Christ. I was reasonably self-aware. My identity was (so I thought) in being "beloved of God." I preached sermons and wrote books on how the true self is found in Christ. This ending, however, carried me into a crucible that burned off yet another false layer—but it was very close to the bone.

God granted me grace during that two-year period. The pain gradually lifted (I am still not sure how) and I found myself slowly moving into resurrection and even exuberance by years three and four. Fifteen months before the official transition, I shared my new role with the congregation. Here is the letter I sent to the church in 2012:

> *My first priority remains the integrity and health of New Life. I will continue to be the "Chief Champion and Cheerleader" for Rich, Redd, the staff, the elders, and all of you. I love New Life! There isn't a church like ours anywhere in the world. I will continue to serve as a teaching pastor, preaching and offering retreats and classes under Rich's leadership. Moreover, I will also mentor, lead small groups, and be a resource to our leadership. While I recognize there will be a normal, healthy grieving process to navigate through during this transition, I also want to invite you to*

join us in our enthusiasm about the future. New Life is called to be a movement of people, not a monument or institution erected around a person or building. For this reason, one of the greatest gifts Geri and I can offer is the investment in a new generation of leaders who can carry forth New Life's mission for the next twenty-five years. We are looking forward to 2039! Here is what I am asking you to do: Begin to embrace Rich as the person God has called to lead us at New Life as of September 2013. Let's join together in what God desires to do in and through our church during what surely will be one of the most exciting, expansive times in our history.

Thank you all for being such a great church.

Pete

Receiving the New Beginning

Fifteen months before the official transition date, Rich and I reversed roles. He functioned as if he were the new lead pastor; I worked as if I were the teaching pastor/pastor-at-large under his leadership. He led all executive team and staff meetings. He reported directly to the elder board. I stopped attending board meetings and executive team meetings. He set the vision, the preaching schedule, and hired new staff. It was a great year. Our excitement for what God was doing only increased during that time. The church continued to grow. By the time we approached the formal installation of Rich in the fall of 2013, there wasn't much change for the staff or the board. We were already living in the new reality.

We had a month-long buildup to the installation. One week, Geri preached a message on her lessons learned from the past twenty-six years of ministry. I preached the following week on the "Four Lessons I Learned from Twenty-Six Years at New Life Fellowship."[14] Our church threw a massive party to celebrate our years at New Life.

As we approached the day of Rich's installation, many of us sensed something profound was about to happen in this transfer of spiritual authority. I realized that the installation of a new pastor has some similarities to a wedding. The church was making a commitment to Rich and Rich was making a commitment to the church. In a sense, I was like a father giving away his daughter (the child I had birthed) in marriage. The first loyalty of New Life was now formally and officially to be with Rich, their new lead pastor. In his seminal book *Generation to Generation: Family Process in Church and Synagogue*, psychologist Edwin Friedman wrote about this kind of transition: "Success depends on the previous partner being able to let go — but stay connected."[15]

We also felt led by God to frame the installation as the making of a covenant, a solemn agreement between two people, each of whom carries responsibilities and obligations. As with a wedding, once that covenant is made, something very significant happens spiritually.

For days, I pondered the kind of commitment I hoped Rich might make to the people of New Life. I also reflected carefully on the kind of commitment I yearned for New Life to make to Rich. After researching a variety of church traditions, I wrote statements of intent for both Rich and for New Life that they publicly declared to one another in the installation service on October 6, 2013.[16]

Nothing changed between Rich and me in terms of our working relationship from what it had been in the previous fifteen months, and yet everything changed. Authority had passed from one leader to another. Everyone present at our three services knew something beautiful and supernatural happened that day. Even though we didn't have words to describe it, it was truly a wonder to behold.[17]

Over the years, Geri repeatedly said to me, "Pete, you think you are so indispensable. People will forget you six months after you are gone."

She was wrong.

Most people forgot me *before* the succession was completed! There was such a sense of God's powerful presence in our midst that it didn't matter who was leading. People met and heard from God in new and fresh ways at Sunday services. People continued to be radically transformed. The church continued to get the best of Geri and me. Only now, New Life was receiving fresh vision, ideas, and energy from Rich and a new generation of leaders.

The fruit of these past couple of years has been far greater than any of us could have imagined. New Life has prospered and is preparing to move into a multisite model. Emotionally Healthy Spirituality functions as a ministry that flows out of New Life and has spread to over twenty-five countries around the world. Geri and I continue to love our working relationship with Rich and New Life.

As I write this, we are near the end of year two in our new roles. Geri and I continue to adjust to our new normal. I find myself disoriented on certain days, but thus far, I would consider our ending and new beginning to be the greatest highlight of my twenty-six years at New Life Fellowship Church.

Rich's Perspective on Succession

The process of becoming lead pastor at New Life Fellowship was nothing short of joyful and life-giving. While I experienced my fair share of fear and inadequacy, I was able to walk through this succession process with clarity and confidence. I attribute this experience to five emotionally healthy leadership gifts I received.

1. Pete created an empowerment culture that positioned New Life to thrive without him as the primary leadership voice. Years before the transition, Pete established a preaching team. This prepared our congregation to hear and respond to additional leadership voices. By the time we reached the transition, our church was already familiar with my voice and leadership.

2. Pete gave me the space to "test-drive" as lead pastor without him being present. In 2012, sixteen months before the transition, he went on a four-month sabbatical. In his absence, I had to make difficult decisions, lead staff, preach often, and absorb the big-picture reality of leading a church. This period of time was indispensible.

3. Pete, Geri, and the elders of New Life Fellowship respected my wife's unique journey and separateness. At no time did Pete, Geri, or the elders pressure Rosie to fit into a certain mold of being a pastor's wife. They respected her own journey and encouraged her to be her true self. If she had been treated in any other way, it would have been difficult for me to move forward in this new role.

4. Having a clear and predictable process was critical. We had a four-year process, and every year was carefully designed to reflect the changing reality of the transition. By the fourth year (which was a "practice year"), we functioned internally as if the transition had already taken effect. Having clear expectations helped guide us in our conversations and planning.

5. What made this transition experience incredibly joyful was the constant affirmation I received from Pete, the elders, and the staff. Hearing encouraging words gave me the confidence of knowing I was doing a good job and leading our church effectively. These words of affirmation provided a great sense of peace that I was on the right track.

Ask the Four Questions

As we close this chapter, I invite you to embrace endings and new beginnings in an emotionally healthy way. Insights, joy, surprising gifts, fruit, revelations, and peace from Jesus await us when we cooperate with him in this process. And they are only a foretaste of what awaits us!

Let's consider again the four major themes of the inner life of emotionally healthy leaders (part 1), specifically applying them to the discernment of endings and new beginnings.

- **Face your shadow.** How might my shadow and issues from my family of origin make it difficult for me to discern endings and new beginnings? How might they also cause me to avoid necessary waiting or dark nights of the soul? What issues from my past might hinder me from letting go and staying with God in seasons of disorientation when things appear to be falling apart?

- **Lead out of your marriage/singleness.** How might my spouse (if applicable) or close friends help me to pay attention to God in the midst of the endings in which I find myself? How might they serve as wise counselors during this time? In what way(s) can my vocation as a living sign of Christ's love — whether as a married or single person — serve as a stabilizing anchor during this time?

- **Slow down for loving union.** How might I make sufficient time to remain in loving union with Jesus during this time so I can discern the endings and new beginnings God might have for me in this season? What spiritual practices can help me to remain in a posture of "waiting on the Lord"? How might I integrate these two questions into my thinking about endings: *What is it time to let go of in my personal life and in my leadership? What new thing might* *be standing backstage waiting to make its entrance in my personal life and in my leadership?*[18]

- **Practice Sabbath delight.** Am I listening to God in the little endings that come out of my weekly Sabbaths? If so, what do I sense God may be saying to me? Do I need a longer sabbatical break to discern the new seasons God may be leading me into? How might I learn from my current Sabbath practice and its imposition of limits and ceasing so that I am better equipped to stop and end things well?

Prayerfully engaging these four issues will help you in your discernment process, enabling you to cooperate rather than resist what God is seeking to do. In addition, being aware of the issues they raise will help you to identify the distinct phases of God's process around endings and new beginnings.

You can be sure that when you face endings and new beginnings in leadership, you will have to deal with multiple fears and questions. If you are like me, your mind may occasionally gravitate to worst-case scenarios. That's when panic can set in. When that happens, let me encourage you to stay the course. There really is a resurrection waiting for you on the other side of endings and death. That is the heart of Christianity — life truly does come out of death. If we stay the course with Jesus, there is always a new beginning.

Understanding Your Practice of Endings and New Beginnings

If you took the endings and new beginnings assessment on pages 273 – 74, here are some observations to help you reflect on your responses.

If you scored mostly ones and twos, it's likely you tend to avoid endings and experience discouragement in the face of change rather than an expectant attentiveness to what God might be doing in and through you. Receive this as an invitation from Jesus to walk through a door to learn what it means to "take up your cross and follow him" (see Luke 9:23). Take time this week to reflect on and write about two questions: What is it time to let go of in my personal life and my leadership right now? What new thing might be standing backstage waiting to make its entrance in both my personal life and my ministry?

If you scored mostly twos and threes, you have likely begun to apply a theology of endings and new beginnings to your personal life and to your leadership. This is an opportunity for you to carve out additional time with God to journal and reflect specifically on areas where he is inviting you to let go. Ask God for discernment to recognize the endings and new beginnings that may be emerging in and around you. And, finally, allow God to do his life-changing work in you as you wait and follow him in the process.

If you scored mostly fours and fives, you can expect God to lead you to a deeper revelation of this powerful truth in the years to come. You are also positioned to serve the rest of the church as a mother or father of the faith. Since Jesus leads all of us to places we don't want to go (John 21:18), you can now serve as a spiritual companion to leaders who will be following in your footsteps.

IMPLEMENTING EHS IN
YOUR CHURCH OR MINISTRY

Emotionally Healthy Spirituality (EHS) is a paradigm that ultimately informs every area of a church, ministry, or organization.
So the one question that continually emerges in our work with leaders
is: "How do I bring EHS into our church—and then how do I keep it
there?"

There are a variety of tools, books, conferences, and curriculums for
leaders who want to teach and train their people in emotionally healthy
spirituality. Three tools in particular are essential to becoming a transformed EHS church: *The Emotionally Healthy Skills Course*, *Emotionally
Healthy Skills 2.0*, and *The Emotionally Healthy Leader*.

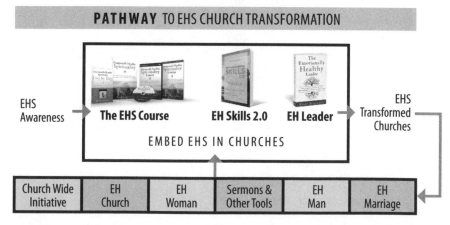

The Three Core Tools

1. The EHS Course. This eight-week spiritual formation course provides a foundational overview of the EHS paradigm for your church or ministry. It includes reading *Emotionally Healthy Spirituality* and learning to cultivate a rhythm of meeting with Jesus twice a day using *Emotionally Healthy Spirituality Day by Day: A Forty-Day Journey with the Daily Office.* Daily devotions correspond with the eight weekly themes of the course. *The EHS Course Workbook* is used by participants during the course. The eight sessions include:

1. The Problem of Emotionally Unhealthy Spirituality (Saul)
2. Know Yourself That You May Know God (David)
3. Go Back to Go Forward (Joseph)
4. Journey Through the Wall (Abraham)
5. Enlarge Your Soul through Grief and Loss (Jesus)
6. Discover the Rhythms of the Daily Office and Sabbath (Daniel)
7. Grow Into an Emotionally Mature Adult (The Good Samaritan)
8. Go the Next Step to Develop a "Rule of Life" (The Early Church)

Many churches around the world, including ours, offer *The EHS Course* at least twice a year in order to reinforce these values in their culture. If possible, we encourage churches to offer it as a church-wide course because of the importance of processing this powerful new content well. To help you lead a high-quality course, we provide additional resources on our website at www.emotionallyhealthy.org. If you're considering offering the course, I encourage you to register online in order to receive ongoing updates and support.

2. Emotionally Healthy Skills 2.0. Over a sixteen-year period, we identified eight essential skills and then developed training to help our leaders and church members grow into emotionally and spiritually mature followers of Jesus Christ:

1. The Community Temperature Reading
2. Stop Mind Reading
3. Clarify Expectations
4. Genogram Your Family
5. Explore the Iceberg

6. Incarnational Listening
7. Climb the Ladder of Integrity
8. Clean Fighting

The formula is simple: new skills + new language + intentional follow-up = transformed community. While *Emotionally Healthy Skills 2.0* can be used in small groups, Sunday school classes, equipping sessions, leadership meetings, or as a church-wide course, the most important factor is intentionally following up in specific situations so people learn to do life differently. *Emotionally Healthy Skills 2.0* is available from our website at www.emotionallyhealthy.org.

3. The Emotionally Healthy Leader. The topics discussed in this book require ongoing discussions, personal and team applications, and nuancing for your particular context. Reading the book alone is not sufficient to make significant shifts in how you and your team lead. To help you engage and apply this material more deeply, we developed a free discussion workbook you can download at www.emotionallyhealthy .com or www.zondervan.com. A number of other podcasts, videos, and additional resources for leaders are also available on our website.

Additional EHS Tools

The Emotionally Healthy Woman book and DVD curriculum focuses on the things we need to quit in order to seriously engage the EHS journey. For example, to quit being afraid of what others think, quit lying, quit over-functioning, and quit living someone else's life. A book for men on this same topic will be released in 2016 as *The Emotionally Healthy Man*.

The Emotionally Healthy Church offers pastors and leaders a theological foundation for EHS principles, such as living in brokenness and vulnerability, embracing grief and loss, and receiving the gift of limits.

We will continue to produce additional materials, including an upcoming book and DVD course for couples on *The Emotionally Healthy Marriage*.

If you are interested in learning more about what it might mean to bring EHS to your church or ministry, I strongly encourage you or a key member of your team to become an EHS Point Person. As you work to slowly and methodically introduce emotionally healthy spirituality in your context, visit our website, www.emotionallyhealthy.org, to learn more about a host of available resources and events, including EHS conferences, web-based training events, and new materials as they are developed.

Appendix 1

Characteristics of Churches Transformed by EHS

What would it look like if Emotionally Healthy Spirituality were fully realized in the life and culture of your organization? The characteristics described below are designed to help you envision EHS as a reality in your context. The descriptions in each of the six categories were developed and refined over a twenty-year span. They are not goals, achievements, or even a list of items to check off as "finished." They are descriptions of what it means in concrete terms to be on an authentic life journey with Christ and to become a missional presence of God in the world.

1. Slowed Down Spirituality

- The rhythms and pace of our personal lives are slower and more deliberate. We operate out of a contemplative activism, with *doing for* Jesus flowing out of *being with* him.
- We commune with and are transformed by Jesus through a consistent, daily practice of reading Scripture.
- We encourage, respect, and value Sabbath observance as a key spiritual discipline.
- We view and practice prayer as part of a lifestyle of loving union with Jesus.

305

- We consider spending time in solitude and silence to be foundational to remaining centered in Christ.
- We believe that discernment of God's will requires sensitivity to what is happening inside of us (consolations and desolations), as well as seeking insights from Scripture and wise counsel.
- We make radical, intentional life changes (adopting a "Rule of Life") in order to cultivate a personal relationship with Jesus and to avoid living off of the spirituality of others.
- We affirm and practice a theology of delight—both personally and corporately.

2. Integrity in Leadership

- Pastors and ministry leaders lead out of a deep interior life with Christ.
- Leaders consider their marriage or singleness to be their loudest gospel message; they intentionally make this aspect of their life a reflection of their eternal destiny of marriage to Christ.
- Pastors and teachers experience Scripture as a deep well for their own soul, and not simply as a tool for teaching others.
- The work of church governance (elder board, leadership team, etc.) flows out of an intentional spiritual discernment process focused on following God's will when making strategic decisions.
- Leaders seek to be appropriately connected to others, yet calmly differentiate their "true selves" from the demands and expectations of those around them.
- The church and its leaders are aware of the complexity of power dynamics and the challenges of navigating dual roles in the course of ministry work and building community.
- Leaders humbly preach and live out of truth and authenticity; they refuse to engage in pretense, impression management, or exaggeration.
- Spiritual authority allows for and encourages people to ask questions and to say "no" when appropriate.

3. "Beneath the Surface" Discipleship

- We go back to go forward, seeking to break negative patterns from our families of origin and cultures that hinder us from following Jesus.
- We acknowledge and respect our personal limits and the limits of others.
- We maintain a profound awareness of and appreciation for our brokenness.
- We seek to integrate a healthy love of self and good self-care with our love for God and others.
- Our measure of what constitutes a mature spirituality is love, humility, and approachability, not gifts, power, or success.
- Losses and disappointments are seen as opportunities to meet God and discover more about ourselves.

4. Healthy Community

- We affirm and practice deep listening as an indispensable means of loving others well.
- We voice our assumptions and expectations about what others might be thinking, rather than relying on "mind reading."
- We seek to use new language that enables us to respectfully articulate our wants, needs, and differences. For example, "I'm puzzled about," "I notice," or "I prefer," rather than making accusations or angry outbursts.
- We continually seek to master the skills and nuances of "clean fighting."
- We maintain a healthy sensitivity to over-functioning (doing for others what they can and should do for themselves) and under-functioning (relying on others to do what they can and should do themselves).
- We pursue the unity of the church by respecting individual differences (valuing different viewpoints, choices, and spiritual journeys).
- We challenge ourselves and encourage others to share out of our weaknesses and vulnerabilities.

- We consistently invite one another to all take responsibility for our own lives and to do so without blaming or shaming.

5. Passionate Marriages and Singleness

- We acknowledge, honor, celebrate, and support both singleness and marriage. This is reflected in everything from regular sermons to retreats and equipping events.
- Married couples and singles understand that they are becoming living signs of God's love for the world, cultivating a love for others that is passionate, intimate, free, and life-giving.
- Our oneness with Christ is closely connected to our oneness with our spouses (for married people) and to our close community (for single people).
- We talk openly about sexuality, recognizing that the beautiful relationship between Christ and his church is to be reflected in the sexual relationship between a husband and wife, or in the chastity of singles.
- We differentiate between "using" and "loving" by monitoring the interior movements of the heart, treating others as unrepeatable and invaluable.
- We accept the marriage paradigm of two differentiated, separate individuals (each with different hopes, values, ideas, and preferences) as the pathway to oneness.
- We can articulate a theology of singleness, and we embrace and value its relationship to each person's spirituality.

6. Missional Workers

- We have a deep sense that our spheres of daily activity — paid or unpaid, work or retirement, in or beyond the home — constitute our ministry and are of equal significance as the activities of those who work in full-time or vocational ministry.
- We view work as an act of worship and consider it part of building God's kingdom and bringing order out of chaos.

- We make no distinction between "sacred" and "secular," and we refuse to compartmentalize work and spirituality.
- We seek to intentionally create and shape community within our spheres of influence, integrating new skills and a new language for loving well.
- We consistently seek to develop slower and more deliberate rhythms in order to practice the presence of Jesus (i.e., be with him) in the context of daily work and activities.
- We take practical steps to give to others and serve others, both within and beyond our own communities.
- Drawing on the deep foundation of the gospel, we seek to combat such evils as racism, classism, and sexism, intentionally engaging the world so our life serves as a gift for others.

Appendix 2

Rule of Life Worksheet

APPENDIX 3

GENOGRAM YOUR FAMILY

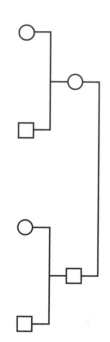

Relationship	Relational Dynamics	Symbol
Conflicted	A consistent pattern where issues do not get resolved between people	
Cut Offs	People in the family stop talking to one another or avoid contact.	
Distant/Poor	Low or minimal emotional connection between family members.	
Enmeshment	Pressure is created for family members to think, feel and act alike. There is low tolerance for people to be separate, to disagree, or be different.	
Abuse	A severe crossing of personal boundaries—whether it be sexual, emotional, or physical, severely injuring the dignity and humanity of another.	

Relationship Status Symbols

Marriage   Living Together   Separated

Divorce   Divorce   Remarried

Themes _____

Earthquake Events _____

313

ACKNOWLEDGMENTS

I may have written this book, but it was birthed in the context of two communities. The first and foremost is with Geri, my best friend and wife of thirty-one years, and our four adult daughters and son-in-law — Maria, Christy, Jesse, Faith, and Eva. Geri's insights, gifts of wisdom, and, most importantly, integrity are spread over these pages.

Secondly, I want to thank the family of New Life Fellowship Church in Queens, New York, where I have served for the last twenty-nine years. This book was written out of the crucible of our life together as a multiracial community committed to bridging racial, cultural, economic, and gender barriers and to serving the poor and marginalized. This book emerged out of this soil; their openness to the Holy Spirit and new beginnings is a gift. I want to express specific appreciation to the elders (particularly Andrew Favilla and Jackie Snape), staff, leaders, the members of New Life, and to all those who read drafts and portions of this book along the way (there are too many to mention by name). Thank you all.

I also want to thank Rich Villodas, the new lead pastor at New Life, for his courageous modeling of emotionally healthy leadership and our many conversations around applying this material to the next generation. Greg Jao, a vice president for InterVarsity and a New Life Fellowship preaching team member, offered numerous insights that made this a better book. Lance Witt, Scott Sunquist, Kathy and Ron Fehrer, Chris Giammona, Steve Treat, and Ken Shigematsu each offered important theological, practical, and historical contributions to this book.

Christine Anderson served as an outstanding editor, challenging me, beyond what I thought possible, to be a better writer. Her perceptive and insightful questions were indispensable throughout the long, arduous writing process. And finally, a heartfelt thanks to Chris Ferebee, my agent, along with the entire Zondervan team for their excellent work and partnership in bringing this manuscript to publication.

Notes

My Journey through Emotionally Unhealthy Leadership

1. To read more about Geri's story, see *The Emotionally Healthy Woman: Eight Things You Have To Quit To Change Your Life* (Grand Rapids, MI: Zondervan, 2010).
2. This story is recounted fully in Peter Scazzero, *The Emotionally Healthy Church: A Strategy for Discipleship that Actually Changes Lives*, updated and expanded edition (Grand Rapids, MI: Zondervan, 2010).
3. See Peter Scazzero, *Emotionally Healthy Church*.

Chapter 1: The Emotionally Unhealthy Leader

1. I was helped by an unpublished paper called "Growth Matters: Numbers Count: Biblical Reflections on Numerical Growth" written by Daniel J. Denk for internal use by InterVarsity Christian Fellowship.
2. Conversations with Scott Sunquist, dean of the School of Intercultural Studies at Fuller Theological Seminary. See Dale T. Irvin and Scott W. Sunquist, *History of the World Christian Movement: Volume 1: Earliest Christianity to 1453* (Maryknoll, NY: Orbis, 2001), 257–88.
3. For two excellent introductory articles, see http://www.nwlink .com/~donclark/hrd/bloom.html and http://thesecondprinciple.com/ instructional-design/threedomainsoflearning/.
4. I am thankful to Wendy Seidman for this simplification of Bloom's taxonomy.

Chapter 2: Face Your Shadow

1. "Leading from Within," by Parker Palmer, in *Insights on Leadership: Service, Stewardship, Spirit, and Servant-Leadership*, Larry Spears, ed. (John Wiley: New York, 1998), 202.
2. Connie Zweig and Jeremiah Abrams, "Introduction: The Shadow Side of Everyday Life," in *Meeting the Shadow: The Hidden Power of the Dark Side of Human Nature* (New York: Tarcher/Penguin, 1991), xvii.
3. It's important to note that churches and organizations can also develop what has been called a "shadow mission." These often flow out of our personal lives as leaders. For example:

- We want to reach people for Jesus Christ. The shadow mission could be that the desire to grow in numbers becomes the *exclusive* way the ministry validates its effectiveness and drives all of its decisions. While growing numbers is part of a legitimate way to measure our effectiveness, it's not enough, and team members can easily become only means to that end.
- We are committed to contextualize the gospel in our rapidly changing culture. We learn from and engage the newest technologies, social media, and ideas. That is good. The possible shadow mission becomes the carving of an identity for the ministry that reacts against others, giving the entire organization a feeling of superiority to those who are more "traditional."

    For further reading, see John Ortberg, *Overcoming Your Shadow Mission* (Grand Rapids, MI: Zondervan, 2008).

4. Travis Bardberry and Jean Greaves, *Emotional Intelligence 2.0* (San Diego, CA: Talent Smart, 2009), 20–21.

5. Travis Bardberry and Jean Greaves, *Leadership Intelligence 2.0* (San Diego, CA: Talent Smart, 2012), 129–34.

6. *The Desert Fathers: Sayings of the Early Christian Monks*, translated by Benedicta Ward (New York: Penguin Classics, 2003), 172.

7. See Ernest Becker, *Denial of Death* (New York: Free Press, Simon and Schuster, 1973), 128.

8. Although by God's grace we can become increasingly free of the shadow's hidden power, it is important to note that the shadow itself never fully goes away. We don't ever "get rid of it." Much like Jacob after his encounter with the Lord in Genesis 32, we walk with a limp. The key difference is that we are now very aware and dependent on God for every step we take.

9. Joshua Wolf Shenk, *Lincoln's Melancholy: How Depression Challenged a President and Fueled His Greatness* (New York: Houghton Mifflin, 2005), 159.

10. See Robert E. Kaplan and Robert B. Kaiser's work on developing versatile leadership, http://sloanreview.mit.edu/article/developing-versatile-leadership/.

11. Jesus asked the demon-possessed man of the Gerasenes, "What is your name?" "My name is Legion," he replied, "for we are many" (Mark 5:9–10). Naming the problem was one of the means Jesus used to take authority over the uncontained, unbounded, evil energy before him.

12. Geri Scazzero, *The Emotionally Healthy Woman* (Grand Rapids, MI: Zondervan 2010), chapter 4; Pete and Geri Scazzero, *Emotionally Healthy Skills 2.0* (New York: Emotionally Healthy Spirituality, 2012); Peter Scazzero, *The Emotionally Healthy Church*.

13. For a fuller treatment of naming emotions, see Geri Scazzero, *Emotionally Healthy Woman*, chapter 4.

14. To learn more about "360," go to The Emotional Quotient Inventory (EQ-I 2.0®) and EQ-360® are recommended feedback tools. For information

on engaging an Executive Coach with these assessments go to www. missiontomeasurement.com.

15. For a summary of the Enneagram and additional resources, see Scazzero, *Emotionally Healthy Woman*, 80–88.

Chapter 3: Lead Out of Your Marriage or Singleness

1. See our *Emotionally Healthy Skills 2.0 Curriculum*, session 5.

2. For a fuller explanation of the I-Thou of Martin Buber, go to Peter Scazzero, *Emotionally Healthy Spirituality* (Grand Rapids, MI: Zondervan, 2006), 183.

3. For a comprehensive treatment of marriage as the least inadequate analogy to depict our relationship with God, see John Paul II's seminal work *Man and Woman He Created Them: A Theology of the Body*, translated by Michael Waldstein (Boston: Pauline Books and Media, 1997, 2006).

4. The early church literature of the third, fourth, and fifth centuries indicates the majority of the church viewed celibacy as superior to marriage. This view was so prevalent that the Council of Paphlogonia (AD 345) had to anathematize those who held that marriage prevented a Christian's entry into the kingdom of God. This did little, however, to check the popular position of the church in which marriage was seen as third class after virginity and widowhood (Carolyn A. Osiek and David L. Balch, *Families in the New Testament World: Households and House Churches* (Louisville, KY: Westminster John Knox Press, 1997).

5. Roman Catholics continue to insist on singleness for priests and monastics. Orthodox churches allow both marrieds and singles to serve as leaders.

6. See Sandra M. Schneider, *Selling All: Commitment, Consecrated Celibacy, and Community in Catholic Religious Life* (Mahwah, NJ: Paulist Press, 2001), 117–59.

7. I am deeply indebted to Ron and Kathy Feher, founders of Living in Love, who significantly share our understanding of marriage as our first ambition, passion, and our loudest gospel message. See their website, www.livinginlove.org.

8. The roots of this rich application of biblical theology go back to the marital "think tank" pioneered by a Jesuit priest, Chuck Gallagher, who gathered a wide spectrum of theologians, couples, and mental health practitioners to develop and articulate a marital spirituality anchored in Christ. For his work, and that of Living in Love ministries (http://livinginlove.org), Geri and I are deeply grateful.

9. Yet as Pope John Paul II highlighted so well, God wanted his marriage plan to be so obvious to us that he stamped it on our bodies as male and female. Sexual union, the becoming of one flesh, is a profound mystery pointing to something beyond itself. It is the foreshadowing of our ultimate union with Jesus Christ, our perfect lover. For the best treatment of this, see John

Paul II, *Man and Woman He Created Them: A Theology of the Body* (Boston: Pauline Books and Media, 2006); Christopher West, *Theology of the Body for Beginners* (West Chester, PA: Ascension Press, 2004).

10. I am thankful to Ron and Kathy Feher of Living in Love marriage ministry for this phrase and for their modeling and mentoring for us what it looks like to live in love with passion.

11. Every Christian is called to a celibate (single) life in the sense that, unless we are married, our bodies and sexuality belong to Christ alone. Christian celibacy is not a rejection of the body or of sexuality, but an affirmation of union and communion with Jesus, the purpose of which is to bear fruit and nurture spiritual children for him. See Christopher West, *Theology of the Body I: Head and Heart Immersion Course* (West Chester, PA: Ascension Press, 2007). I attended this five-day seminar with Christopher West in 2012.

12. One of the unfortunate consequences of the Protestant Reformation in the sixteenth century was the elimination of all monasteries in Protestant-controlled areas of Europe. From 1536–1540, for example, Henry VIII abolished the entire monastic system in England, closing over 800 monasteries, abbeys, nunneries, and friaries that were home to more than 10,000 monks, nuns, friars, and canons. By April 1540, none were left.

13. In addition to hundreds of Anglican monastic communities around the world, we find vowed celibates in Protestant monastic orders in Germany, such as the Communität Christusbruderschaft Selbitz (Community of Christ Brotherhood in Selbitz), which is part of the Evangelical Lutheran Church in Bavaria, and the Evangelical Sisterhood of Mary, an ecumenical religious order founded by Mother Basilea Schlink. In France, Brother Roger Schütz, a Lutheran pastor, founded the ecumenical community of Taizé. There is the Holy Transfiguration Monastery founded by the Baptist Union in Australia, and in the United States, we find the Community of Jesus, and Holy Wisdom Monastery, both ecumenical communities of women — to name a few.

14. Only the prophet Jeremiah was called to observe celibacy as a prophetic sign to Israel.

15. Rodney Clapp, *Families at the Crossroads* (Downers Grove, IL: InterVarsity Press, 1993), 95–98.

16. Sandra M. Schneiders, I.H.M., *Selling All: Commitment, Consecrated Celibacy, and Community in Catholic Religious Life* (Mahway, NJ: Paulist Press, 2001), 29–30.

17. Parker Palmer, *Let Your Life Speak* (San Francisco: Jossey-Bass, 2000), 30–31.

18. Rodney Clapp, *Families at the Crossroads*, 101.

19. This prayer is adapted from a pamphlet distributed by Ron and Kathy Feher's Living in Love ministry.

20. Caring for the quality of both married and single leaders requires us to take male/female relationships seriously (not just as a potential source

of temptation). Not caring too often results in single women remaining underdeveloped as leaders and under-invested in. This is a large topic, but vitally important if we are to create environments where both singles and marrieds relate to each other in mature ways so they both can flourish in their vocations.

See Ruth Haley Barton, *Equal to the Task: Men and Women in Partnership* (Downers Grove, IL: InterVarsity Press, 1998); Carol E. Becker, *Becoming Colleagues: Women and Men Serving Together in Faith* (San Francisco: Jossey-Bass, 1998).

Chapter 4: Slow Down for Loving Union

1. Frederick Dale Bruner, *Matthew: A Commentary, Volume 1* (Dallas: Word, 1987), 287.
2. To read more of Edwards' sermon on "Love More Excellent than the Extraordinary Gifts of the Spirit" based on 1 Corinthians 13:1, see www. biblebb.com/files/Edwards/charity2.htm.
3. Hans Urs von Balthasar, *Prayer* (San Francisco: Ignatius Press, 1976), 171.
4. Jesus was God in the flesh. Yet we must remember, he was also fully human. And he models for us a fully redeemed human life in the Spirit as it was meant to be lived — in loving union with the Father.
5. Geri and I like to say, "The body is a major, not a minor prophet." In other words, the body often knows before the mind when our life is out of alignment with God. For example, my stomach gets knotted, my neck tightens, I sweat, I clench my fists, my shoulders stiffen, I can't sleep, etc.
6. Numbers 2:32.
7. "You did not trust in me" (Numbers 20:12) and "you rebelled" (Numbers 20:24).
8. It is important to note that Aaron's sons died on the spot for offering incense that was not commanded. Moses and Aaron receive a much lighter consequence.
9. The scholar J. de Vaulx suggests that, in striking the rock, Moses was striking God. "God is often likened to a rock (e.g., Ps. 18:2; 31:3; 42:9). The apostle Paul, in writing about the wilderness years, says, 'They drank from the supernatural Rock which followed them, and the Rock was Christ' (1 Corinthians 10:4)," quoted in Gordon J. Wenham, *Numbers: An Introduction and Commentary* (Downers Grove, IL: InterVarsity Press, 1981), 151.
10. I recommend a great book on this theme, Alicia Britt Chole, *Anonymous: Jesus' Hidden Years and Yours* (Nashville: Nelson, 2006).
11. For more detail, see Richard Peace, *Conversion in the New Testament: Paul and the Twelve* (Grand Rapids, MI: Eerdmans, 1999), 52, 67, 89–91.
12. Henri Nouwen, *In the Name of Jesus: Reflections on Christian Leadership* (New York: Crossroad, 1991).

13. Robert C. Gregg, *Athanasius: The Life of Antony and the Letter to Marcellinus*, Classics of Western Spirituality (Mahwah, NJ: Paulist Press, 1980), 81.
14. *The Sayings of the Desert Fathers: The Alphabetical Collection*, translated by Benedicta Ward (Kalamazoo, MI: Cistercian, 1975), 8.
15. I devote an entire chapter to developing a Rule of Life in *Emotionally Healthy Spirituality*. Two additional excellent books on the topic are Ken Shigemastu, *God in My Everything* (Grand Rapids, MI: Zondervan, 2013) and Steve Macchia, *Crafting a Rule of Life* (Downers Grove, IL: InterVarsity Press, 2012).
16. Praying the Daily Office typically includes silence, Scripture, prayer, and perhaps a devotional reading. For additional guidance, see Peter Scazzero, *Emotionally Healthy Spirituality Day by Day: A 40-Day Journey with the Daily Office* (Grand Rapids, MI: Zondervan, 2014).
17. See "Reflection and Our Active Lives," www.ignatianspirituality.com/ignatian-prayer/the-examen/reflection-and-our-active-lives/ and "The Daily Examen," ignatianspirituality.com, accessed December 10, 2014.

Chapter 5: Practice Sabbath Delight

1. Wayne Muller, *Sabbath: Finding Rest, Renewal, and Delight in Our Busy Lives* (New York: Bantam, 1999), 69.
2. I still smile when I remember Eugene Peterson's Sabbath article in *Leadership* magazine many years ago. It contained a picture of him behind bars dressed in a prison uniform with a sign hanging on his chest that read, "Sabbath Breaker."
3. For a fuller explanation of these four qualities of Sabbath, go to Peter Scazzero, *Emotionally Healthy Spirituality*, 165–71.
4. Abraham Heschel, *The Sabbath: Its Meaning for Modern Man* (New York: Farrar, Straus, Giroux, 1951).
5. Adapted from Brene Brown, *I Thought It Was Just Me (But It Isn't): Making the Journey from "What Will People Think?" to "I Am Enough"* (New York: Gotham, 2012); Ernest Kurtz, *Shame & Guilt*, 2nd ed. (New York: iUniverse, Kindle edition), location 211.
6. Kurtz, *Shame & Guilt,* location 211.
7. "How Do I Know If I'm a Workaholic?", www.workaholics-anonymous.org. Accessed November 15, 2014.
8. See "Pull the Plug on Stress," www.hbr.org/2003/07/pull-the-plug-on-stress. Accessed February 2015.
9. David N. Laband and Deborah Hendry Heinbuch, *Blue Laws: The History, Economics, and Politics of Sunday-Closing Laws* (New York: Lexington, 1987), 45–46. For an excellent, well-documented discussion of the Jewish Sabbath in Jesus' time, see C. S. Keener, *The Gospel of John: A Commentary, Volume One and Two* (Grand Rapids: Baker, 2003), 1:641–45.
10. The irony was that in Geri's family the mantra was, *Go out and play*. Play was first; homework was second. The expectation was that she would return

from school, change her uniform, and play. While she struggled initially to set a boundary around her twenty-four-hour Sabbath and to refrain from work during that time, she didn't experience any guilt around her newfound practice like I and so many others I know did.

11. See http://www.kwiat.com/diamond-education/diamond-facets/5815; and http://www.hardasrocks.info/diamond-facets.htm.

12. Francine Klagsbrun, *Jewish Days: A Book of Jewish Life and Culture around the Year*, illustrated by Mark Podwal (New York: Farrar Straus Giroux, 1996), 9–10.

13. I owe this insight to Eugene Peterson and his many books and articles on this theme and his careful exegetical work in *Christ Plays in Ten Thousand Places: A Conversation in Spiritual Theology* (Grand Rapids, MI: Eerdmans, 2005).

14. I am indebted to Walter Brueggemann, *Sabbath as Resistance: Saying No to the Culture of Now* (Louisville, KY: Westminster John Knox Press, 2014) for his exegesis on the exodus and the title of this section.

15. Walter Wink, *Naming the Powers: The Language of Power in the New Testament*, (Minneapolis, MN: Fortress Press, 1984), 5.

16. Brueggemann, *Sabbath as Resistance*, 10.

17. Gary Sterns, "How B&H Photo thrives in Amazon's jungle using both bricks and clicks—and without Black Friday," *Business Journal*, November 27, 2012, accessed at www.bizjournals.com on November 15, 2014; Associated Press, "New York's B&H Camera Shop Mixes Yiddishkeit and Hi-Tech Savvy," accessed at www.jpost.com on November 15, 2014.

18. Elie Wiesel, *All Rivers Run to the Sea: Memoirs* (New York: Alfred A. Knopf, 1995), 87.

19. Jürgen Moltmann, *Theology of Play* (New York: Harper and Row, 1972), 17.

20. R. Paul Stephens, *Seven Days of Faith: Every Day Alive with God* (Colorado Springs: NavPress, 2001), 211.

21. Ben Witherington III, *The Rest of Life: Rest, Play, Eating, Studying, Sex from a Kingdom Perspective* (Grand Rapids, MI: Eerdmans, 2012), 49. See also Ben Witherington III, *Work: A Kingdom Perspective on Labor* (Grand Rapids, MI: Eerdmans, 2011).

22. Moltmann, *Theology of Play*, 18.

23. Moltmann, *Theology of Play*, 13.

24. Witherington, *Rest of Life,* 52–53.

25. For free resources and FAQs, see www.emotionallyhealthy.org/sabbath.

Chapter 6: Planning and Decision Making

1. Deuteronomy 17:14–17; 1 Kings 10:23–11:6.

2. Malcolm Muggeridge, "The Fourth Temptation of Christ," in *Christ and the Media* (Grand Rapids, MI: Eerdmans, 1977).

3. Summarized by Jeannine K. Brown, Carla M. Dahl, and Wyndy Corbin Reuschling, *Becoming Whole and Holy: An Integrative Conversation about Christian Formation* (Grand Rapids, MI: Baker Academic, 2011), 188.

4. To read more about a theology on "Receiving the Gift of Limits," see chapter 8 in Peter Scazzero, *Emotionally Healthy Church*.

5. Robert Barron, *And Now I See: A Theology of Transformation* (New York: Bantam, 1999), 37.

6. Bernard of Clairvaux, *Five Books on Consideration: Advice to a Pope* (Kalamazoo, MI: Cistercian, 1976), 27–28.

7. As discussed in chapter 4, the Examen, or Daily Examen, is a practice developed by Ignatius of Loyola (1491–1556) to help Christians reflect on the events of the day in order to detect God's presence and discern his direction.

8. I am indebted to Russ Nitchman for patiently spending time with me to explain to this urban, slow-to-learn New Yorker the intricacies of plant life.

9. Ignatius, *Spiritual Exercises*, 12.

10. Kevin O'Brien, SJ, *The Ignatian Adventure: Experiencing the Spiritual Exercises of Saint Ignatius in Daily Life* (Chicago: Loyola Press, 2011), 57–58.

11. Joan Chittister, *Wisdom Distilled from the Daily: Living the Rule of St. Benedict Today*, reprint ed. (New York: HarperCollins, 2013).

12. Judy Brown, "Fire," in *The Art and Spirit of Leadership* (Bloomington, IN: Trafford, 2012), 147–48. Used by permission.

13. For a great example of this, see Jesus' parable of the shrewd manager in Luke 16:1–12.

14. For a rich description of the parts of prudence, read Thomas Aquinas, *Summa Theologica*, II-I, q. 23, a.1, ad.2; Joseph Pieper, *The Four Cardinal Virtues* (Notre Dame, IN: University of Notre Dame, 1966), 3–40.

15. Ruth Haley Barton, *Pursuing God's Will Together: A Discernment Practice for Leadership Groups* (Downers Grove, IL: InterVarsity Press, 2012), 187–200.

16. "Flog a mocker, and the simple will learn prudence" (Proverbs 19:25).

17. "Blows and wounds scrub away evil, and beatings purge the inmost being" (Proverbs 20:30).

18. "Plans fail for lack of counsel, but with many advisers they succeed" (Proverbs 15:22).

19. See chapter 8, "Receive the Gift of Limits," in Peter Scazzero, *Emotionally Healthy Church*.

20. See http://bobbiehl.com/quick-wisdom2/questions-to-ask/decide-to-make-any-major-decision/.

Chapter 7: Culture and Team Building

1. Edwin H. Friedman, *Friedman's Fables* (New York: Guilford Press, 1990), 25–28. Reprinted with permission of Guilford Press.

2. Developed by Murray Bowen, the founder of modern family systems theory, *differentiation* refers to a person's capacity to, in Bowen's words, "define his or her own life's goals and values apart from the pressures of those around them." The degree to which you are able to affirm your distinct values and goals apart from the pressures around you (separateness) while remaining close to people important to you (togetherness) helps determine your level of differentiation. People with a high level of differentiation have their own beliefs, convictions, directions, goals, and values apart from the pressures around them. They can choose, before God, how they want to be without being controlled by the approval or disapproval of others. Intensity of feelings, high stress, or the anxiety of others around them does not overwhelm their capacity to think intelligently.

3. Scott W. Sunquist, *Understanding Christian Mission: Participation in Suffering and Glory* (Grand Rapids, MI: Baker, 2013), 244.

4. This is journalist Ken Myers's definition of culture as summarized by Andy Crouch in *Playing God: Redeeming the Gift of Power* (Carol Stream, IL: InterVarsity Press, 2013), 17.

5. I want to express gratitude to the Pairs Foundation for their development of the tool called the "Dialogue Guide," which served as a prototype for us in developing The Ladder of Integrity; see http://emotionallyhealthy.org/theladderofintegrity.

6. Pete Scazzero and Geri Scazzero, *Emotionally Healthy Skills 2.0.*

7. Note that this tool is used for small annoyances, not large conflicts. These two phrases are more fully explained as part of a larger tool we teach at New Life Fellowship called "The Community Temperature Reading," which is the first skill found in the course curriculum called *Emotionally Healthy Skills 2.0.*

8. If a church has more than 800 people who meet the three criteria, they expand from thirty to a larger number. It is possible to have 10,000 attenders in five services, but still have only 800 who meet the criteria. NCD recommends separate assessments be done for different campuses in a multisite context or with very different types of worship services (e.g., different languages, traditional vs. contemporary, youth vs. elderly, etc).

9. This was based on conversations with Canadian leaders and practitioners of Natural Church Development. See: "How to Take the NCD survey" at http://ncd-canada.com or at the NCD global website, http://www.ncd-international.org/.

10. See Peter Scazzero, *Emotionally Healthy Church*, 34–35.

11. See Jim Loehr and Tony Schwartz, *The Power of Full Engagement* (New York: Free Press, 2003), 4–5, 41.

12. For a fuller explanation of a leadership theology for marrieds and singles, see chapter 3, "Lead Out of Your Marriage or Singleness."

Chapter 8: Power and Wise Boundaries

1. Richard M. Gula, *Just Ministry: Professional Ethics for Pastoral Ministers* (Mahwah, NJ: Paulist Press, 2010), 123.
2. I am thankful to Kaethe Weingarten from the Department of Psychiatry at Harvard Medical School for the idea of her helpful grid and work on how people unaware of their power are the most dangerous people on earth, transmitting trauma from one generation to the next. This applies to politics, parenting, government, churches/synagogues. See Kaethe Weingarten, "Witnessing, Wonder, and Hope," Magnum, Family Process, Winter 2000, 39, no. 4.
3. This is my adaption from Richard Gula's discussion on the dynamics of power in *Just Ministry*, 117–55.
4. Stanley Hauerwas and William H. Willimon, *Resident Aliens: A Provocative Christian Assessment of Culture and Ministry for People Who Know Something Is Wrong* (Nashville, TN.: Abingdon, 1989), 121–27.
5. Richard A. Blackmon and Archibald D. Hart, "Personal Growth for Clergy," in *Clergy Assessment and Career Development*, eds. Richard A. Hunt, John E. Hinkle Jr., and H. Newton Maloney (Nashville: Abingdon, 1990), 40.
6. Steve, a mentor of mine, is a well-respected CEO with a doctorate in marriage and family counseling. He doesn't hire anyone who has significant, unresolved issues with their parents or caregivers. Why? He believes these issues will inevitably be replayed and projected onto authority figures in the workplace. If a person's relationship with a parent was highly conflicted and reactive, that conflict will be replayed with future authority figures— unless they have done their own internal work. His perspective helped me to understand the seemingly irrational behavior I would occasionally experience from people over whom I had a position of authority.
7. This phrase comes from an excellent book on power by Andy Crouch, *Playing God: Redeeming the Gift of Power* (Downers Grove, IL.: InterVarsity, 2013), 14.
8. See Marilyn Peterson, *At Personal Risk: Boundary Violations in Professional-Client Relationships* (New York: Norton, 1992) for her thesis that professionals who refuse to embrace their authority that comes with their role are most at risk to hurt others.
9. Gula, *Just Ministry*, 137.
10. See Marilyn Peterson, *At Personal Risk: Boundary Violations in Professional-Client Relationships* (New York: Norton, 1992) for her thesis that professionals who refuse to embrace the authority that comes with their role are most at risk to hurt others.
11. See, for example, Robert G. Jones, ed., *Nepotism in Organizations* (New York: Routledge, 2012).
12. For a recent tragic example, see "Where Are the People? Evangelical Christianity in America Is Losing Its Power: What Happened to Orange

County's Crystal Cathedral Shows Why," *The American Scholar*, www.
theamericanscholar.org/where-are-the-people/#.VO–ejr2102g. Accessed
February 2015.

13. Martha Ellen Stortz, *PastorPower* (Nashville: Abingdon, 1993), 111–17.

14. The Rule of Life for pastoral staff can be found in its entirety in the
appendix of *The Emotionally Healthy Church: Updated and Expanded*, or at
www.emotionallyhealthy.org/resources.

Chapter 9: Endings and New Beginnings

1. See Henry Cloud, *Necessary Endings: The Employees, Businesses, and
Relationships That All of Us Have to Give Up in Order to Move Forward* (New
York: HarperCollins, 2010).

2. See Peter Scazzero, chapter 5, *Emotionally Healthy Church*, 159–79, for a
more extensive biblical explanation of these three phases.

3. I am grateful to William Bridges, *Transitions: Making Sense of Life's Changes:
Strategies for Coping with the Difficult, Painful, and Confusing Times in Your
Life* (Cambridge, MA: Da Capo Press, 2004) for this initial insight that
opened up so many biblical texts on endings for me.

4. It is important to note that not every ending feels like a death. Some are
actually welcome, depending on a number of factors. For example, if an
underperforming team member who resists your leadership at every turn
finally leaves, you may feel relief. Yet he or she may feel a terrible loss. One
of our New Life staff recently left to enter a monastery. We as a leadership
team and church viewed it like a painful death and felt the great loss of her
presence; her primary emotion was elation as she courageously stepped into
God's calling for her life. There have been occasions when I felt relief and a
new beginning when a key leader or volunteer moved on, yet they have felt
enormous sadness.

5. Adapted from Bridges, *Transitions*, 87.

6. St. John of the Cross, *Dark Night of the Soul*, translated by E. Allison Peers
(New York: Image, Doubleday, 1959).

7. For a fuller treatment of this material, see chapter 6, "Journey through the
Wall," Peter Scazzero, *Emotionally Healthy Spirituality*.

8. Parker J. Palmer, *Let Your Life Speak: Listening to the Voice of Vocation* (San
Francisco: Jossey-Bass, 2000), 54.

9. See William Vanderbloemen and Warren Bird, *Next: Pastoral Succession
that Works* (Grand Rapids, MI: Baker, 2014); Carolyn Weese and J. Russell
Crabtree, *The Elephant in the Boardroom: Speaking the Unspoken about
Pastoral Transitions* (San Francisco: Jossey-Bass, 2004).

10. See Timothy Fry, ed., *RB 1980: The Rule of St. Benedict in English*
(Collegeville, MN: Liturgical Press, 1981).

11. The mission statement of New Life Fellowship specifies that the way we do our mission is through five unique values. We call them the 5 "M's".
12. See also Proverbs 12:15; 15:12; 15:22; 19:11; 28:26.
13. See Henri Nouwen, *In the Name of Jesus: Reflections on Christian Leadership* (New York: Crossroad, 1991), 53–73. I learned that reading and preaching about this is easier than living it.
14. These sermons can be found at www.emotionallyhealthy.org/sermons.
15. Edwin Friedman, *Generation to Generation: Family Process in Church and Synagogue* (New York: Guilford Press, 1985), 250–73.
16. We framed the installation similar to the making of a covenant, i.e., a solemn agreement between two people, each with responsibilities and obligations. As with a wedding, once that covenant is made, something significant happens spiritually. We found that to be true. To access the covenant exchanges, go to www.emotionallyhealthy.org/succession.
17. You can watch this service on Youtube at http://emotionallyhealthy.org/succession.
18. Adapted from Bridges, *Transitions*, 87.

The Emotionally Healthy
Spirituality Course

Go beneath the surface
and transform your life ...

85% of Christians today admit to being stuck
in their walk with Christ.

FIND A SOLUTION!

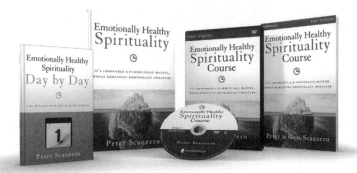

Take a powerful 8-week journey of transformation
that will equip you with tools on how to have
a deep, interior life with Christ.

Learn more:
www.emotionallyhealthy.org

Emotionally Healthy Spirituality Day by Day

A 40-Day Journey with the Daily Office

Peter Scazzero

In this groundbreaking devotional book, Peter Scazzero introduces the ancient spiritual discipline of the Daily Office. The basic premise of the Daily Office is simple: We need to intentionally stop to be with God more than once a day so that practicing the presence of God becomes real in our lives.

Each day offers two Daily Offices—Morning/Midday and Midday/Evening—where each pause can last from five to twenty minutes.

Available in stores and online!

Emotionally Healthy Church, Updated and Expanded Edition

A Strategy for Discipleship that Actually Changes Lives

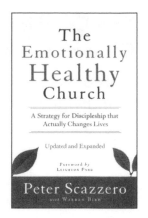

Peter Scazzero with Warren Bird

Emotional health and spiritual maturity are inseparable

Our churches are in trouble, says Pete Scazzero. They are filled with people who are unsure how to biblically integrate anger, sadness, and other emotions. Sharing from New Life Fellowship's painful but liberating journey, Scazzero reveals exactly how the truth can and does make you free—not just superficially, but deep down.

This updated and expanded edition of *The Emotionally Healthy Church* takes the original six principles further and deeper, adding a seventh crucial principle. You'll acquire knowledge and tools that can help you and others look beneath the surface of problems and break the power of past wounds, failures, sins, and circumstances to live a life of brokenness and vulnerability.

Available in stores and online!

The Emotionally Healthy Church Workbook

8 Studies for Groups or Individuals

Peter Scazzero

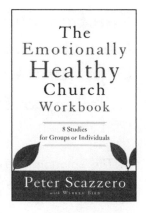

Emotional health and spiritual maturity are inseparable: that is the premise of the award-winning book *The Emotionally Healthy Church*. This stand-alone workbook helps leaders and lay persons alike apply the biblical truths in Peter Scazzero's revolutionary book to their personal lives, small groups, and churches. Eight studies take you beyond merely reading about emotional health to actually cultivating it as a disciple of Jesus. Step-by-step, you'll discover what it means to have Christ transform the deep places hidden beneath the surface so that you might become more authentic and loving toward God, others, and yourself.

Available in stores and online!

The Emotionally Healthy Woman

Eight Things You Have to Quit
to Change Your Life

Geri Scazzero with Peter Scazzero

In *The Emotionally Healthy Woman*, Geri Scazzero provides you a way out of an inauthentic, superficial spirituality to genuine freedom in Christ. This book is for every woman who thinks, "I can't keep pretending everything is fine!"

The Emotionally Healthy

Woman

EIGHT THINGS YOU HAVE to
QUIT to CHANGE YOUR LIFE

Previously titled *I Quit*

Geri Scazzero
with Peter Scazzero

Contents:

- Quit Being Afraid of What Others Think
- Quit Lying
- Quit Dying to the Wrong Things
- Quit Denying Anger, Sadness, and Fear
- Quit Blaming
- Quit Overfunctioning
- Quit Faulty Thinking
- Quit Living Someone Else's Life

DVD Study and Workbook Also Available

ZONDERVAN®
.com